The Santa Cruz Mountains Trail Book

by Tom Taber

TENTH EDITION

Exploring the parks and trails of the mountains of San Mateo, Santa Clara, and Santa Cruz Counties, and the adjacent coast.

The Oak Valley Press

ISBN: 0-9609170-9-8
978-0-9609170-9-9

First Edition 1976
Second Edition 1979
Third Edition 1982
Fourth Edition 1985
Fifth Edition 1988
Sixth Edition 1991
Seventh Edition 1994
Eighth Edition 1998
Ninth Edition 2002

Cover, design, maps, and illustrations by Tom Taber.
Photo on page 30 courtesy Sempervirens Fund
Front cover photo by Regina Taber
All other photos by Tom Taber
Front cover photo: Long Ridge Open Space Preserve
Back cover photo: Mori Point Unit, Golden Gate National Recreation
Area.

THE OAK VALLEY PRESS

1643 Fillmore Avenue
San Mateo, CA 94403

Table of Contents

Introduction **8**
General Area Map **10**
Almaden Quicksilver County Park **13**
Alpine Road Trail **17**
Ano Nuevo State Reserve **18**
Arastradero Preserve **23**
Bear Creek Redwoods Open Space Preserve **24**
Big Basin Redwoods State park **27**
Bonny Doon Ecological Preserve **38**
Burleigh Murray Ranch State park **40**
Butano State Park **42**
Calero County Park **45**
Castle Rock State Park **49**
Chitactac-Adams Heritage County Park **55**
Coal Creek Open Space Preserve **57**
Edgewood County Park & Preserve **58**
El Corte de Madera Creek Open Space Preserve **60**
El Sereno Open Space Preserve **63**
Fall Creek Unit, Henry Cowell Redwoods State Park **90**
Filoli Estate **65**
Foothills Open Space Preserve **66**
Foothills Park **67**
Forest of Nisene Marks State Park **69**
Fremont Older Open Space Preserve **75**
Golden Gate National Recreation Area
    Sweeney Ridge **78**
    Fort Funston **80**
    Mori Point **82**
    Phleger Estate **84**
Henry Cowell Redwoods State Park
    Southern Unit **86**
    Fall Creek Unit **90**
Hidden Villa Ranch **94**
Huddart County Park **96**
Jasper Ridge Biological Preserve **99**
La Honda Creek Open Space Preserve **100**
Loch Lomond Recreation Area **102**

Long Ridge Open Space Preserve **105**
Los Trancos Open Space Preserve **109**
McNee Ranch State Park **113**
Monte Bello Open Space Preserve **115**
Mount Madonna County Park **119**
Pescadero Creek County Park **122**
Pescadero Marsh Preserve **127**
Picchetti Ranch Open Space Preserve **129**
Pogonip Open Space Preserve **131**
Portola State Park **133**
Portola Valley Trails **137**
Pulgas Ridge Open Space Preserve **139**
Purisima Creek Redwoods Open Space Preserve **141**
Quail Hollow Ranch County Park **147**
Rancho Canada del Oro Open Space Preserve **149**
Rancho San Antonio Open Space Preserve & County Park **150**
The Ridge Trail **154**
Russian Ridge Open Space Preserve **156**
Saint Joseph's Hill Open Space Preserve **159**
Sam McDonald County Park **162**
San Bruno Mountain County Park **164**
San Francisco Fish and Game Refuge **166**
    Sawyer Camp Trail **167**
San Mateo County Memorial Park **170**
San Pedro Valley County Park **172**
Sanborn Skyline County Park **175**
Santa Teresa County Park **179**
Saratoga Gap Open Space Preserve **181**
Sawyer Camp Trail **167**
Sierra Azul Open Space Preserve **182**
Skyline Ridge Open Space Preserve **186**
Skyline-to-the-Sea Trail **190**
The Skyline Trail **195**
Soquel Demonstration State Forest **197**
Stevens Canyon Ranch Open Space Preserve **200**
Stevens Creek County Park **201**
Teague Hill Open Space Preserve **203**
Thornewood Open Space Preserve **203**
University of California, Santa Cruz Campus **204**

Upper Stevens Creek County Park **207**
Uvas Canyon County Park **209**
Villa Montalvo Arboretum & County Park **211**
Wilder Ranch State Park **213**
Windy Hill Open Space Preserve **218**
Wunderlich County Park **221**
Coastal Access Guide **224**
   San Mateo County Coast **225**
   Santa Cruz County Coast **234**

SPECIAL SECTIONS:
Mountain Charlie's Acorn Cookies **16**
Mountain Charlie **26**
Andrew P. Hill, Conservation Pioneer **30**
The Last Grizzly **35**
Coast Redwoods **36**
Santa Cruz Mountains Geology **39**
Walk For Health **44**
"Wandering Man" words and music **48**
Poison Oak **62**
Watch Out For Ticks **85**
Are There Bears In The Santa Cruz Mountains? **93**
An Ohlone Legend of the Winter Solstice **108**
A Short Guide to Earthquake Faults **110**
Where to Walk Your Dog **118**
Sudden Oak Death Syndrome **121**
The Great Logging Boom **126**
Banana Slugs **136**
The Fog Forest **145**
Wild Pigs **161**
Off-Road Bicycling **174**
The Joy of Bay Nuts **189**
Acorn Woodpeckers **199**
Mountain Lions **206**
Mountain Charlie's Tree **240**
Resources **241**
The Best of the Santa Cruz Mountains **243**
Wildlife Tracks **246**
Intertidal Life **247**

Introduction

When this book was first published in 1976 it was only 64 pages, and the acreage of public lands and the mileage of trails was only a fraction of what we enjoy today. The Santa Cruz Mountains are now part of one of the most splendid greenbelts next to any major metropolitan area in the world.

Though this book is a celebration of the parks and trails of the mountains south of San Francisco, there is still plenty of room for improvement. Here is my wish-list for the future:

A) First, we need more trails, especially between public lands.

There are some abandoned road alignments, usually dating back to the nineteenth century, which should be researched to determine if there are public right-of-ways. If so, they could become trails. If not, trail easements could possibly be negotiated with property owners. One example is the old La honda Road route which runs north of the current road of the same name between La Honda Creek Open Space Preserve and Sam McDonald County Park. Another example is the Page Mill Road route west of Skyline Boulevard between Skyline Ridge Open Space Preserve and Portola State Park. This scenic route was built by William Page in the 1870's as a logging toll road. It could become part of an extraordinary loop encompassing Skyline Ridge and Long Ridge Open Space Preserves, and Portola State Park.

I would also like to see a short loop trail into the rugged Devil's Canyon in Long Ridge Open Space Preserve. With its dramatic rock outcroppings and series of rainy season waterfalls, this is an area that has long attracted rock climbers and adventure seekers. Unfortunately, without a good trail, cross-country access to this steep canyon is both dangerous and hard on the landscape. The solution is to provide a well-designed trail that will allow visitors to safely enjoy the wonders of this wonderful place.

B) There should be more public access to the San Francisco Watershed property.

It is a time to allow far more public access to the San Francisco Watershed lands around Crystal Springs and San Andreas Reservoirs. The San Francisco Water Department should be commended for opening part of this 23,000-acre property to docent-led walks. However, these walks are much too limited. Trail users should be allowed to travel the 10-mile Cahill Ridge Trail from Sweeney Ridge to Highway 92. This would be the perfect route for the Ridge Trail. There are other gravel roads that could also be opened to public use to form loop trails. Why is the City & County of San Francisco so much more afraid of the public using the trails on the ridge above their reservoirs than is the City of Santa Cruz of people fishing, picnicking, hiking, and even boating on and around the city's water supply at Loch Lomond Reservoir? I don't get it.

You can rent a boat on Loch Lomond Reservoir, which is Santa Cruz's drinking water supply.

C) There should be more places to camp in the Santa Cruz Mountains. It has been decades since a new campground has been established. The Bay Area population has grown and the public land acreage has multiplied, yet the list of places for car camping is the same today as it was in the 1970's. Have you tried reserving a campsite at Butano State Park on a weekend between May and October? Good luck.

It's the same story for backpacking. A vast network of trails is developing in this range, yet trailcamps and hikers huts aren't keeping pace. Where are people supposed to spend the nights while traveling the Ridge Trail through the Santa Cruz Mountains? There should be some place to camp at least every eight miles along the route. The Midpeninsula Regional Open Space District could help by adding more trailcamps. Today it operates only one, at Monte Bello.

Today there is only one hikers hut in the entire Santa Cruz Mountains. I would like to see a series of them placed approximately a day's walk apart for people who prefer indoor accomodations.

D) More public land should be open to the public.

The Midpeninsula Regional Open Space District should open the southern part of La Honda Creek Open Space Preserve to the public. There is plenty of room for parking along La Honda Road, and existing ranch roads could easily be converted into trails. It is also time for the airforce to clean up the summit of Mount Umunhum so the public can enjoy the stunning views. The formidable airforce blockhouse on top should be preserved as a relic of the cold war. See item B for my opinion about the San Francisco Watershed property.

E) Fire has been an essential part of Santa Cruz Mountains ecology for eons. Evidence is found in the form of fire scars on virtually every old-growth redwood. The suppresion of fire is resulting in excess buildup of fuel that could result in catastrophic fires. Occasional prescribed burning would prevent this disaster and also enhance the natural qualities of public lands. Prescribed burning has been conducted succesfully at Big Basin Redwoods State Park and Russian Ridge Open Space Preserve. On the Sunset Trail in Big Basin you will find thousands of young knobcone pine

9

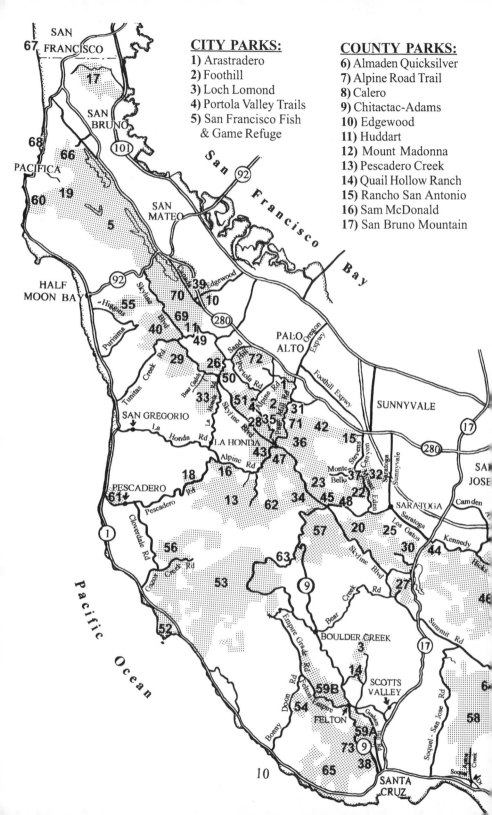

CITY PARKS:
1) Arastradero
2) Foothill
3) Loch Lomond
4) Portola Valley Trails
5) San Francisco Fish & Game Refuge

COUNTY PARKS:
6) Almaden Quicksilver
7) Alpine Road Trail
8) Calero
9) Chitactac-Adams
10) Edgewood
11) Huddart
12) Mount Madonna
13) Pescadero Creek
14) Quail Hollow Ranch
15) Rancho San Antonio
16) Sam McDonald
17) San Bruno Mountain

10

18) San Mateo County
  Memorial
19) San Pedro Valley
20) Sanborn Skyline
21) Santa Teresa
22) Stevens Creek
23) Upper Stevens Creek
24) Uvas Canyon
25) Villa Montalvo
26) Wunderlich

OPEN SPACE PRESERVES:
27) Bear Creek Redwoods
28) Coal Creek
29) El Corte de Madera
30) El Sereno
31) Foothills
32) Fremont Older
33) La Honda Creek
34) Long Ridge
35) Los Trancos
36) Monte Bello
37) Picchetti Ranch
38) Pogonip
39) Pulgas Ridge
40) Purisima Creek
41) Rancho Canada
  Del Oro
42) Rancho San Antonio
43) Russian Ridge
44) St. Joseph's Hill

45) Saratoga Gap
46) Sierra Azul
47) Skyline Ridge
48) Stevens Canyon Ranch
49) Teague Hill
50) Thornewood
51) Windy Hill

STATE PARKS:
52) Ano Nuevo
53) Big Basin Redwoods
54) Bonny Doon
55) Burleigh Murray
56) Butano
57) Castle Rock
58) Forest of Nisene Marks
59A) Henry Cowell Redwoods
  Southern Unit
59B) Henry Cowell Redwoods
  Fall Creek Unit
60) McNee Ranch
61) Pescadero Marsh
62) Portola
63) Skyline-to-the-Sea Trail
64) Soquel Demonstraion Forest
65) Wilder Ranch

GOLDEN GATE NTL RECREATION AREA:
66) Sweeney Ridge
67) Fort Funston
68) Mori Point
69) Phleger Estate

PRIIVATE
70) Filoli
71) Hidden Villa
72) Jasper Ridge

UNIVERSITY OF CALIFORNIA
73) Santa Cruz Campus

11

trees which sprouted soon after a burn. Knobcone pine are one of several native plants that require fire in order to reproduce.

F) Wildlife habitat should be restored and enhanced. Salmon and steelhead could be restored to major streams by clearing obstacles, preventing siltation, and restoring riperian vegetation. The creeks of the Santa Cruz Mountains have been badly degraded by 150 years of logging. Coho salmon are an indicator of watershed health. I look forward to the day when our streams have been restored enough to welcome them back.

Tule elk, pronghorn antelope, and other native wildlife could be re-introduced. Non-native wild pigs should be reduced. Obstacles to wildlife migration should be mitigated wherever possible. There should be wide wildlife overpasses and underpasses crossing Highway 17 and 92. Fences could guide wildlife toward these safe crossings. These structures are being used in Europe and along the Trans Canada Highway to encourage the safe migration of wildlife.

G) Shut down the rod and gun club next to Castle Rock State Park. People shouldn't have to feel like they are passing through a war zone when they take a walk through this beautiful park.

H) Increase geographic awareness about the Santa Cruz Mountains. I am amazed by how many people live in and next to the Santa Cruz Mountains and don't know it. Many people in Pacifica, San Bruno, San Mateo, and Palo Alto think the Santa Cruz Mountains are those mountains near Santa Cruz. I hope this book will educate people in those and other cities that they live just as close to the Santa Cruz Mountains as do people in the city of Santa Cruz. It's as if people thought that the biggest river in the United States is only called the Mississippi River where it flows next to the state of Mississippi.

Photographs from space clearly show that the Santa Cruz Mountains are one distinct geographic unit; probably the most clearly defined range in the California Coast Range. Because of San Francisco Bay, it is the only unit of the Coast Range that is partly separated from the mainland of North America.

Almaden Quicksilver County Park

TO GET THERE... there are 4 entrances to this park. From Highway 85 take Almaden Expressway 5 miles south and turn right on Almaden Road. You can then turn right on Mockingbird Hill Lane for one of the access points or continue for about 3 miles on Almaden Road to the Hacienda Trailhead Staging Area. To reach the McAbee Road entrance from Highway 85 take the Camden Avenue exit, go south on Camden for about 3 miles and turn right on McAbee Road. There is street parking at the end of the road. To reach the westside entrance, from Highway 17, take Camden Avenue south and turn right on Hicks Road and continue south about 6 miles. Where Hicks Road intersects Mt. Umunhum Road turn left (east) on a short road to a large parking lot with plenty of room for horse trailers.

This 3,977-acre park in the dry eastern foothills of the Santa Cruz Mountains is well known for its colorful mercury mining history and for its extraordinary display of spring wildflowers. Despite many years of mining and settlement, much of this land still feels wild. For safety reasons some of the mining sites are closed to the public.

This park, which is covered mainly with oak, grasslands, and chaparral, has 29 miles of hiking trails, 23 miles of equestrian trails, and 10 miles of bicycle trails. There are also dirt roads which are not official trails and are not on the map. To keep from getting confused look for trail markers that identify established routes. Dog owners will be pleased to know that their leashed canine companions are welcome on all trails.

Be aware that summer is often hot in this park, so bring lots of water. From early March until the middle of May is the perfect time to visit, when the hills are green and the wildflowers are abundant.

Of the 5 entrances to this park, my favorite is the Mockingbird Hill entrance. There are numerous loop options to choose from depending on your level of fitness and time requirements. Just add up the distance between trail junctions on the map to determine which loop is best.

The map reveals many loop options from each of the 4 park entrances. From the Almaden Road (Hacienda) entrance hikers and equestrians can enjoy a 5.9 mile loop by charging up the steep Mine Hill Trail. Take the short side trip to look into the San Cristobal Mine and then loop back to where you started via the Castillero and English Camp Trails. You can take an additional 1 mile sidetrip to the cemetary, though there are no headstones.

From the Hicks Road entrance travel east on the Wood Road Trail through oak woodland, chaparral, and grassland, with dramatic views to the west of the highest peaks in the Santa Cruz Mountains. This trail is part of the 400-mile-long Bay Area Ridge Trail. You can make a great 5.15-mile loop, with lots of mining era relics along the way, by combining the Wood Road, Castillero, and Mine Hill trails. The map reveals lots of opportunities to expand this route.

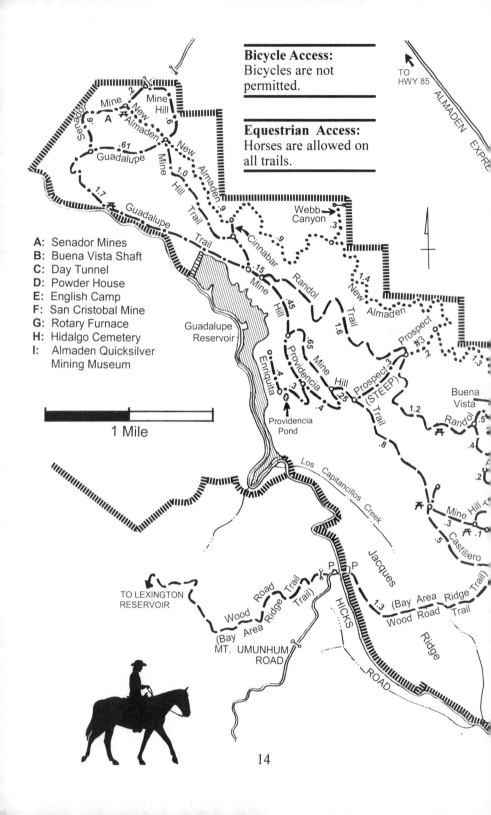

Bicycle Access:
Bicycles are not permitted.

Equestrian Access:
Horses are allowed on all trails.

TO
HWY 85

ALMADEN EXPR

Mine
Senador Mine
Mine Hill
New Almaden
A
.6
.2
.61
Guadalupe
New Mine Hill Trail
1.0
New Almaden
1.7
Guadalupe Trail
.9
Webb Canyon
.3
Cinnabar
.9
1.4
New Almaden

A: Senador Mines
B: Buena Vista Shaft
C: Day Tunnel
D: Powder House
E: English Camp
F: San Cristobal Mine
G: Rotary Furnace
H: Hidalgo Cemetery
I: Almaden Quicksilver Mining Museum

Randol Trail
.15
Mine Hill Trail
.45
1.6
Prospect #3
.3
.2
1.3
Providencia
.65
Mine Hill
Prospect (STEEP)
Buena Vista
Randol
.5
Enriquita
.4
.3
.25
.4
Prospect Trail
1.2
.4
Guadalupe Reservoir
Providencia Pond
.8
.2

1 Mile

Los Capitancillos Creek

Mine Hill T.
.3 .1
.5
Castillero

Jacques

TO LEXINGTON RESERVOIR

Wood Road Trail
(Bay Area Ridge Trail)
P P
1.3 (Bay Area Ridge Trail)
Wood Road Trail

HICKS

MT. UMUNHUM ROAD

Ridge

ROAD

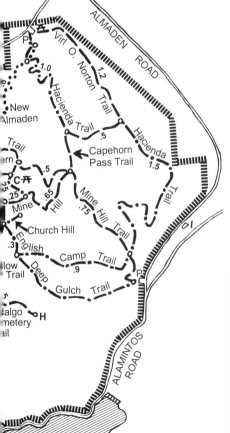

P

Vir O. Norton Trail 1.2

1.0

New Almaden

Hacienda Trail

Hacienda Trail 1.5

.5

Trail

ern

Capehorn Pass Trail

C

.5

.25

.65

Mine

Hill

Mine Hill Trail .75

Church Hill

.3

English

low Trail

Deep

Camp Trail .9

Gulch Trail

P

dalgo metery ail

H

ALMADEN ROAD

HARRY

ALAMINTOS ROAD

Almaden Reservoir

Dogs on leash are allowed on all trails in Almaden Quicksilver County Park.

15

From the McAbee Road trailhead you can travel an easy and scenic 7-mile loop by combining the Mine Hill and Guadalupe Trails over a ridge and past Guadalupe Reservoir. You will see remnants of quicksilver (mercury) mining along the way.

The discovery of quicksilver here in 1845 by Mexican cavalry captain Andres Castillero soon resulted in the development of one of the world's greatest mercury mines. The boom went bust in the early twentieth century as the ore was exhausted and the Quicksilver Mining Company declared bankruptcy in 1912. Qicksilver, or mercury, had many uses, including the processing of gold ore. It is derived from a red rock called cinnabar, which is heated to 1000 degrees until the mercury vaporizes. As the vapor cools it assumes a liquid form.

Cinnabar was derived from an ore rock called silica carbonate. A ton of ore yields 12-15 pounds of mercury. Cinabar is a heavy red rock mined from deep mine shafts and is rarely seen on the surface.

The New Almaden Quicksilver County Park Association is a nonprofit corporation which offers guided interpretive tours, sponsors an annual Pioneer Day, and operates the New Almaden Mining Museum (open Saturdays from noon-4 pm) on Almaden Road in the historic Casa Grande building. For more information call (408)323-1107 or write them at P.O. Box 124, New Almaden, CA 95042.

This park, only 11 miles south of San Jose, is open from 8 am until sundown. For more information, call the Santa Clara County Parks and Recreation Department at (408)268-3883 (www.parkhere.org).

SPECIAL SECTION
Mountain Charlie's Acorn Cookies

Acorns were the one food Ohlone people ate nearly every day of their lives. They are high in fat, protein, and carbohydrates, and they have a unique nutty taste. Here's how to make them edible:

First, gather acorns in early fall. Discard those that feel light (they're rotten) or have small holes (they're worm infested). Then break open the acorns with pliers and remove the husks. The next step is to break the nuts into small pieces by using the pliers or by striking them with a hammer. Bring a pot of water to a boil and turn off the heat just before adding the acorn chunks. Stir occasionally, as the water turns increasingly brown when the tanic acid is leached from the acorns. Repeat this process until the water is only a light brown.

Pour a little water into your blender and add the acorns. Blend until the mixture has a smooth consistency. Add more water if needed to make it blend. Then drain off any excess water.

To make cookies, find your favorite oatmeal cookie recipe and just replace oatmeal with acorn mush.

Alpine Road Trail

TO GET THERE... From Highway 280 take Alpine Road about 3 miles south and west to a metal gate where it becomes a trail.

Where the pavement ends at the southwestern end of Alpine Road you can continue uphill on foot, horse, or bicycle for 2.5 miles to where it intersects Page Mill Road.

This dirt road trail gently ascends 1,000 feet through a forest of oak, bay, maple, and madrone, paralleling Corte Madera Creek which flows through the fracture zone of the San Andreas Fault.

For a more extended outing you can take connecting trails through adjacent Coal Creek Open Space Preserve and from there on to Russian Ridge and Skyline Ridge Open Space Preserves.

This road, built in 1894, is particularly popular with mountain bikers.

Near the downhill trail entrance gate you can find thin veins of coal in the roadcut on Alpine Road. This explains the the local place names "Coal Mine Ridge" and "Coal Creek".

Bicycle Access:	**Equestrian Access:**
Bicycles are allowed.	Horses are allowed.

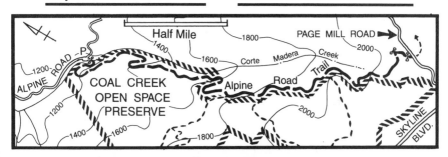

Ano Nuevo State Reserve

TO GET THERE... the main entrance is west of Highway 1 about 19 miles north of Santa Cruz and about 23 miles south of Half Moon Bay. The reserve begins just south of the Pigeon Point Lighthouse. The Cascade Ranch Unit can be reached from the Whitehouse Creek Road and the Gazos Creek Road.

PLEASE NOTE: To protect wildlife, access to the Wildlife Protection Area (south of Cascade Creek) may be restricted at any time of year.

Ano Nuevo is truly one of America's great marine wildlife preserves.

Cormorants nest on ocean cliffs, tidepools abound with intertidal life, sea lions and harbor seals are commonly seen and heard on the beaches and rocks here, and sea otters are seen offshore. The reserve is most popular, however, from December through March when a colony of elephant seals visits the island and peninsula for mating and bearing young. To protect these enormous mammals, and the people who come to see them, the wildlife protection area of the reserve, which covers the sand dune area south of Cascade Creek, is open only through naturalist guided walks at that time of year.

The optimal time to see the most activity among adult males, adult females, and their pups, is around the middle of February (near Valentine's Day).

Male elephant seals arrive in early December to establish a breeding hierarchy and are followed in late December by the females who join the harems of the dominant males. Male elephant seals are enormous, reaching lengths of up to 16 feet and weighing 3 tons. Females are much smaller, at 1,200 to 2,000 pounds. Slaughtered for their oil-rich blubber, by 1892 fewer than 100 seals remained. In the 1920's the Mexican and United States

18

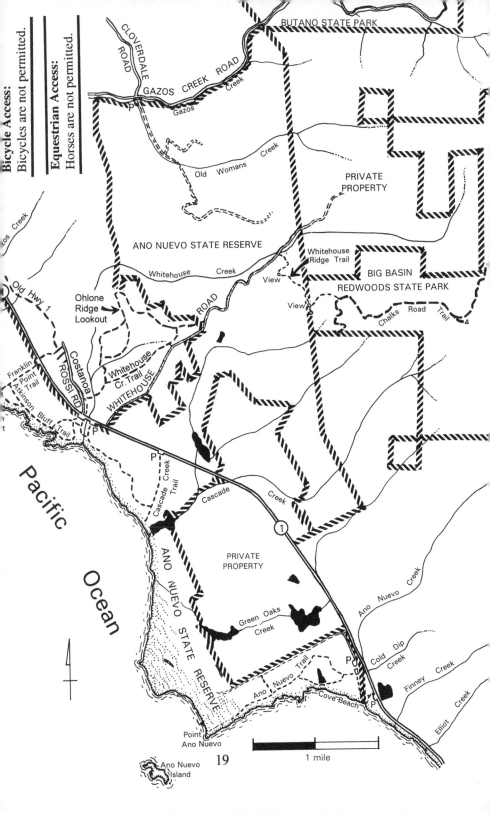

BUTANO STATE PARK

CLOVERDALE ROAD

GAZOS CREEK ROAD

Creek

Gazos

Old Womans Creek

PRIVATE PROPERTY

ANO NUEVO STATE RESERVE

Whitehouse Ridge Trail

Whitehouse Creek

View

BIG BASIN REDWOODS STATE PARK

Los Creek

Old Hwy 1

Ohlone Ridge Lookout

ROAD

View

View

Chalks Road Trail

Franklin Point Trail

Costanoa

ROSSI RD

Atkinson Bluff Trail

Whitehouse Cr. Trail

WHITEHOUSE

P

P

Cascade Creek Trail

Cascade Creek

1

Pacific

Ocean

ANO NUEVO STATE RESERVE

PRIVATE PROPERTY

Green Oaks Creek

Ano Nuevo Creek

Cold Dip Creek

Finney Creek

Ano Nuevo Trail

P

Cove Beach

P

Elliot Creek

Point Ano Nuevo

Ano Nuevo Island

19

1 mile

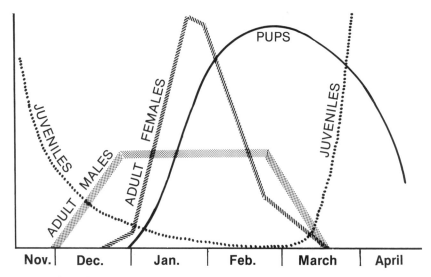

Nov. | Dec. | Jan. | Feb. | March | April

This chart shows the relative abundance of elephant seals during the breeding and pupping season at Ano Nuevo.

governments gave them legal protection, allowing their numbers to rapidly increase since then. They first returned to Ano Nuevo Island in 1955 and are now also breeding on the peninsula. These animals, the largest members of the seal family, seem awkward on land, but they are excellent swimmers, able to dive as deep as 5,000 feet to feed mainly on rays, squids, skates, and fish.

This fascinating peninsula is worth exploring all year; and in fact, can be most enjoyable when most of the elephant seals and their hordes of loyal admirers are gone, and walking may be done without ranger escort. Ano Nuevo is one of the few places on the San Mateo County coast where it is possible to do some real hiking west from Highway 1.

From the parking lot it is about 1.5 miles to the end of the peninsula, depending on your route. Half a mile off the peninsula is .5-acre Ano Nuevo Island, breeding ground for elephant seals, Steller sea lions, and harbor seals, and a nesting place for western gulls, pigeon guillemots, and black oystercatchers. Because of its importance to coastal wildlife, public access to the island is prohibited. This cherty shale island was part of the mainland until relatively recently in geologic time, when it was separated by wave erosion and by the gradual rising of the sea level when the ice age glaciers melted over the past 10,000 years.

This area was uplifted from the sea a mere 70-100,000 years ago, creating treacherous rocky obstacles for ships. Several major shipwrecks resulted in the construction of a lighthouse on the island in 1890. Difficult to maintain, the storm-battered station was replaced by an automated signal buoy on the island in 1948. Today the weathered lightkeepers' house still stands clearly visible from the mainland, now inhabited only by seals, sea lions, and birds.

Tidepools exposed near the tip of the peninsula have an extraordinary abundance of marine life, though access is sometimes restricted to prevent disturbing seals and sea lions. At low tide you may notice what appears to be spherical boulders several feet in diameter fastened to the tidepoool rocks. Closer inspection will reveal that these objects, covered with countless tiny holes, are actually tube masses, created by calciferous tube worms. Nourished largely by sea lion and seal waste, the waters of Ano Nuevo have some of the world's largest tube worm formations. Each calcium carbonate tube mass is a community of worms and a vast network of tubal tunnels.

Harbor seals are often seen lounging on the rocks offshore, and are seen bobbing their heads above water near shore. Their short, plump, spotted bodies are easily distinguished from other seals. They mate on the island in April and May.

Humans have been visiting this area for thousands of years, as evidenced by shell mounds left by a once large Ohlone Indian habitation. For many centuries Indians lived a relatively easy life, thriving on the coast's abundance of seafood, game, acorns, and other wild edibles, and had no need for agriculture. Their discarded seashells form numerous shell mounds on the peninsula. Along with shell fragments you will find chips of a glassy rock called chert, which was used for cutting edges and arrow heads. It is illegal to disturb these mounds.

Ano Nuevo has one of the oldest place names in the country, named "La Punta Del Ano Nuevo" (The Point of the New Year) by the Spanish explorer Sebastian Vizcaino on January 3, 1603. It was used for shipping redwood timber from the Santa Cruz Mountains between 1853 and 1920, and the peninsula and vicinity was part of a cattle ranch established by Isaac Steele. The residence south of the main parking lot was built in 1870 for Isaac's daughter, Flora Dickerman Steele. The barn now houses the visitors' center.

North of Cascade Creek the reserve can be explored all year without a permit from the parking area on the west side of Highway 1.

Park rangers and volunteers conduct walks in the reserve when elephant seals are in their greatest numbers between December 15 and March 31. The 2.5 hour 3-mile walk is conducted rain or shine. As of this writing, reservations may be made by calling (800)444-4445. Because of the popularity of these walks, make your reservations early; as much as 8 weeks in advance. For more information call the state park office at (650)879-0227. Information is also available on the World Wide Web at www.anonuevo.org and www.parks.ca.gov .

San Mateo County Transit (SamTrans) offers weekend guided walk packages between January 6 and February 25. Call (650)508-6448 for information or visit its web site at www.samtrans.com.

Cascade Ranch Unit (Ano Nuevo State Reserve)

People usually associate 3,986-acre Ano Nuevo State Reserve with sand dunes, pounding surf, and seals. For this reason the 2,500-acre Cascade Ranch part of the preserve, which is east of Highway 1, deserves to be treated as a separate entity with its own unique qualities.

This land slopes uphill to the east as it approaches Big Basin Redwoods State park, which can be reached by trail from Whitehouse Creek Road. This is a dirt road that passes through Cascade Ranch and then enters private property on the other side.

Just before entering private property on the east side of the reserve you will find the beginning of the Whitehouse Ridge Trail, which makes a scenic 1.5 mile ascent into Big Basin Redwoods State Park. Be aware that the trailhead is unmarked. The trail begins on the south side of Whitehouse Creek Road 2.4 miles from Highway 1. There is parking for only a few cars. The trail makes a steep ascent, first through second-growth redwoods, then through Douglas fir, and upward to a rocky ridge covered with knobcone pine and manzanita, and then intersects Chalk Mountain Road in Big Basin. There are 2 vista points offering excellent views of Ano Nuevo Island, Pigeon Point Lighthouse, and other sights on the coast.

From Gazos Creek Road, on the north side of Cascade Ranch, you can access the property from an old ranch road that goes south from near the intersection of Gazos Creek Road and Cloverdale Road. Following Old Woman's Creek, this route passes under an extraordinarily large redwood limb that reaches over the trail. This route doesn't form a loop.

The Ohlone Indians thrived in this abundant land, feasting on acorns and other edible plants, deer and other game in the mountains, salmon and steelhead in the streams, and mussels, abalone, clams, and other bounty from the sea. This area was home to the largest settlement of Ohlone on the coast between Monterey and San Francisco. This is also the place where these Indians first made contact with Spanish explorer Gaspar de Portola during his long trek through California in 1776.

Costanoa

Costanoa is a lodge and campground next to the Cascade Ranch Unit on Rossi Road just east of Highway 1. A stay here is an excellent base for exploring the southern San Mateo County coast, Ano Nuevo State Preserve, Wilder Ranch State Park, Butano State Park, and Big Basin Redwoods State Park. Tent camping, RV sites, canvas bungalows, cabins, and lodge rooms are available. Mountain bike and horse rentals are also available. From the lodge there is a 3-mile trail loop to Franklin Point on the coast; and a 3.5-mile scenic uphill loop on the Whitehouse Creek and Ohlone Ridge Lookout Trails. This route offers a fine vista of the southern San Mateo County coast. For reservations call (877) 262-7848, or visit their web site at: www.costanoa.com.

Arastradero Preserve

TO GET THERE... From Highway 280 take Page Mill Road south and turn right on Arastradero Road to the preserve parking lot on the right side of the road.

The city of Palo Alto owns this gentle 613 acres of grassy foothills

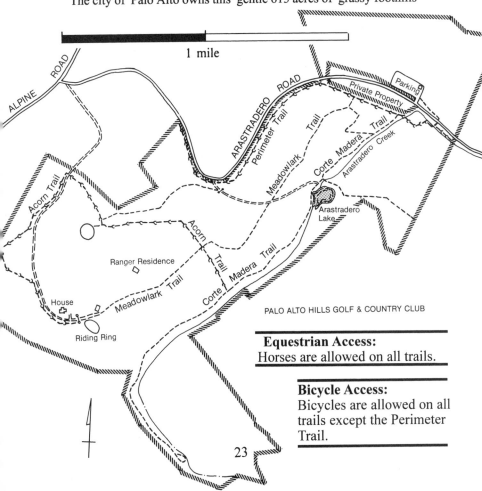

PALO ALTO HILLS GOLF & COUNTRY CLUB

Equestrian Access:
Horses are allowed on all trails.

Bicycle Access:
Bicycles are allowed on all trails except the Perimeter Trail.

landscape. The 6 miles of trails are relatively level-- ideal for small children and relaxed saunters.

Be advised that you will find little refreshing shade during hot weather, though stately old oaks seem to be scattered conveniently for the benefit of weary travelers.

Offroad bicycles are allowed in the preserve, but not on the Perimeter Trail, which is popular with equestrians. Dogs are permitted Monday through Friday only and must be leashed and restrained at all times.

Arastradero Lake is a small reservoir just over half a mile from the parking lot by way of the Corte Madera Trail. It's a good place to pause and watch ducks, coots, and redwing blackbirds. Boats and swimming are not allowed.

For a moderate 4-mile loop around the preserve, combine the Corte Madera Trail, the Acorn Trail, and the Meadowlark Trail to the uphill (west) side of the preserve and then swing back to the parking lot via the Acorn and Perimeter trails.

Bear Creek Redwoods
Open Space Preserve

TO GET THERE... Take the Bear Creek Road exit west from Highway 17 near Lexington Reservoir. Hikers enter at gate BC 04. Equestrians enter at gate BC 02.

PLEASE NOTE: As of this writing access is only allowed with a permit from the Midpeninsula Regional Open Space District. A master plan is being developed which could change access policies.

Despite its name, much of this preserve consists of oak, bay, maple, douglas fir, and grassland, in addition to second-growth redwood. The preserve's 1,343 acres include 5 ponds and three perennial creeks which flow through the preserve on their way to nearby Lexington Reservoir. Fishing and swimming are prohibited in the ponds. Bicycles and dogs are not allowed in the preserve.

This preserve has a ready-made trail system of ranch roads. At this time none of them are marked. However, this area is too small for you to get lost. The preserve is primarily used by equestrians from the Bear Creek Stable, which is inside the preserve. Because the stable offers boarding, riding circles, and horse trailer parking, this could be the most equestrian oriented of all the open space preserves.

Throughout Bear Creek Redwoods you will see evidence that this land has been used for more than 100 years. The sound of traffic on nearby Highway 17 will remind you that civilization is not far away.

General James Fremont camped on this land in 1846. It was home to a stage driver named Charley Parkhurst, who was thought to be a man until her death. She was probably the first California woman to vote in an election. In the 1830's, when the water presure failed, a fire was doused here with wine. A radio tower here was the first to receive news of the

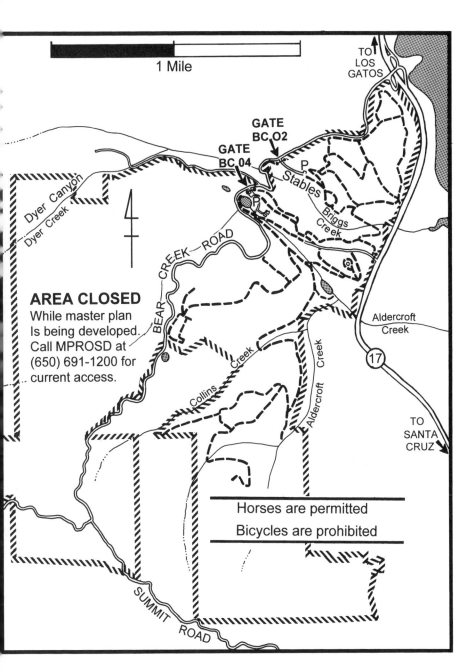

Japanese attack on Pearl Harbor in 1941. The abandoned Alma College campus still stands, but is closed to the public.

25

Mountain Charlie
Hunter, Rancher, Teamster, & Road Builder

"RIGHT WRONGS NOBODY"

Born in 1825, Charlie McKiernan left hard times in his native Ireland for a life of adventure. After serving in the British army in Australia he headed for the unsettled wilds of California.

In 1850 Charlie built a small cabin, along what is now Mountain Charlie Road, and raised sheep near the Skyline summit between Santa Clara and Santa Cruz Counties. Back in those days the Santa Cruz Mountains were wild and remote. Grizzly bears were still common, and they discovered that sheep were easy to catch and good to eat.

Considering grizzlies to be vermin, Charlie made a name for himself as a bear hunter. In 1854 he and a friend made the mistake of sneaking up on a sow bear with 2 cubs. When she suddenly charged, Charlie aimed and fired his rifle, but only wounded the bear. In the hand-to-hand combat that followed, Mountain Charlie swung his muzzle loader at the bruin until it broke. After the bear left him for dead his friend carried the unconscious mountain man back to his cabin. The grizzlie cost Charlie his left eye and left a gaping hole in his skull that a San Jose doctor covered with a flattened Mexican silver dollar. For many years to come he was embarrassed enough about the silver plate to wear his hat cocked over his forehead.

In 1862, at the age of 37, Charlie married Barbara Bercary, the nurse who helped him recover from the bear attack. They had 7 children. He died in 1892 at the age of 67.

Today, Charlie is memorialized by Mountain Charlie Road, just south of Highway 17, which he helped build as a toll road, and by the Mountain Charlie Tree, a large redwood near Glenwood (see page 240).

Big Basin Redwoods State Park

**TO GET THERE... From Skyline Boulevard take Highway 9 southwest
and turn west on Highway 236 at Waterman Gap or at Boulder Creek.
There is also an entrance on Highway 1 about 18 miles northwest of
Santa Cruz.**

Big Basin is a large and diverse land of dark redwood groves, sunny
ridges, and rocky peaks. This is the largest park in the Santa Cruz Mountains, with 80 miles of trails to escape the crowded paved areas and explore
some of the range's most beautiful semi-wilderness. Not all trails are open
to bicyclists and equestrians.

The wildest and most spectacular hike in Big Basin is the 11.5-mile
Skyline-to-the-Sea/Berry Creek Falls/Sunset Trail loop to Berry Creek Falls.
Take an entire day and enjoy the waterfalls and remote old-growth redwood groves, stopping often to appreciate the wonderful variety of scenery. This is not an easy walk, and it has plenty of ups and downs to
encourage you to slow down and enjoy your ramble. The trail has a million
rewards any time of year, but most people like it best in the late winter and
early spring when everything is fresh and green and Berry Creek Falls is
an awesome torrent, plunging more than 65 feet over mossy and fern-
adorned sandstone cliffs. Upstream are Silver, Golden, and Cascade Falls.

This loop wanders about as far from a paved road as you can get in
the Santa Cruz Mountains as it passes through all the park's ecological
communities. To find this route from park headquarters, take the Redwood
Trail past the campfire circle and across Opal Creek to the Skyline-to-the-
Sea Trail, which connects with the Berry Creek and Sunset trails. Allow at
least 6 hours to walk this trail. You can make a 2-day trip out of this route

by camping at Sunset Trailcamp. it is about 5.5 miles from park headquarters.

For a longer and more strenuous alternative, take the Hihn Hammond dirt road trail up Mount McAbee and turn right on the Howard King Trail. This route has some great views, especially of the Waddell Creek canyon (Rancho del Oso) and the ocean to the southwest.

The trail to Pine Mountain and Buzzards Roost is a strenuous but scenic 5-mile round trip climb of more than 1,000 feet from park headquarters. The climb to the 2,208-foot summit of Buzzards Roost and Pine Mountain is a journey above the redwoods to an ecological island of madrone, knobcone pine, and chaparral. The weathered sandstone summit of Buzzards Roost offers the best views of the two peaks. You can see all the way from the Skyline Ridge to the ocean. A more primitive, unmaintained path goes to the top of Pine Mountain. To take this route from park headquarters, take the Redwood Trail toward the Skyline-to-the-Sea Trail across Opal Creek. Then follow the trail south along Opal Creek to the Hihn Hammond Road. Cross the creek at the bridge and turn right on the Pine Mountain Trail. Be sure to bring water, as there is none available along the way.

The knobcone pine is well suited for these dry and rocky ridgetops. It is found mostly in dry areas with poor soil, where most other trees do

(ABOVE)
Horse and rider on the Westridge Trail.

(RIGHT)
This article from the March 3, 1935 San Francisco Chronicle explains why bears weren't released into Big Basin during the 1930's.

(LEFT)
Berry Creek Falls is at its best in late winter and early spring.

BEARS BANNED IN BIG BASIN

SANTA CRUZ, March 2-- In the interest of nudists and huckleberry pie the San Lorenzo Chamber of Commerce has dropped its plan to import bears into the Big Basin State Park.

At first the San Lorenzo folk thought it would bring fame to the local park to cultivate bears after the manner of Yosemite valley.

"Then we got to thinking," said Frank Pimentel. "Last summer they went nudist in portions of the park, and I for one wouldn't want 'em any more bear. More important still, the directors of the San Lorenzo Chamber of Commerce are mighty fond of huckleberry pie. Now it's a cinch none of our wives are going to go out and gather huckleberries if there's danger of their meeting up with a bear.

There will be no bears."

Andrew P. Hill- Conservationist

Big Basin Redwoods State Park has the largest and grandest old-growth redwood forest anywhere in the Bay Area. We owe an immense debt of gratitude to one man, Andrew P. Hill, for the existence of this amazing park.

Born in 1853, Hill came to California at the age of 14 and learned portrait painting at the California School of Design. He opened a portrait studio in San Jose, and added photography to supplement his income.

In 1899 Hill was commissioned by a London newspaper to photograph giant redwood trees. By this time the logging boom left few large old-growth redwoods in the Bay Area. The owner of the Big Trees Grove near Felton (now part of Henry Cowell Redwoods State Park) kicked Hill off his property when he attempted to photograph the trees. On his train ride back to San Jose, Hill dedicated himself to starting a movement to establish a public redwood park. He wrote that: *"the thought flashed through my mind that these trees, because of their size and antiquity, were among the natural wonders of the world and should be saved for posterity."*

When Andrew heard rumors of a large isolated forest of ancient redwoods in the Big Basin area, he organized an expedition into the remote area. All the participants were amazed by what they saw. Hill photographed the trees, and they returned to launch a campaign to create California's first state park.

Hill established the Sempervirens Club to arouse interest in the park. He travelled back and forth between San Jose and Sacramento to successfully lobby the governor and legislature for the $250,000 needed to buy the property.

Even after the park was established in 1902 Hill's work was not finished. He returned to Sacramento years later to fend off efforts to open the park to logging. He was instrumental in passing legislation to build Highway 236 into the park so that the public could enjoy and protect this new wonderland. The Sempervirens Fund continues his work today by purchasing new land for the park.

poorly. This hardy pine needs the direct sunlight of peaks and ridges and is dependent on fire to remove competing vegetation and for generating sufficient heat to release seeds from the cones. You will see knobcone pines on the Sunset Trail and the Hihn Hammond Road.

There is a strenuous one-day hike, or a moderate 2-day backpacking trip on a scenic and diverse 14-mile loop through the park's northern mountains. From park headquarters walk the Skyline-to-the-Sea Trail north and east to the Basin Trail, which climbs north and west to the Lane Trailcamp. This is a spectacular place to spend a night, with a remote wilderness feel to it. Call park headquarters for reservations. To complete the loop follow the ridge westward to the Middle Ridge Trail, which is actually a dirt road that goes southbound on the ridge. Take Sunset Trail east to the Skyline-to-the-Sea Trail and back to park headquarters. This route passes through all the park's ecological zones and involves a climb of more than 1,300 feet. Don't forget to bring drinking water, especially in warm weather.

You can travel north on the Basin Trail on a 1.5-mile easement through private lumber company land and on to Pescadero Creek County Park, and then to Sam McDonald County Park, and Portola State Park.

If that one is too tough, you might want to go to the other extreme and take the easiest trail in the park. Just west of the parking lot near park headquarters begins the .6 mile Redwood Trail loop, an easy self-guiding nature trail by some of the largest trees in the park. It makes an easy, and nearly level, stroll past the Father of the Forest and the Mother of the Forest, which is probably the tallest tree in the Bay Area.

The Sequoia Trail takes a gentle 1.8-mile walk to 25-foot Sempervirens Falls. Inquire at park headquarters about ranger guided walks.

Big Basin has a seasonal grocery store and a nature museum. Car camping may be reserved by calling (800)444-7275 or logging on to www.reserveamerica.com. There are 146 family campsites, each with a picnic table and fire ring. There are 4 group camps for groups up to 100. For more information about trailcamp reservations call (831)338-8861. This park has the only tent cabins in the Bay Area. Each includes a wood stove, bed, and table. Restrooms with coin showers are nearby. Call (800)874-8368 to make reservations. For other information call (831)338-8860 (www.parks.ca.gov).

RANCHO DEL OSO

The southern part of Big Basin Redwoods State Park stretches all the way to the ocean, encompassing the broad valley of Waddell Creek. Called Rancho Del Oso (Spanish for "Ranch of the Bear"), this area offers a beautiful stream, forests of second-growth redwood, Douglas fir, and Monterey pine, as well as meadows and a freshwater marsh.

Equestrians with horse trailers and backpackers with reservations may drive to the trailhead near the ranger office. All others use the beach parking lot.

There are 3 easily accessible trail camps in this valley. Leave your car

Equestrian Access:

Equestrians may ride their horses on the following routes: Rogers Road, Lane Sunset Rim Trail, Middle Ridge Road, Gazos Creek Road, Johansen Road, Hihn Hammond Road, McCrary Ridge Trail, Canyon Road, and the "Skyline-to-the-Sea" Trail south of Berry Creek.

Bicycle Access:

Bicycles are allowed on paved and dirt roads, and prohibited on foot trails. They are allowed on the following routes: Rogers Road, Gazos Creek Road, Middle Ridge Road, Johansen Road, Chalks Road, Canyon Road, Anderson Landing Road, Hihn Hammond Road, Pine Mountain Road, and the "Skyline-to-the-Sea" Trail south of Berry Creek.

1 mile

Johansen Road

Gazos Creek Road

Canyon Road

Whitehouse Road

West Sunset Trail Camp

Sunset Trail

Trail

Timms Creek Trail

Suns

Golden Falls

Silver Falls

Berry Creek Falls Trail

Henry Creek

Henry Creek Trail

Berry Creek

Berry Creek Falls

West Waddell Creek

Skyline to the Sea Trail

Kell

Howard King Trail

Chalks Road

Chalks Road

Chalk Mtn. Overlook 2250

Westridge Trail

Ano Nuevo Creek

Skyline to the Sea Trail

Mt. Mc Overl 1730

Hi

McCrary Ridge Trail

SEE SEPARATE MAP FOR SOUTHERN PART OF PARK

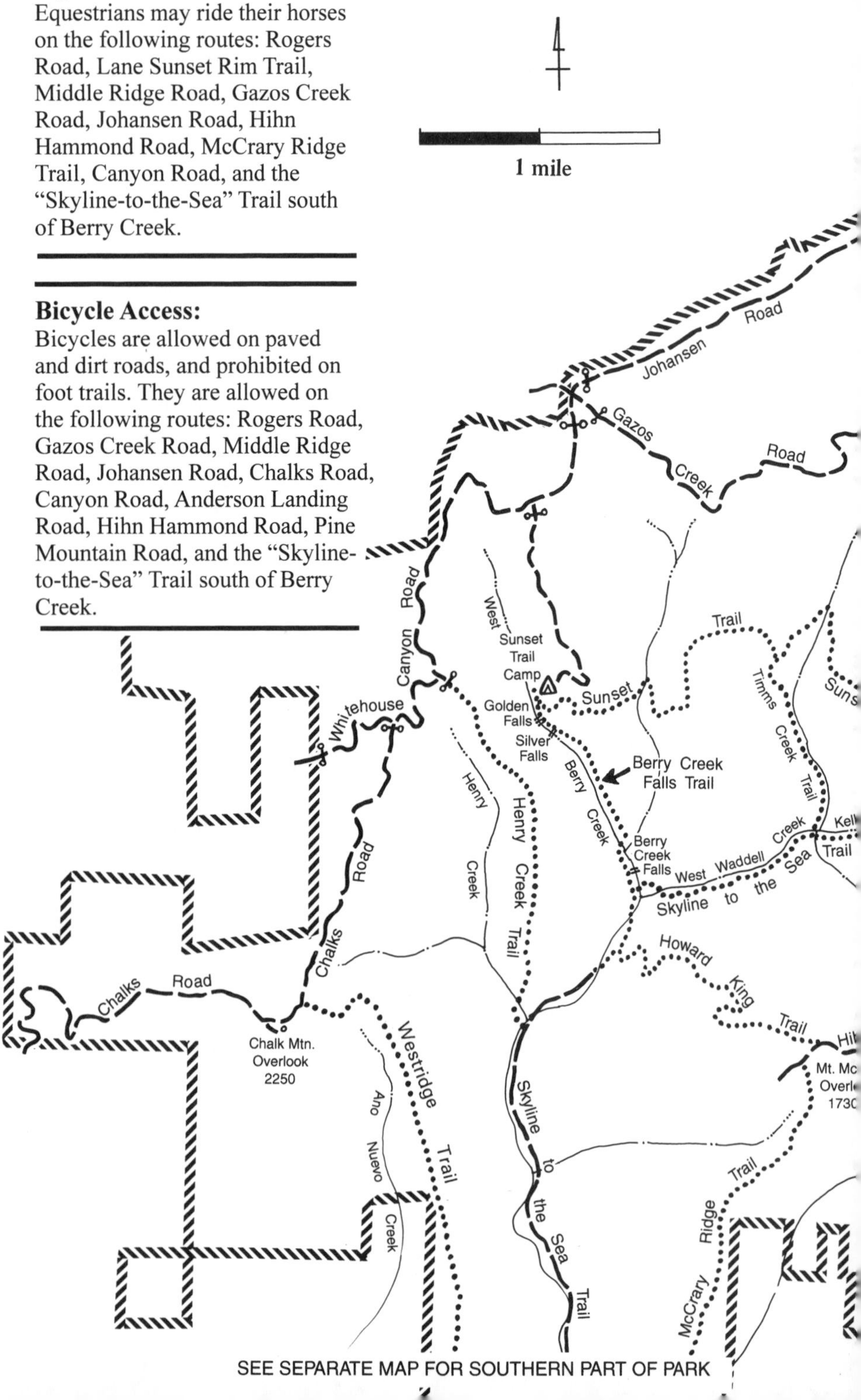

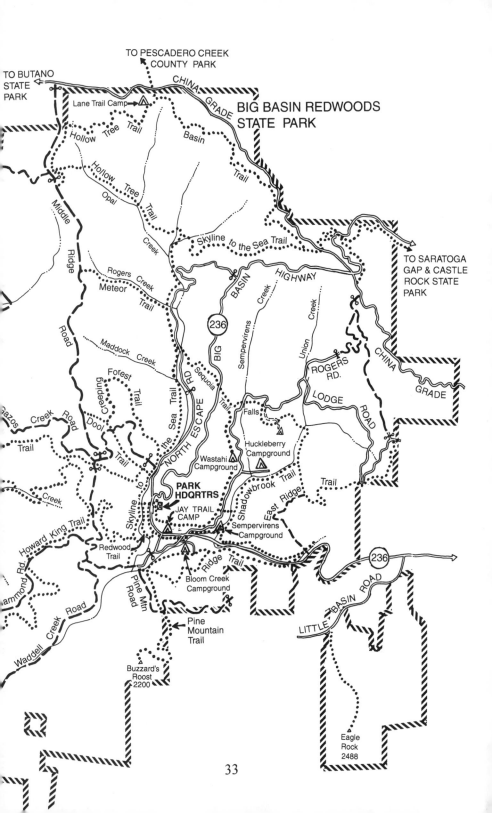

TO PESCADERO CREEK COUNTY PARK

TO BUTANO STATE PARK

CHINA GRADE

Lane Trail Camp

BIG BASIN REDWOODS STATE PARK

Hollow Tree Trail

Basin Trail

Hollow Tree

Opal

Creek

Middle

Ridge

Rogers Creek

Meteor Trail

Road

Maddock Creek

Skyline to the Sea Trail

BIG BASIN HIGHWAY

236

Sempervirens Creek

Union Creek

TO SARATOGA GAP & CASTLE ROCK STATE PARK

ROGERS RD.

CHINA GRADE

LODGE

BIG

Sequoia Trail

ROAD

Forest Trail

Creeping

Dool

Trail

Gazos Creek Road

Trail

Creek

NORTH ESCAPE RD.

to the Sea Trail

Falls

Huckleberry Campground

Wastahi Campground

PARK HDQRTRS

JAY TRAIL CAMP

Shadowbrook Trail

East Ridge Trail

Trail

Howard King Trail

Hammond Rd.

Skyline to

Redwood Trail

Sempervirens Campground

236

Pine Mtn Road

Bloom Creek Campground

Ridge Trail

LITTLE BASIN ROAD

Waddell Creek Road

Pine Mountain Trail

Buzzard's Roost 2200

Eagle Rock 2488

TO
CHALKS ROAD   TO
PARK HEADQUARTERS   TO
HIHN HAMMOND ROAD

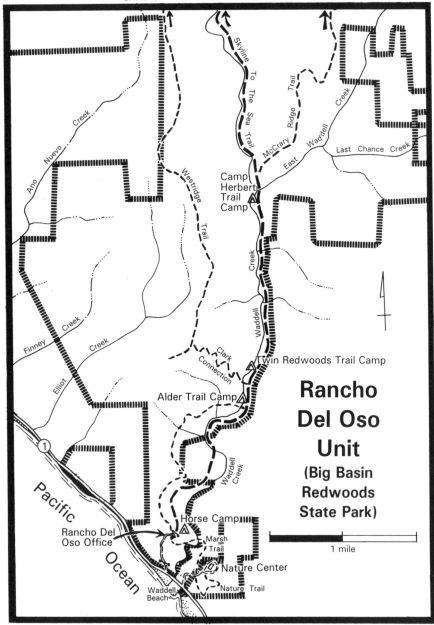

**Rancho
Del Oso
Unit**
(Big Basin
Redwoods
State Park)

1 mile

at the ranger office parking lot and backpack in about 1.2 miles to Alder Camp, 1.5 miles to Twin Redwoods Camp, and 2.7 miles to Camp Herbert. Sunset Camp is 6.5 miles. Make trailcamp reservations by calling park headquarters at (831)338-8861 at least 2 weeks in advance for summer weekend use. Ground fires are prohibited. Equestrians can reserve the Horse Camp at Rancho Del Oso by calling (831)425-1218.

For travelers on the Skyline-to-the-Sea Trail from Big Basin park head-quarters, the distance to Camp Herbert is 7.5 miles, Twin Redwoods is 9 miles, Alder Camp is 9.8 miles, and Highway 1 is about 11 miles.

Just south of Waddell Creek on Highway 1 a narrow road leads to the Rancho del Oso Nature and History Center, where you can see natural and human history exhibits and join guided walks. The center is managed by the non-profit Waddell Creek Association in cooperation with the state park system. There is an adjacent self-guided nature trail. The center is open Saturdays and Sundays 1-4 pm. Guided nature walks are on Sundays at 1 pm. For information call (831)427-2288; www.santacruzstateparks.org.

Waddell Creek was named for lumber mill owner William Waddell, who was killed in this valley by a grizzly bear in 1875.

SPECIAL SECTION

The Last Grizzly

Grizzly bears were once common in the Santa Cruz Mountains, feast-ing on berries and acorns, digging for roots, and gathering along streams to fish during the annual runs of salmon and steelhead. They were seen along the coast feasting on dead whales that washed ashore. California probably had more grizzlies than anywhere else.

When the Spanish grazed cattle over their vast ranchos in the late eighteenth and early nineteenth centuries the opportunistic bears ac-quired a taste for beef. The gold rush of 1850's, however, began a process that resulted in the extinction of the California grizzly. Gold, timber, and land brought hordes of immigrants to the Bay Area, including loggers and ranchers who claimed the Santa Cruz Mountains for their commer-cial value, leaving dwindling habitat for the great bears. Grizzlies were shot on sight into the 1880's, when the last one was killed.

Around Bonny Doon Mountain lived an old sow bear who had ac-quired a taste for pork. Late one night in November 1885 she made the mistake of carrying off a 300-pound hog that rancher Orrin Blodgett had been fattening for market. When Orrin found the remains that the bear had stashed away for later consumption, he readied his rifle and waited. Several nights passed before the bear returned; and when she did, the rancher met up with her unexpectedly, with barely time to raise his muzzle-loaded rifle and fire. The dead bear weighed in at 642 pounds; the last grizzly ever reported in the Santa Cruz Mountains.

Coast Redwoods
(The "Ever-living" Sequoias)

When you enter a redwood grove you will see an environment similar to one inhabited tens of millions of years ago by dinosaurs.

Close relatives of today's redwoods are found in the fossil record over much of the northern hemisphere dating back to the Jurassic period more than 150 million years ago. As the climate changed these trees retreated to a narrow strip along the Northern California coast where the climate is both mild and moist.

The scientific name for our coast redwoods is Sequoia Sempervirens, the "ever-living" Sequoia. Ever-living may seem like an overstatement until you consider the facts.

The maximum age of individual redwood trees is more that 2,000 years; but in some ways they are truly ever-living. Though these trees produce seeds, the most common means of reproduction is by sprouting new shoots

Forest debris rolls downhill and accumulates against the uphill side of the tree. The burning debris produces flames hot enough to penetrate the bark. A succession of fires can hollow out a tree.

Redwoods have amazing re-generative powers. They can survive severe fire scars, sprout from a stump after being cut down, and routinely reproduce by sprouting from a parent tree.

from the base of existing trees. These shoots are clones, not offspring of the parent tree; and they often continue to use the root system of the parent tree long after it has fallen and disintigrated. Could it be that these sprouts, which can grow into full-size trees, are the same plant as the parent tree? If this is true, and if the parent tree sprouted from an older tree which sprouted from a still older tree, then redwoods may be as close to immortal as any living thing on this planet.

Though sprouting is the most common form of reproduction, these trees also produce cones, the smallest produced by any evergreen. It is ironic that the world's tallest trees can grow from seeds so small that it takes 120,000 to make one pound.

The redwood's ability to survive is enhanced by a thick, fibrous, and fire-resistant bark containing tanin, which is a natural fungicide and insec-ticide.

When you visit an old-growth redwood grove you will notice that virtually every large tree has fire scars, indicating that fire is a natural and beneficial part of redwood ecology. It has been proposed, however, that because the native people intentionally set fire as a way of promoting vegetation growth and hunting opportunities, most of these fire scars could be considered archaeological artifacts. Occasionally flames are hot enough to breach the thick bark, especially on the tree's uphill side where forest debris accumulates as it rolls downhill. As this happens, a cavity may be burned into the heartwood that might become quite large over a period of centuries with a succession of fires. But even hollowed trees, with only thin connections of living tissue, still bear green foliage testi-mony to their amazing will to survive.

I have seen redwoods that have been hollowed out by fire and then chopped down; yet they have sprouted anew and are thriving. Redwoods are one of the few connifers with the ability to sprout from a stump. More than any other tree they deserve their title as the "ever-living" sequoia.

Bonny Doon Ecological Preserve

TO GET THERE... from Highway 1 take Bonny Doon Road to Pine Flat Road and turn right on Martin Road. Park at the parking lot next to the Bonny Doon Volunteers fire station on Martin Road.

This small area of strange sandstone formations and sandy soil is one of the most unique and interesting natural places in California.

It supports an extraordinary variety of unusual life, including the endangered Santa Cruz cypress tree, which survives in only a few groves, and the endangered Santa Cruz wallflower. The silver-leaved manzanita and Rattan's mimulus grow nowhere else in the world. You will also find a forest of stately ponderosa pine, a tree that is rarely seen in the coastal ranges, but common in the middle altitudes of the Sierra Nevada. It grows in sandy soil because there is less competition with other trees.

Also found here is the world's largest known nesting site for the colletes kincaidii, the solitary bee. Unlike other bees, which are highly social, the female solitary bee builds a single nest in the ground without help from other bees and then seals her eggs inside with a food supply. She then dies without encountering her offspring. This primitive bee is considered to be an evolutionary link between ancestral wasps and modern bees.

Other wildlife includes peregrine falcons, long-eared owls, Cooper hawks, Santa Cruz kangaroo rats, golden eagles, purple martins, and California tiger salamanders.

What makes this 545-acre preserve a mecca for uniquely Californian plants and animals is its Zayante sandstone outcroppings and sandy soil, which is unique to Santa Cruz County.

These sandstone formations have eroded into strangely beautiful shapes, different in form and texture from Castle Rock sandstone. From atop these outcrops are seen broad panoramas of mountains and ocean.

The preserve is open to the public for day use, though there is no formal trail system. There are some unmarked trails, but it is difficult to know when you have left the preserve boundary. Because of its unique natural qualities you are required to be careful not to disturb any natural features. As of this writing a self-guided nature trail is being developed.

Until a real trail system is established, the best way to see this reserve is with a docent-led walk. Guided nature walks are sometimes offered on the last Saturday of each month. For more information, call docent coordinator Valerie Haley at (831)425-1587. You can also call the California Department of Fish and Game at (831)649-2870.

SPECIAL SECTION
Santa Cruz Mountains Geology

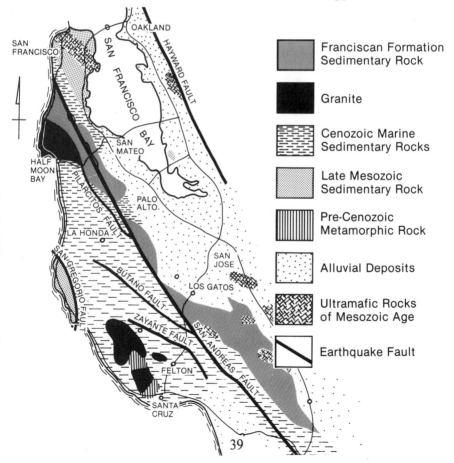

Burleigh Murray Ranch State Park

TO GET THERE... take Highway 1 just south from Half Moon Bay and turn east on Higgins Road. There is a parking lot on Higgins Road about 1.6 miles from Highway 1.

Mills Creek tumbles more than a thousand feet down the steep western slopes of Cahill Ridge and then meanders through a broad and gentle valley as it approaches Higgins Road.

This perennial stream flows through the middle of this 1,325-acre state park, which is just 2 watersheds north of redwood-forested Purisima Creek Open Space Preserve. But unlike Purisima, the hills and mountains of Burleigh Murray are covered mainly with coastal scrub and chaparral, as well as grasslands, riperian woodlands, and scattered groves of eucalyptus. Because this is ideal rabbit and rodent habitat, bobcats and coyote abound. Birds of prey are commonly seen, including a variety of hawks and owls.

As of this writing, the only real trail in this park is the ranch road along Mills Creek, which is a well-maintained dirt road between Higgins Road and the house. Past the old 1860's barn it more resembles a real trail, and beyond the water tanks it rapidly deteriorates, becoming progressively more difficult to follow through the brush. Someday this route may extend uphill all the way to Skyline Boulevard, where it will connect with the Bay Area Ridge Trail. There are several road cuts that have the potential of forming an excellent trail system once a route is cut through the brush.

The large wooden cow barn is an extraordinary example of a nineteenth century English bank barn. Constructed into a hillside in 1889, it is notable for both its size and its construction. Notice that the second floor is suspended from the ceiling by metal rods. This barn is being stabilized and restored, and will someday be the center of an agricultural history

exhibit. Barn owls nest there in the spring. Nearby, 2 graceful sandstone arch bridges span Mills Creek, built by the same Italian stone mason who constructed the retaining wall for the barn.

The park is named for a former owner, Burleigh Murray, who was born on the ranch in 1865.

For more information, call the state park office at (650)726-8820 (www.parks.ca.gov).

Equestrian Access:
Horses are allowed.

Bicycle Access:
Bicycles are allowed.

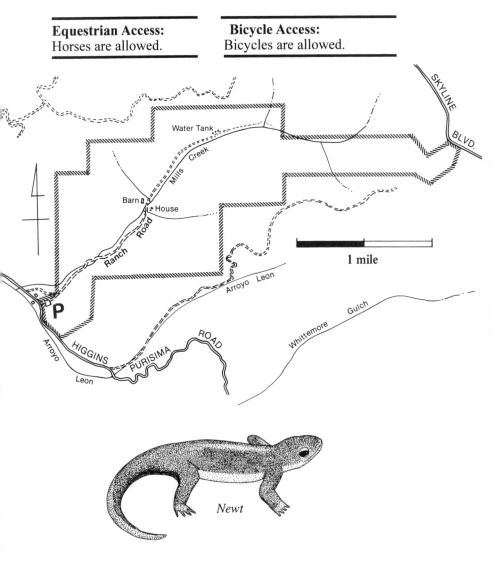

Newt

41

Butano State Park

TO GET THERE... From Highway 1 take Pescadero Road east for about 3 miles and turn right on Cloverdale Road. The park is about 5 miles south of the town of Pescadero.

It is hard to overstate the charm of this cool, green canyon park. It has a magical rainforest garden of redwoods and ferns cupped between steep ridges, which can be climbed for sweeping vistas.

The easiest walk in the park is on the Creek Trail, which can be started on the left side of the road just before reaching the campfire center. This trail is short and mostly level and follows the creek as it flows through a shady forest of second-growth redwoods. More strenuous paths take hikers to the Olmo Fire Trail on the south ridge and the Butano Fire Trail on the north ridge. The Ano Nuevo Trail offers a view of the ocean on clear days.

Serious backpackers may consider hiking to Butano Trailcamp, which can be reached by following several routes on both sides of the canyon. Bring your own water. It makes a good half-way stop on an 11-mile loop formed by combining the Butano Fire Road and the Olmo Fire Road. This loop, requiring some vigorous uphill, rims Butano canyon mostly on dirt roads. Be sure to make reservations in advance to use the trailcamp between May and October by calling park headquarters. A glimpse at the map will show that many variations on this loop are possible. By combining the Doe Ridge, Indian, Canyon, and Jackson Flats Trails you may enjoy a less strenuous version of this loop.

For a scenic 6.5-mile loop and an ideal moderate outing on the south side of the canyon, combine the Goat Hill Trail, the Doe Ridge Trail, and the Olmo Fire Trail. Atop the ridge is a cluster of knobcone pines and views of the Gazos Creek canyon to the south. The Ano Nuevo Trail can be added to this loop, but it is very steep.

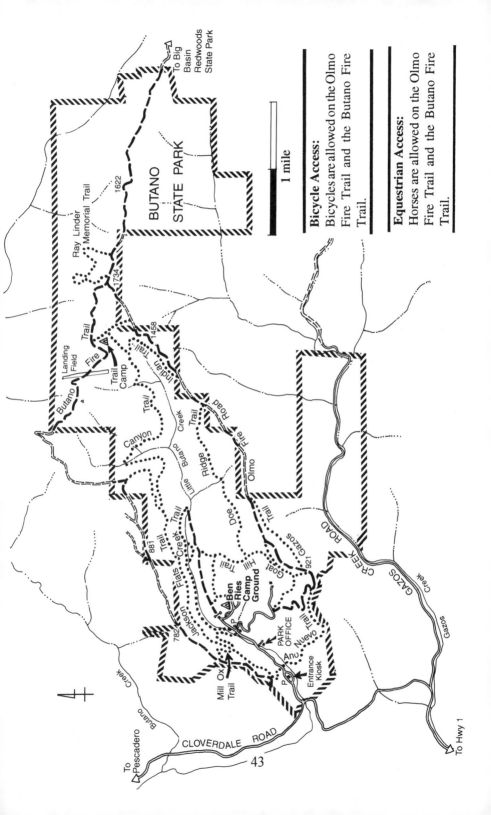

Bicycle Access: Bicycles are allowed on the Olmo Fire Trail and the Butano Fire Trail.

Equestrian Access: Horses are allowed on the Olmo Fire Trail and the Butano Fire Trail.

1 mile

BUTANO STATE PARK

To Big Basin Redwoods State Park

Ray Linder Memorial Trail

1622

1734

Landing Field

Butano Fire Trail

Trail Camp

1458

Indian Trail

Canyon Trail

Little Butano Creek

Ridge Trail

Olmo Fire Road

Doe Trail

881 Trail

Flats Trail

Jackson Creek Trail

782

Mill Ox Trail

Ben Ries Camp Ground

Goat Hill Trail

921

Gazos

Nuevo Trail

Ano

PARK OFFICE

Entrance Kiosk

GAZOS CREEK ROAD

Gazos Creek

To Hwy 1

CLOVERDALE ROAD

To Pescadero

Butano Creek

43

The Mill Ox Trail will take you to the Butano Fire Road, where you can turn right (east) and connect with the Jackson Flats Trail, which will take you back where you started. This is a 5-mile loop.

Mountain bikers aren't allowed on hiking trails, but they can gain access to the Butano Fire Trail just outside the park on Cloverdale Road. Ask a ranger for directions. There are many miles of mountain biking possibilities. You can take Butano Fire Road to the Olmo Fire Road or to the China Grade Road, to the east, which goes all the way to Big Basin Redwoods State Park.

A free, ranger-guided bicycle tour of the park is sometimes offered. Call park headquarters for information and reservations.

Butano (pronounced "Bute-Uh-No") is a 3,200-acre enclave of mostly second-growth redwoods in the coastal fog belt. One of its joys is the absence of crowds. Because of its out-of-the-way location you can often travel for hours without passing another person.

The Ohlone Indians usually avoided the shady redwood groves for both practical and religious reasons. They felt the same life force that many people still experience today, and were convinced that redwoods were haunted by powerful spirits. Also, because edible plants, for both man and deer, are rare in the redwood groves, the Indians found happier hunting grounds elsewhere.

The park campground has 38 campsites, each with a table and camp-fire ring and nearby restrooms. Twenty-one are drive-in sites, and the rest are walk-in. Because this is one of the most attractive and popular camp-grounds in the Santa Cruz Mountains, reservations are advised. Reserva-tions may be made through Reserve America at (800)444-7275 (www.reserveamerica.com) for camping from from May 18 through Labor Day weekend.

For more park information call park headquarters at (650)879-2040.

SPECIAL SECTION
Walk for Health

Our bodies are perfectly designed for walking. There is no other form of excercise that is safer and more beneficial. Vigorous walking maintains the heart muscle in healthy tone, lowers blood presure, con-trols weight, reduces tension, headaches, and backaches. It benefits the heart and lungs as much as jogging, but without orthopedic problems.

Because walking is a weight-bearing excercise, it helps prevent bond-thinning and helps to build bone mass.

A Veterans Administration study of elderly people found that a regu-lar walking program actually resulted in improved memory, vision, and reasoning powers. It also reduces the risk of developing Alzheimer's disease later in life.

Doctors recommend taking a post-walk stroll for a few minutes after a vigorous outing to give the heart a chance to slow down gradually.

Calero County Park

TO GET THERE. . . from Highway 101 southbound take Bernal Road west, Santa Teresa Boulevard south, and Bailey Avenue west. Northbound take Cochrane Road in Morgan Hill west, north on Monterey Highway, and west on Bailey Road

This park has two distinct personalities. The reservoir itself is noisy with urban refugees and their power craft, making this the last place you might expect to find a little quiet and solitude.

A quick study of the map, however, reveals that most of this 3,466-acre park lies south of the reservoir and is accessible by 12 miles of exceptionally well-maintained trails, most of which are old ranch roads.

Hikers and equestrians can enter this backcountry part of the park by heading south on McKean Road, less than a mile from Bailey Road, and turning right into the Calero Park entrance. Here you will find a ranger station/visitors center, stables, parking lot, and an equestrian staging area. For horse rental call (408)268-2567.

The trails in this park are for hikers and equestrians only. No bicycles are allowed.

Calero Park has an extraordinary variety and display of California oaks. White, blue, black, and coast live oaks grow in abundance, and in most of the park they grow in an open grassy savanna, with lots of space between the trees. Sweeping views of Calero Reservoir to the north, the

Equestrian Access:
Horses are allowed on all trails.

Bicycle Access:
Bicycles are not permitted.

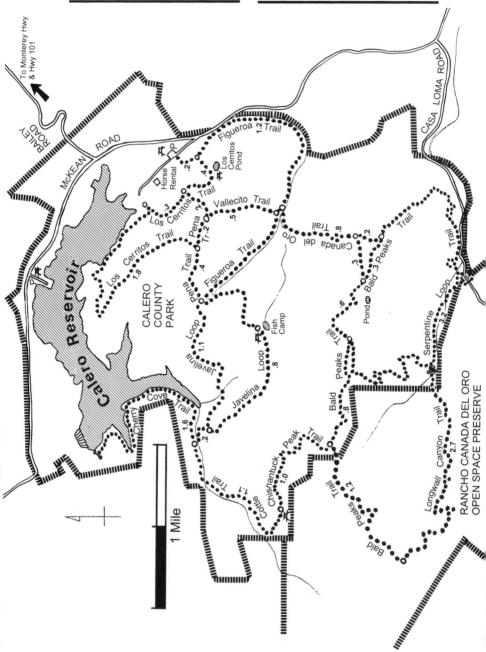

46

Santa Clara Valley to the east, and Mount Umunhum and Loma Prieta to the west, will reward your efforts.

Located in the dry eastern foothills of the Santa Cruz Mountains, the character of this park changes dramatically between the cool and moist winters and the hot and dry summers. Between early March and mid-May the park is green and the wildflowers are spectacular.

Just south of this park is 1,485-acre Rancho Canada Del Oro Open Space Preserve, which is owned and managed by the Santa Clara County Open Space Authority. Because this mountainous property can only be accessed by crossing through Calero County Park, it adds 3.8 miles of additional trails to the Calero trail system. They combine to form a total of 4,951 acres and 22.4 miles of trails.

TRAIL OPTION 1: For a 6.1-mile figure 8 route with views of the reservoir, take the Los Cerritos Trail uphill to the Pena Trail and head west to include the Javelina Loop and then take the Figueroa Trail back.

TRAIL OPTION 2: For a shortened, 3.5-mile version of the above route, just leave off the Javelina Loop.

TRAIL OPTION 3: For the ultimate 11.1-mile backcountry tour, which includes some steep climbs and an 800-foot elevation range, head south on the Vallecito and Canada del Oro Trails, turn left on the Bald Peaks Trail, loop south and to the west and then north on the Serpentine Loop Trail, turn west on the Bald Peaks Trail, north on the Chisnantuck Peak and Cottle Trails, and then east on the Javelina Loop and Pena Trails.

TRAIL OPTION 4: You can add 2.3 miles to Option 3 by adding the Longwall Canyon and Bald Peaks Trails in the Rancho Canada De Oro Open Space Preserve.

Be aware that poison oak is common here, but easily avoided by staying on the trails. Also keep in mind that rattlesnakes are active in warm weather. Because of mercury in the reservoir, fish are unsafe to eat.

This park is open from 8 a.m. until half an hour past sunset. For more information, call park headquarters at (408)355-2201 (www.parkhere.org).

Wandering Man

By Tom Taber with help from Marita & Joan Taber.

I wrote this song while hiking up Montara Mountain in February 2002.

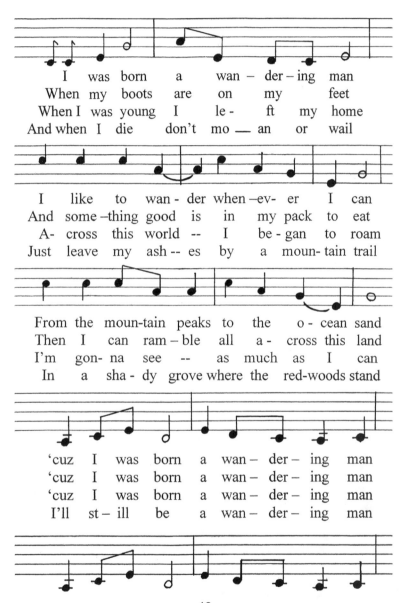

I was born a wan – der – ing man
When my boots are on my feet
When I was young I le - ft my home
And when I die don't mo — an or wail

I like to wan - der when –ev- er I can
And some –thing good is in my pack to eat
A- cross this world -- I be - gan to roam
Just leave my ash -- es by a moun- tain trail

From the moun-tain peaks to the o - cean sand
Then I can ram – ble all a - cross this land
I'm gon- na see -- as much as I can
In a sha - dy grove where the red-woods stand

'cuz I was born a wan – der – ing man
'cuz I was born a wan – der – ing man
'cuz I was born a wan – der – ing man
I'll st – ill be a wan – der – ing man

Castle Rock State Park

TO GET THERE. . . take Skyline Boulevard about 2.5 miles south from its intersection with Highway 9 (Saratoga Gap).

Spectacular views in all directions, rock outcroppings ideal for climbing, shallow caves, and beautiful groves of oak, madrone, and Douglas fir make this one of my favorite parks.

Castle Rock itself is one of the Bay Area's most popular climbing rocks because of its challenging overhangs and impressive posture on the crest of the range. You can see the ocean and San Francisco Bay from the top. This 80-foot Chico sandstone outcropping, however, is sometimes so congested that climbers must wait their turn to rappel off the summit.

This park covers 4,900 acres and has more than 30 miles of excellent trails. Hiking, picnicking, rock climbing, and backpacking are favorite activities here. To reach some of the outlying areas, take the Ridge Trail heading uphill (north) from Saratoga Gap Trail east of the waterfall. Goat Rock, with its formidable south face for climbers, is easily ascended on the uphill side by hikers who marvel at the extraordinary views of Monterey Bay, the Monterey Peninsula, and the Santa Lucia Mountains 80 miles to the south. Continue west on the Ridge Trail for more views and lesser known rocks, and on to Castle Rock Camp.

The Travertine Springs Trail offers a short cut to the Skyline to the Sea Trail and connects the eastern and western parts of the park. It takes a forested route, mainly through Douglas fir, bay, oak, and madrone woods.

What is Tafoni?

The shallow caves and honeycomb texture (called "tafoni") in the sandstone outcroppings of the Santa Cruz Mountains are the result of what geologists call "cavernous weathering", a phenomenon that occurs only in a few places in the world. First, there has to be outcroppings of sandstone cemented together with calcium carbonate in the form of mineral calcite. Next, the extent of cementation has to be variable, so that some parts of the rock are harder than others. And most importantly, this strange weathering only happens where there is a moderately dry climate with a prolonged dry season.

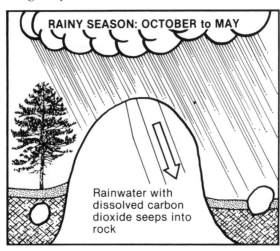

RAINY SEASON: OCTOBER to MAY

Rainwater with dissolved carbon dioxide seeps into rock

Castle Rock is less than half a mile south of the parking lot. The park's main trail, the Saratoga Gap Trail, begins at the opposite end of the parking lot from Skyline and continues through most of the park. About a mile from the parking lot is l00-foot Castle Rock Falls, which can be viewed from an observation platform.

A walk to Castle Rock Camp, about 2.6 miles from the parking lot is a moderate 6.4- mile loop via the Ridge and Saratoga Gap trails. A shorter version of this loop can be made by taking the connecting trail between these two routes.

The Saratoga Gap Trail is on the west slope of the ridge, offering a wonderful chance to see the role of topography on mountain ecology. Compare the deep green of the moist evergreen valleys with the drought-resistant vegetation of the dry and rocky west and south facing ridgetops. Some of the most beautiful oak, madrone, and chaparral in the Santa Cruz Mountains are in this park.

From the trailcamp, the Saratoga Gap Trail heads north to Saratoga Gap, at the intersection of Highway 9 and Skyline Boulevard; or you can take the Travertine Springs Trail to the Skyline-to-the-Sea Trail. Much of

---

Heavy winter rains seep into the sandstone along cracks and planes of soft rock. The rainwater contains carbon dioxide from the air, which dissolves the calcium carbonate that holds the sandstone grains together. The dry season allows the rock to dry out, and the calcium carbonate is then drawn to the surface by the capillary action of water. As the water evaporates, the calcium carbonate is deposited within a few feet of the surface to form a hard shield that resists erosion. The interior of the rock, however, is left without much cement and easily crumbles away and is removed by water, wind, and animal activity, including people.

Look for spheres of hard rock in the sandstone. These concretions are masses of complete rather than partial cementation. The reddish-brown color is the result of small amounts of iron oxide.

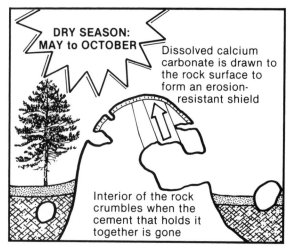

DRY SEASON: MAY to OCTOBER

Dissolved calcium carbonate is drawn to the rock surface to form an erosion-resistant shield

Interior of the rock crumbles when the cement that holds it together is gone

Equestrian Access:
Horses are allowed access to the trail camp via the Saratoga Gap Trail from Saratoga Gap and via the Service Road Trail. Horses are also allowed on the Toll Road part of the "Skyline-to-the-Sea" Trail which goes through the western part of the park.

Bicycle Access:
Bicycles are allowed on the Service Road Trail to the trail camp.

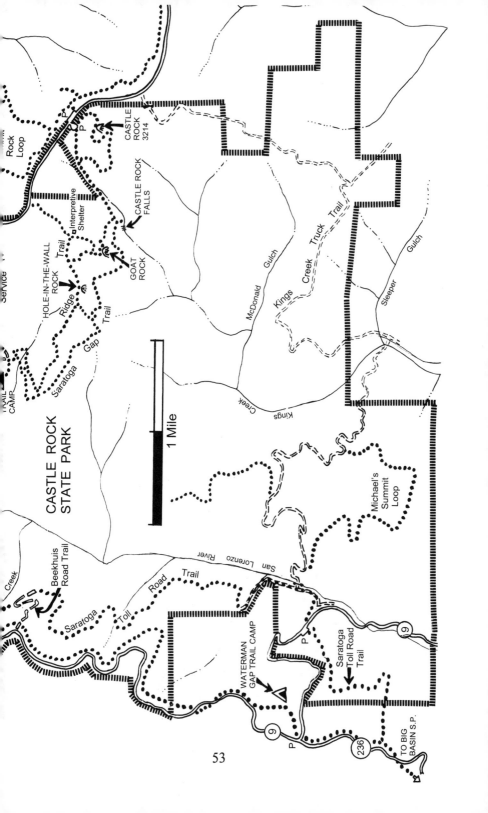

CASTLE ROCK
STATE PARK

CASTLE ROCK 3214

CASTLE ROCK FALLS

Interpretive Shelter

HOLE-IN-THE-WALL ROCK

GOAT ROCK

Trail

Ridge

Saratoga Gap Trail

TRAIL CAMP

Rock Loop

Service

McDonald Gulch

Kings Creek Truck Trail

Sleeper Gulch

Kings Creek

1 Mile

Michael's Summit Loop

Beekhuis Road Trail

Creek

Saratoga Toll Road Trail

San Lorenzo River

WATERMAN GAP TRAIL CAMP

Saratoga Toll Road Trail

P

P

9

9

236

TO BIG BASIN S.P.

53

the park was acquired with the help of the Sempervirens Fund. With its grassy promontories and groves of Douglas fir, madrone, and oak, and plenty of pleasing vistas, the Summit Meadows property may be explored by trail from Highway 9 west of Skyline Boulevard.

In 2004 the 1,340-acre San Lorenzo River property was added to the park. Purchased with donations to the Sempervirens Fund, this property expands Castle Rock State Park to the south, near the intersection of Highways 9 and 236. It consists mostly of second-growth redwoods, with areas of chaparral, madrone, oak, Douglas fir, and knobcone pine. At this time there is only one trail, the Michael's Summit Trail loop, which is about 5 miles . The route is steep in places and there isn't much of a view from the summit. It can be reached via the Saratoga Toll Road Trail, which is an alternative route for the Skyline-to-the-Sea Trail. Be aware that there is only trailhead parking for a few cars along Highway 9.

Castle Rock State Park has an exceptional abundance and variety of spring wildflowers. The parking lot area is a good place to look for the exotically beautiful spotted coral root, a member of the orchid family that has no green, chlorophyll-producing parts. Instead, it absorbs energy from decaying organic material in the soil. Castle Rock's grasslands explode with vibrant displays of mule ear, buttercup, baby blue eyes, larkspur, Douglas iris, and many others. Because it is one of the highest ridges in the Santa Cruz Mountains, you can continue to enjoy native flowers here long after they have wilted in lower parks.

Because this park can get hot and dry be sure to carry water. Sturdy footwear will be useful on the rocky sections of trail.

The park's trailcamp has 23 sites, available on a first-come, first-served basis, or by calling (831)338-6132 for reservations. There is a camping fee; and because there is an extra charge for making reservations, it's a good idea to ask if the trailcamp is likely to be full before reserving a site. Water is available. There is also an inclement weather shelter with a fireplace.

For more information, call park headquarters at (831)338-8860 (www.parks.ca.gov).

Chitactac Adams Heritage County Park

TO GET THERE... From Highway 101 take the Tennant Avenue exit in Morgan Hill and go west. Turn left on Monterey Highway and go about half a mile to Watsonville Road. Turn right on Watsonville Road and travel about 5.5 miles to the park, which is at the intersection of Watsonville Road and Burchell Road.

At only 4 acres, this is by far the smallest park in this book. Chitactac Adams Heritage County Park, on the banks of Uvas Creek, has a short paved loop trail with views of the creek, some interesting rock outcroppings, and artifacts of ancient Ohlone Indian life.

The self-guided interpretive walk will take you to 8 stations with interpretive panels. You will see acorn mortar stones and rare petroglyphs carved in a sandstone rock in the creek. What these concentric circle markings mean is not known. Your guess is as good as anybody's. The interpretive shelter contains 7 additional interpretive panels and a petroglyph.

Radio carbon dating has revealed that this site was inhabited by Mutson Ohlone for over 3,000 years. Chitactac was the village name.

This park is open from 8:00 am until sunset all year. Picnic tables, restrooms, and water are available. You can find out about staff and docent interpretive walks by calling (408) 323-0107 (www.parkhere.org).

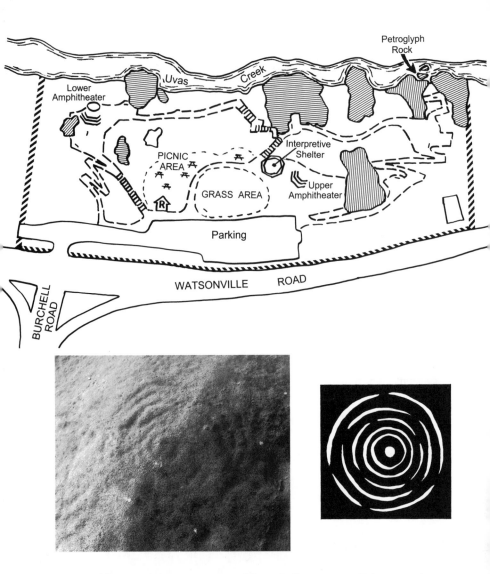

In addition to mortar stones, used for grinding acorns, Chitactac Adams also has several ancient Ohlone cup-and-ring petroglyphs. Possibly several thousand years old, these faint, weathered sandstone carvings consist of concentric circles with a center depression. Their meaning is a mystery. However, similar stone symbols in other parts of the world are associated with puberty rites, fertility, rain making, fishing, and hunting.

Coal Creek Open Space Preserve

TO GET THERE... Park at the Vista Point on Skyline Boulevard 1.2 miles north of Page Mill Road and walk down the Clouds Rest Trail that intersects Skyline just to the north. Another access is at the intersection of Skyline and Crazy Pete's Road, 1.8 miles north of Page Mill Road. It can also be reached from the end of Alpine Road in Portola Valley.

This 493-acre preserve slopes eastward from Skyline Boulevard to form a pleasant place to ramble on about 4 miles of trails, most of which are old ranch roads.

A liesurely 2.6-mile loop can be taken from the Vista Point on Skyline Boulevard via the Clouds Rest and Meadow Trails to Alpine Road to the northeast. Head north (downhill) on Alpine Road about .5 miles to an unnamed trail on the left side of the road. Take this trail .5 miles uphill to the Clouds Rest Trail and then back to your starting point. The area is covered with oak, bay, some very large madrone, and grasslands. A clear day will reveal some great views of the south Bay Area. You can connect with Monte Bello Open Space Preserve by heading uphill on the Alpine Road Trail.

A scenic 1.6-mile ramble can be started from Skyline Boulevard where it intersects Crazy Pete's Road, which can be combined with the Valley View Trail to form a loop. A footbridge crosses a cascading series of small waterfalls that are delightful during the rainy season.

The preserve is named for Coal Creek, at the north end of the preserve, which was named for thin veins of coal seen in the nearby streambeds and roadcuts.

Dogs on leash are allowed on all trails.

See map in Russian Ridge Open Space Preserve chapter.

Edgwood County Park & Preserve

TO GET THERE... From Highway 280 take the Edgewood Road turnoff and park at the park and ride lot just east of the freeway. Then walk across Edgewood Road, go under the freeway, and connect with the trail into the park. You can also take this entrance by parking at the intersection of Edgewood Road and Canada Road. To reach the Old Stage Day Camp entrance, take Edgewood Road about 1.5 miles east of Highway 280. Here you will find restrooms and picnic facilities. You can also enter the park from a trailhead along Canada Road east of Highway 280. The east side entrance is near the intersection of Hillcrest Way and Sunset in the Emerald Hills area of Redwood City.

The serpentine grasslands of this 467-acre park are famous for some of the Bay Area's most spectacular displays of springtime wildflowers. Because of its easy access to the Redwood City area, this is a wonderful place for picnics and short walks that take only a few hours out of the day.

The serpentine grasslands, which make up about a third of the park, support 7 rare and endangered plant species and the endangered Bay Checkerspot Butterfly. Serpentine, associated with fault zones, provides poor soil for non-native plants because of its high toxicity and low water-holding capacity, but encourages the growth of indigenous flowering plants in great abundance. In April people come from all over the Bay Area to witness dazzling displays of goldfields, blue-eyed grass, tidy tips, larkspur, and buttercups, to name a few. Though most of the wildflower activity is in April, there are beautiful flowers such as shooting stars which blossom in February and March, and others, such as Mariposa lilly, which bloom in May and June.

Edgewood has about 8 miles of clearly-marked trails, popular with walkers and equestrians, that climb the forested 800-foot high ridge and circle the grassland perimeter. The Serpentine Loop Trail gently circles the central ridge, offering some of the best exhibitions of wildflowers. The map reveals many other loop options. There is also a trail connection along Edgewood Road to the Crystal Springs Trail and on to Huddart Park and from there to Wunderlich Park and Purisima Creek Open Space Preserve.

For more information, call (650)363-4020 (www.eparks.net).

Equestrian Access:
Horses are allowed on all trails, subject to closure when wet.

Bicycle Access:
Bicycles are not permitted.

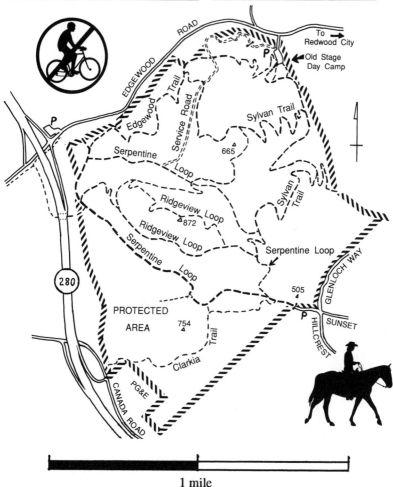

1 mile

El Corte de Madera Creek
Open Space Preserve

TO GET THERE... From Highway 92 take Skyline Boulevard south 8.6 miles to the Caltrans Rest Stop at Skegg's Point. It is 3.9 miles north of Woodside Road. From Skegg's Point walk north about .25 miles on Skyline Boulevard to a gate on the west side of the road where a sign marks the entrance to the preserve. There is another access .5 miles south of Skegg's Point, across from the Methuselah Tree. See map for other access points.

At the headwaters of El Corte de Madera Creek, this 2,821-acre preserve combines scenic ridgetops and ocean views with deep verdant valleys filled with second-growth redwood and Douglas fir.

This preserve's most popular attraction is a large sandstone formation with shallow caves and strange honeycomb depressions reminiscent of outcroppings at Castle Rock State Park, though it seems to be made of a softer and more fragile material. For this reason climbing is not allowed. The rock is 2.5 miles from the trailhead near Skegg's Point. You will find a description of how these features were formed in the Castle Rock chapter.

Some spectacular views are revealed along the ridgetop near the rock, especially at Vista Point, where low brush allows a good panorama to the south and west, stretching out to sea on a clear day. This is a fine place for a lunch break, wind and fog permitting.

From Skegg's Point you can take a scenic 3.8-mile loop by combining the Tafoni and El Corte de Madera Creek Trails. A short spur trail, for

---

The process of cavernous weathering (see Castle Rock chapter) results in rocks eroding from the inside out.

walkers only, will take you to and from the sandstone formation.

An extensive system of old logging roads, some quite steep and eroded, make this preserve a favorite with mountain bikers. The haphazard layout of some of these old roads has contributed to erosion of sediments into El Corte de Madera Creek, which is a tributary of San Gregorio Creek. In order to restore stealhead and coho salmon spawning

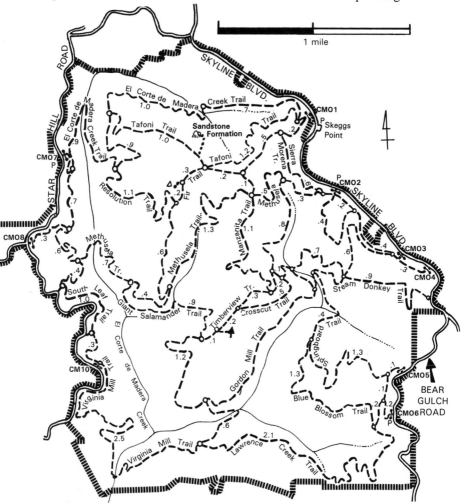

Equestrian Access:
Horses are allowed on all trails except the footpath to the sandstone formation.

Bicycle Access:
Bicycles are allowed on all trails except the footpath to the sandstone formation.

habitat, some of the trails are being realigned. Among these are parts of the Blue Blossom Trail, Crossover Trail, Gordon Mill Trail, Timberview Trail, and the Methuselah Trail.

This land was repeatedly logged between about 1850 and 1988. One of the few old-growth redwoods to survive is a fire-scarred 14-foot diameter giant at the end of a short spur trail off the Timberview Trail. Relics of the crash of a DC-6 can still be seen along the Resolution Trail. The rescue base was on the knoll off the Fir Trail. A look at the map will show that there are many loop options possible.

For more information, call the Midpeninsula Regional Open Space District at (650) 691-1200; www.openspace.org.

SPECIAL SECTION
How to live with Poison Oak

The bad news is that poison oak is common in the Santa Cruz Mountains. It grows as a shrub or a vine and its leaves often turn bright red in Fall. Plants commonly lose their leaves in the winter, making them hard to identify.

The good news is that poison oak is usually easy to identify, with its distinctive glossy lobed leaves arranged in groups of three, and the ill effects can normally only be acquired by physical contact with the plant. Their are two exceptions to this rule: 1) Inhaling poison oak smoke; 2) Touching objects, pets, or people who have rubbed against it.

Fortunately for the 75% of the population that is at least mildly sensitive to the urushiol oil found in this shrub, contact is easily avoided. The Santa Cruz Mountains have many broad trails which will allow you to keep a safe distance.

If you do accidentally rub against poison oak leaves or stems, a washing with soap and water will reduce the severity of the rash if done soon after contact.

El Sereno Open Space Preserve

TO GET THERE... from Highway 17 take the Bear Creek Road offramp and follow the signs to Montevina Road. Drive uphill on Montevina Road 3.5 miles west to to a locked gate where a turnout provides parking for a few cars.

This 1,083-acre preserve spans 2 miles of scenic ridgetop and steep canyons on the east side of the range. Chaparral covers most of the area, with oak, madrone, and bay scattered through the area, providing islands of shade for summer visitors. Beautiful groves of madrone and bay grow on the north and east sides of the ridge.

A good time to visit is in early spring, when chemise, ceanothus and other chaparral vegetation burst forth with new growth and are adorned with an abundance of flowers. Use your nose often here to appreciate the spicy aromas that offer a special appeal in this kind of plant community. You will see and hear lots of birds as they feed off the many seeds and berries that grow here.

Another advantage of chaparral is that it's low enough that it doesn't obstruct the commanding vistas of the Santa Cruz Mountains and the urbanized Santa Clara Valley. To the north you will see Black Mountain,

Bicycle Access:
Bicycles are allowed on all trails.

Equestrian Access:
Horses are allowed on all trails.

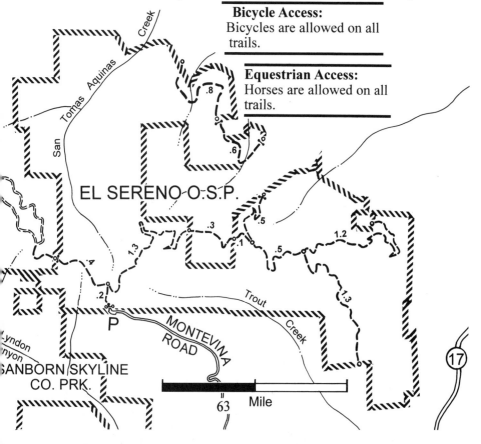

EL SERENO O.S.P.

San Tomas Aquinas Creek

Trout Creek

P

MONTEVINA ROAD

Lyndon Canyon

SANBORN/SKYLINE CO. PRK.

63

Mile

17

El Sereno Ridge drops off to the west into deep and straight Lyndon Canyon, which was formed by the San Andreas Fault.

Oakland, and even Mount Tamalpais, and to the southeast stands Mount Umunhum. The views are particularly stunning on those cold crystal clear days of winter when the smog and haze are gone from the valley below. The San Andreas Fault runs through deep and straight Lyndon Canyon just to the west.

Most of the trails through this preserve are dirt roads, and if you have ever tried cross-country hiking through chaparral you will appreciate why this is a good place for sticking to the established trails. Trail users should also be aware that this is one of the region's driest parks and water should be carried. Animals you might see here include woodrats, black-tail deer, rabbits, and coyotes.

El Sereno is open for day use only. For more information, call the Midpeninsula Regional Open Space District at (650)691-1200.

Mountain Charley's Law:

FOR EVERY UPHILL THERE IS AN EQUAL AND OPPOSITE DOWNHILL*

* and vice versa

Filoli Estate

TO GET THERE... from Highway 280 in Woodside, take Edgewood Road west and turn right on Canada Road.

The magnificent Georgian-style mansion and adjoining 27 landscaped acres are one of San Mateo County's premier tourist attractions. What many visitors don't realize is that the undeveloped majority of the estate, which climbs all the way up the ridge to Skyline Boulevard, is also worth exploring.

Be aware that this is not a public park. It is owned by the National Trust for Historic Preservation and is accessible only through docent-led group tours. All walks are by advance reservations only and there is a fee.

Nature walks are offered weekdays and Saturday mornings, visiting the Ohlone Indian dig, the San Andreas Fault, a small reservoir, and the Bourn family cemetery, among other sights. The 654-acre estate, which is surrounded by the San Francisco Fish & Game (watershed) property, has a wonderful variety of habitats, including grasslands, oakwoods, second-growth redwoods, and chaparral. It is ideal wildlife habitat and is a great place to see a wide variety of birds. One of the trails is the original Canada Road. William Bourn influenced the county to re-route it to its current location for privacy reasons. Notice how the ecology abruptly changes, with a lot more redwood trees, when you cross to the west side of the San Andreas Fault.

The liesurely 2 1/2-hour nature walks cover about 3 miles. Groups of ten or more may arrange for private personalized walks. Because the trail system can be combined to form a variety of routes, you can take the tour several times without repeating exactly the same route.

The name "Filoli" comes from the Bourn family motto: "To Fight, To Love, To Live." The mansion was constructed between 1915 and 1917 for William B. Bourn II and his wife Agnes and was their home until they died

in 1936. William Bourn made his fortune with the Empire Gold Mine, in the Sierra foothills near Grass Valley. It was then occupied by Mr. and Mrs. William Roth, owner of Matsun Navigation. Mrs. Roth donated the estate to the National Trust for Historic Preservation in 1975. The Georgian revival mansion was modeled after Muckross House in Killarney, Ireland.

A walking tour of the mansion and the gardens takes about 2 hours. House and garden tours are conducted Tuesdays through Saturdays from mid-February until mid-November. Advance reservations are necessary and there is an admission charge.

For more information about nature hikes, classes, and house and garden tours call Friends of Filoli at (650) 364-8300, Monday through Friday 9 a.m. to 3 p.m. ; www.filoli.org.

SEE MAP ON SAN FRANCISCO FISH & GAME REFUGE CHAPTER.

Foothills Open Space Preserve

TO GET THERE... it is along Page Mill Road, about a mile uphill from the entrance to Foothills Park. Enter at a brown metal gate.

This small preserve is covered mainly with chaparral and oak. From the Page Mill road entranc an easy half-mile trail goes to a rounded grassy knoll with a wide view of the southern Bay Area.

Dog walking is allowed in this preserve. Be sure to keep your pet on a leash.

Be aware that there are only a few parking places at the preserve entrance along Page Mill Road. Call the Midpeninsula Regional Open Space District at (650) 691-1200 (www.openspace.org) for additional information.

SEE MAP IN FOOTHILL PARK CHAPTER.

Foothills Park

TO GET THERE. . . take Page Mill Road in Palo Alto about 3 miles south and west of Highway 280.

PLEASE NOTE: Unfortunately for most Bay Area exploreres, this park is open only to Palo Alto residents and their guests, and you will be asked for identification at the gate. So if you don't live in Palo Alto, make friends with someone who does.

The city of Palo Alto operates this "nature preserve" in the foothills west of town. The park, on the steep eastern slopes of the Santa Cruz Mountains, is characterized by grasslands, chaparral, oak, madrone, bay, buckeye, meadows, and 7 picnic areas. You may also appreciate the small reservoir for fishing and non-motorized boating near the park entrance and the nature interpretive center that has an educational exhibit of native plants and animals. Campsites can be reserved for groups or individuals.

The patchwork ecology of this park provides home to a wide variety of birds and other wildlife-- so bring binoculars.

The park changes dramatically between the dry season (May through October) when the grasslands are brown and the wet season (November through April) when the flora does most of its growing. The park has about 15 miles of hiking trails, including the 7.5-mile Los Trancos Loop.

The park is open for day use only. For information about the regularly scheduled nature walks and other events, and camping reservations, call park headquarters at (650)329-2423.

1 mile

Equestrian Access:
Horses are not permitted.

Bicycle Access:
Bicycles are not permitted.

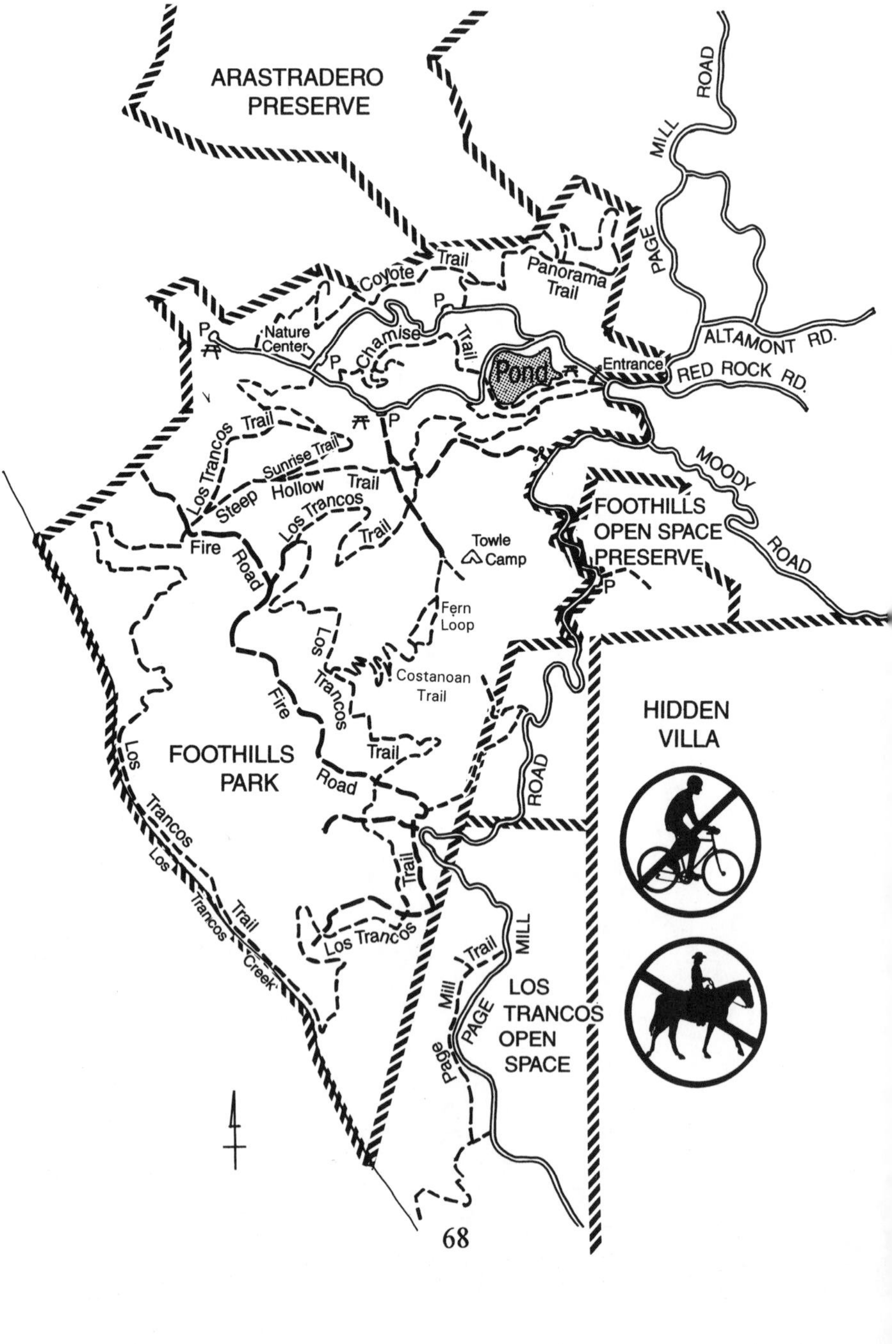

ARASTRADERO PRESERVE

PAGE MILL ROAD

Coyote Trail

Panorama Trail

Nature Center

Chamise Trail

P

Pond

Entrance

ALTAMONT RD.

RED ROCK RD.

P

Los Trancos Trail

Sunrise Trail

Steep Hollow Trail

Los Trancos Trail

Trail

Towle Camp

MOODY ROAD

FOOTHILLS OPEN SPACE PRESERVE

P

Fire Road

Fern Loop

Los Trancos

Costanoan Trail

HIDDEN VILLA

Fire Road

FOOTHILLS PARK

Trail

Los Trancos Trail

ROAD

Los Trancos Trail

Los Trancos Creek

Los Trancos

Trail

MILL

Page Mill Trail

PAGE MILL

LOS TRANCOS OPEN SPACE

68

Forest of Nisene Marks State Park

TO GET THERE... To reach the main entrance from Highway 1 take State Park Drive north (inland), turn right on Soquel Drive, and left on Aptos Creek Road in Aptos. The park can also be accessed from Olive Springs Road (from the west side), Soquel Demonstration State Forest (from the north), and from Buzzard Lagoon Road (from the east).

The Forest of Nisene Marks State Park is a vast and rugged semi-wilderness. It's a diverse land of redwood forests, riperian woodlands, oak groves, knobcone pine, and chaparral; and it has a robust pioneer history whose remnants are rotting away and becoming part of the landscape.

This park has more than 40 miles of trails. Camping is permitted only at the trailcamp near the Sand Point Overlook, which is 6 miles from the Aptos Creek Road trailhead via the West Ridge Trail. It can also be reached by traveling 5.4 miles up Buzzard Lagoon Road and the Aptos Creek Fire Road past the locked gate off Eureka Canyon Road. The trailcamp has no water, and fires are prohibited. There is an outhouse. Advance reservations are required.

Because of a Marks family deed restriction, horses are only permitted downstream from the steel bridge. In 2004 a Superior Court ruled that the Marks family deed also bans bicycles from the 9,000-acre upper portion of the park, which was given to the state in 1963. A compromise in effect as of this writing allows bicycles on the dirt road trails.

From the parking lot on Aptos Creek Road climb up the Aptos Creek Fire Road. Be sure to stop at the Sand Point Overlook for the best view in the park. Look for fossil seashells in the road cut as the route climbs above the redwoods and into oak, madrone, and chaparal. You can continue into Soquel Demonstration State Forest just north of the park.

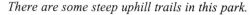

There are some steep uphill trails in this park.

The view from Sand Point Overlook.

The Loma Prieta Grade and West Ridge Trails wind through some steep terrain for about 7 miles, revealing evidence of old logging camps and a railroad. You can hike north on the West Ridge Trail to the trailcamp. This loop can be extended by adding on the Bridge Creek Trail. A .5-mile side trip through a steep gorge to 25-foot Maple Falls is worth the effort, especially during the rainy season. Be aware that the trail to the falls is difficult and unimproved.

The most interesting hiking route is an 11-mile loop that combines the Aptos Creek Fire Road, the Aptos Creek Trail, and the Big Slide Trail. Along this route you will visit the epicenter of the October 17, 1989 ("Loma Prieta") earthquake, including some remnant fissures from the quake, a massive landslide, and a beautiful creek and canyon. This loop involves an elevation gain of more than 1,000 feet and is quite steep in places. For an additional 2 miles (round trip) you can continue up Aptos Creek to see Five Fingers Falls. This loop can be further extended by continuing uphill to the Sand Point Overlook on the Aptos Creek Fire Road.

Uphill (north and east) from the Sand Point Overlook the park takes on a very different appearance. The redwoods are mostly left behind as you climb into oak and madrone woodlands. You will, however, pass a large old-growth redwood that was spared the logging boom because of severe fire scars. From the overview at 2,500 feet elevation you can enjoy views of Monterey Bay, Monterey Peninsula, and the Santa Lucia range to the south. From here you can enter the Soquel Demonstration State Forest. The Aptos Creek Fire Road continues west to Buzzard Lagoon Road and then leaves the park as it approaches Eureka Canyon Road. Be aware that this route is not clearly marked.

In the 1880"s Southern Pacific built a broad-guage railroad line up Aptos Creek to log this area. Then the Loma Prieta Lumber Company built the largest lumber mill in Santa Cruz County and a company town that included a telegraph office, hotel, and school.

This park covers more than 10,000 acres, and all the creeks that flow through it originate within its boundaries. These brawling arteries support their own plant communities. They are characterized by vertical gardens of five finger ferns hanging from moist, shady banks.

Because most of this park has been heavily logged, it is a pleasant surprise to enjoy a recent acquisition of largely old-growth trees in Marcel's Forest, near the park entrance station on Aptos Creek Road. From the entrance station parking lot take the trail west from the picnic tables and follow the signs to the Old Growth Trail. At the Aptos Creek crossing is the Pourroy Picnic Area, named for Marcel Pourroy, who preserved what is now the most beautiful forest in the park. Don't miss the Twisted Grove of "intoxicated" redwoods bending in different directions. Also of interest is a fire-scarred giant called "The Advocate"; which is the largest redwood in the park.

Forest of Nisene Marks State Park is open from 6 a.m. until sunset. For more information and trailcamp reservations, call (831)649-2810 (www.parks.ca.gov).

Don't miss the old-growth redwoods in Marcel's Forest.

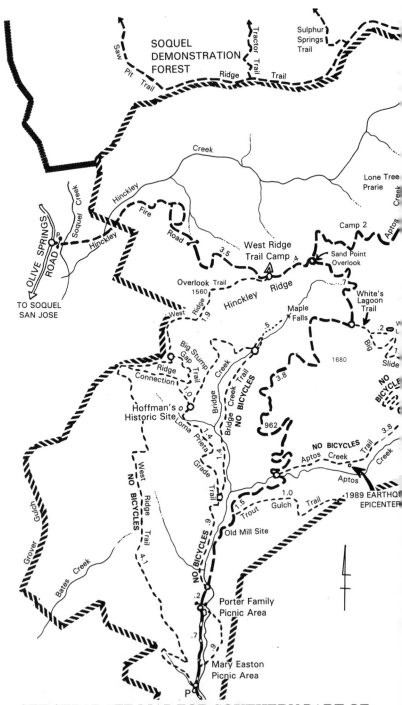

SOQUEL
DEMONSTRATION
FOREST

Saw Pit Trail

Tractor Trail

Sulphur Springs Trail

Ridge Trail

Creek

Lone Tree Prarie

Hinckley Creek

Soquel Creek

Hinckley Fire Road

3.5

West Ridge Trail Camp

Camp 2

Aptos Creek

OLIVE SPRINGS ROAD

P

Hinckley

Sand Point Overlook

TO SOQUEL SAN JOSE

Overlook Trail
1560

Hinckley Ridge

.7

White's Lagoon Trail

West Ridge
1.9

.5

Maple Falls

.2

W L

Big Stump Gap Trail

Bridge Creek

Bridge Creek Trail
NO BICYCLES

3.8

1680

Big

1

Slide

NO BICYCLE

Ridge Connection

1.0

Hoffman's Historic Site

Loma Prieta Grade Trail

1.4

1.4

962

NO BICYCLES

Aptos Creek

NO BICYCLES

3.8

Trail

Creek

Aptos

1989 EARTHQ EPICENTER

West Ridge
NO BICYCLES
Trail
4.1

NO BICYCLES

1.5

Old Mill Site

1.0

Trout Gulch Trail

Grover Gulch

Bates Creek

.2

Porter Family Picnic Area

.7

.6

Mary Easton Picnic Area

P

SEE SEPARATE MAP FOR SOUTHERN PART OF PARK ON PAGE 74

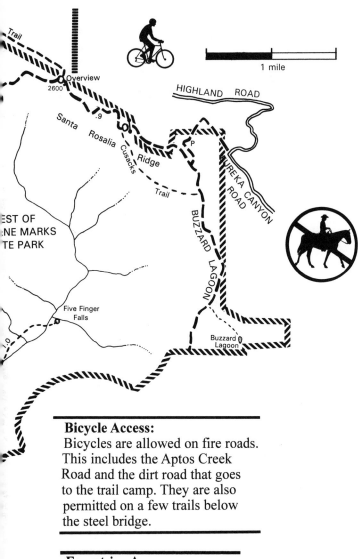

Bicycle Access:
Bicycles are allowed on fire roads.
This includes the Aptos Creek
Road and the dirt road that goes
to the trail camp. They are also
permitted on a few trails below
the steel bridge.

Equestrian Access:
Horses are only allowed on trails
south (downstream) from the steel
bridge.

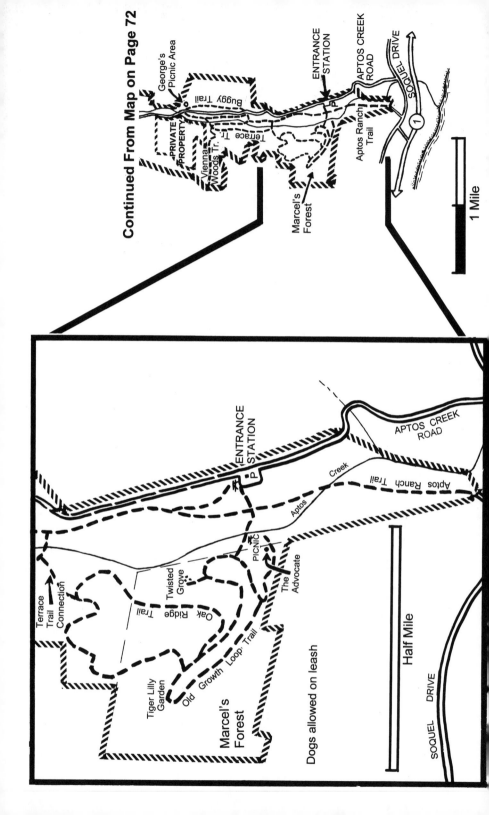

Continued From Map on Page 72

George's Picnic Area

Buggy Trail

PRIVATE PROPERTY

Vienna Woods Tr.

Terrace Tr.

ENTRANCE STATION

P

APTOS CREEK ROAD

Aptos Ranch Trail

Marcel's Forest

SOQUEL DRIVE

1

1 Mile

ENTRANCE STATION

P

APTOS CREEK ROAD

Aptos Ranch Trail

Aptos Creek

Terrace Trail Connection

Oak Ridge Trail

Twisted Grove

PICNIC

The Advocate

Old Growth Loop Trail

Tiger Lilly Garden

Marcel's Forest

Dogs allowed on leash

Half Mile

SOQUEL DRIVE

Fremont Older Open Space Preserve

TO GET THERE... From Highway 280 take route 85 south, exit on De Anza Boulevard and turn right (west) on Prospect Road. The preserve entrance is at the end of Prospect Road. You can also reach the preserve by trail from Stevens Creek County Park.

This 739-acre foothill preserve near Cupertino is a land of gentle hills, with about 9 miles of trails that ramble through oakwoods, grasslands, chaparral, hayfields, and remnant walnut and apricot orchards that still bear fruit. Since 1870 this land has produced grapes, apricots, prunes, walnuts, and olives. It is now popular with hikers, bicyclists, and equestrians.

This preserve is a gentle blend of natural and agricultural qualities; but it still hosts a wonderful abundance of wildlife. Deer roam freely, squirrels trapeze across the the green leafy forest canopy, and acorn woodpeckers are heard tapping holes in oak trees. Expensive homes and a quarry come right up to the preserve, testifying to the preserve's role as a boundary to urban sprawl.

There is a pleasurable 3.4-mile loop from the parking lot, up to a scenic hilltop and around the Seven Springs Loop Trail and back. This moderately easy route takes you up 900-foot Hunters Point, with a great view of the Santa Clara Valley, and then downhill to complete the loop. The Seven Springs Trail is named for the many springs that once provided water for nearby agriculture. The abandoned apricot groves along the way bear fruit around late June.

For a fairly strenuous 7.5-mile workout, with some steep ups and downs and some extraordinary views and a close look at Stevens Creek Reservoir, take a grand loop through this preserve and into the adjoining Stevens Creek County Park. From the parking lot at the end of Prospect

Equestrian Access:

Horses are allowed on all trails except the short footpath near the Prospect Road entrance.

Bicycle Access:

Bicycles are allowed on all trails except the short footpath near the Prospecrt Road entrance.

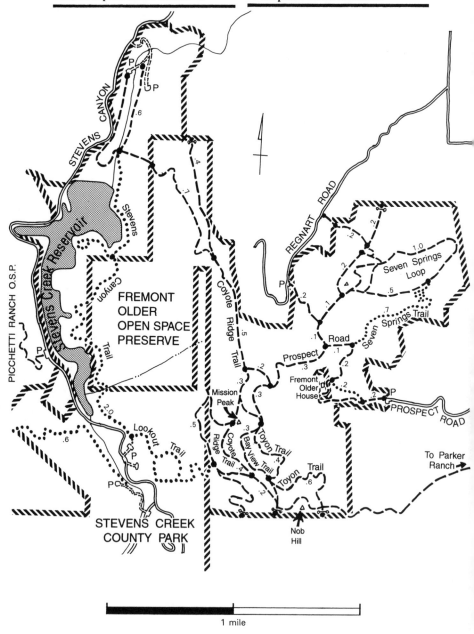

76

Road, head uphill and to the west on the Hayfield Trail, turn right on the Coyote Ridge Trail, and follow it up the ridge and down the other side into Stevens Creek County Park. Turn left on the Lakeside Trail and on Stevens Canyon Trail, and back up the ridge and into Fremont Older Open Space via the Lookout Trail. On the way back be sure to take the few extra steps required to reach the highest point in the preserve, Maisie's Peak. Named for Maisie Garrod, a past owner of the property, this summit has the best views in the preserve. Then head downhill and back to Prospect Road.

The home of distinguished San Francisco newspaper editor Fremont Older, which was built in 1911, has been faithfully restored and is open to the public occasionally for group tours. The property was purchased by the Midpeninsula Regional Open Space District in 1975, and the house is under private lease.

Be aware that this preserve can be hot in summer and early fall and that rattlesnakes are especially active in warm weather. Bring plenty of water.

Dogs on leashes are allowed on all trails.

This preserve is open from dawn to dusk. Most of the trails are old ranch roads. For more information, call the Midpeninsula Regional Open Space District at (650)691-1200 (www.openspace.org).

Golden Gate National Recreation Area

SWEENEY RIDGE

TO GET THERE . . . from Highway 280 in San Bruno, take Sneath Lane west to a locked gate. The road continues as a trail. The park is also accessible from the south side of Skyline College, which is at the end of College Drive, off Skyline Boulevard in San Bruno. Park at parking area #2. A dirt road runs south from the college to Sweeney Ridge. From Pacifica take Highway 1 south of Sharp Park to Shelldance Nursery .5 miles south of Sharp Park Boulevard. Continue up the driveway past the nursery to a wide dirt lot. Park there and walk up the fire road past the locked gate.

This is a place to go for breathtaking Bay Area views and spring wildflowers. On a clear day you can see the Pacific Ocean, the Farallon Islands, Mount Tamalpais, San Bruno Mountain, Mount Diablo, San Francisco Bay, Mount Hamilton, Moffett Field, San Andreas Lake, and many cities ringing the bay. This is a good place to become familiar with Bay Area geography.

Be aware that Sweeney Ridge is often foggy, especially in summer, and usually windy, especially in the afternoon; so dress appropriately.

Of course, these spectacular views can only be seen on clear days; and when the ridge is shrouded in ocean fog, trail users can easily become disoriented, and even lost.

From the gate on Sneath Lane, the trail climbs about 600 feet and 1.9 miles to the Portola Discovery Site at an elevation of 1280 feet. The road itself is on national park land, but both sides are in the San Francisco watershed, where public access is prohibited. The actual discovery site is marked by 2 stone monuments, one to Portola.

Equestrian Access:
Horses are allowed on the fire roads and the horse trail from the Linda Mar stables. There is no horse access via Sneath Lane.

Bicycle Access:
Bicycles are allowed on paved and dirt roads.

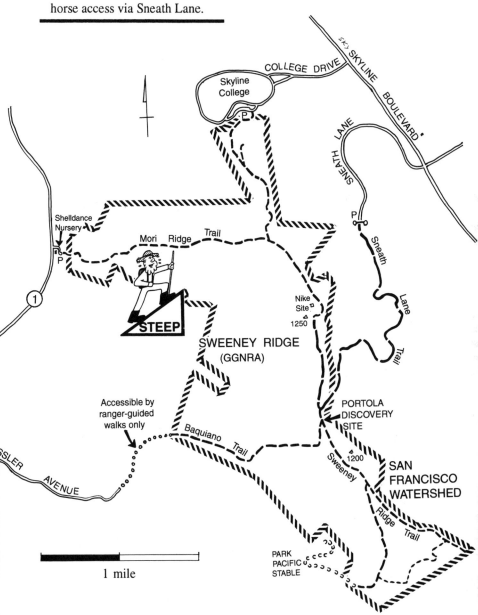

At this place, on November 4, 1769, Captain Gaspar de Portola, seeking Monterey Bay, accidentally found the large arm of the ocean which was named San Francisco Bay. Portola thought that this inland sea was Drakes Bay, near Point Reyes, and was disappointed to have missed Monterey Bay. After returning to San Diego he realized that this bay, one of the world's best natural harbors, was a new discovery and a perfect place for a Spanish presidio.

Covering 1047 acres, Sweeney Ridge is covered mostly with coastal scrub and grasses. Wildflowers are abundant especially in April and May, including checkermallow, Indian paintbrush, lupine, columbine, and blueeyed grass. This is also an excellent place to see a wide variety of birds.

From near the discovery site, the paved Sneath Lane trail veers sharply north to an abandoned Nike missile site. From here, a dirt road continues north and downhill to Sharp Park and Skyline College. South from the discovery site a dirt road traces the ridgetop to the boundary with the watershed property, which is off limits.

The Mori Ridge Trail from Highway 1 makes a steep 1,600-foot ascent up the ridge with lots of ocean views. You can take this route 2.5 miles to the Portola Discovery Site. The distance is 2 miles from Skyline College to the Discovery Site with an elevation gain of 500 feet. This ridge is an imprtant segment of the 400-mile-long Bay Area Ridge Trail.

The National Park Service offers ranger-guided walks on Saturdays dealing with natural and human history. Rangers also lead walks from Fassler Avenue in Pacifica. For more information, call (415)556-8371.

Mileage to Portola Discovery Site:
From Sneath Lane: 1.8 miles
From Skyline College: 2 miles
From Shelldance Nursery: 2.4 miles
From Fassler Avenue: 1.5 miles

FORT FUNSTON

TO GET THERE. . . from Highway 280 take John Daly Boulevard west and turn north on Skyline Boulevard (Highway 35). It's in the southwest corner of San Francisco, just west of Lake Merced.

The hills of San Francisco are actually the northernmost foothills of the Santa Cruz Mountains. At Fort Funston you can see one of the few places in this city that is still anything close to its natural condition.

Covered with sand dunes, as most of western San Francisco was originally, this 116-acre area was spared from development by the army in the early 1900's. Named for General Frederick Funston, a hero of the Spanish-American War, the fort was established to help defend the coast against foreign invasion.

Fort Funston is ideal for easy walks and for exploring relics of military history. It also has a wheelchair-accessible paved trail. Be sure to watch for hang gliders soaring along the bluffs above the beach.

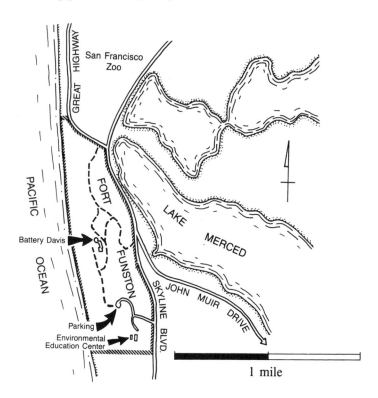

Mori Point

TO GET THERE... Mori Point is just west of Highway 1 in Pacifica. (1) From Highway 1 take Rockaway Beach Road west, turn right on Dondee, and left on San Marco to a large parking lot; (2) From Highway 1 turn west at the stop light on Reina Del Mar to a parking lot; (3) From Highway 1 turn west on Westport and left on Bradford. There is room along the street for a few cars near the entrance gate.

As of this writing the land owned by the Golden Gate National Recreation Area is only 105 acres. Because the GGNRA boundaries are not marked, many of the trails take you south through land owned by the city of Pacifica. This is a relatively small area of rounded hills, wetlands, an abandoned quarry, and dramatic cliffs plunging into the Pacific, with wave-battered offshore rocks .

There is no real trail system. Instead, there are unmarked dirt roads and trails formed by years of off-road motorcyle use. Despite severe erosion, there are efforts by the GGNRA staff and volunteers to restore the land. This small area can be explored in a couple of hours.

Mori Point is a popular place for dog walkers to exercise their pets. Leashes are required. Look for an explosion of wildflowers (goldfield, lupine, and checkerbloom) at the tip of the point in April and early May.

On the north side of the point, bordering Sharp Park, is a freshwater wetland, home to the endangered red-legged frog and the San Francisco garter snake, which feeds on the frog. You will notice efforts underway to restore and enhance their habitat.

Fans of the 1971 movie, Harold & Maude, may recognize the cliffs just south of the point as the place where Harold's Jaguar plunged off the cliff and landed upside on the beach in the final scene.

For more information, call the Golden Gate National Recreation Area at (415) 556-8642 (www.nps.gov).

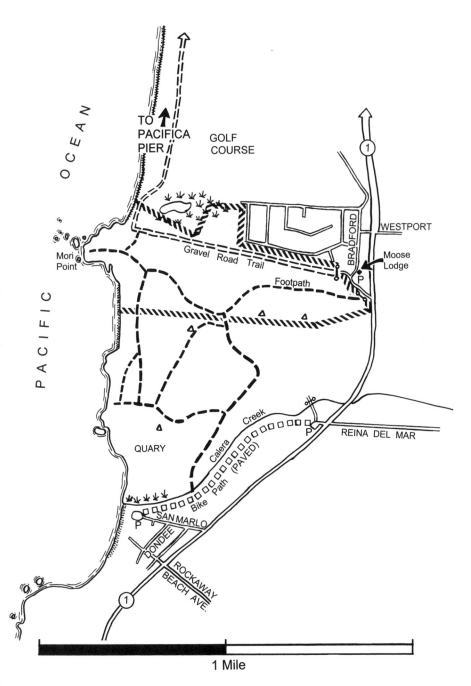

OCEAN

TO
PACIFICA
PIER

GOLF
COURSE

1

WESTPORT

BRADFORD

Moose
Lodge

P

Mori
Point

Gravel Road Trail

Footpath

PACIFIC

Creek

Calera

P

REINA DEL MAR

QUARY

Bike Path (PAVED)

P

SAN MARLO

DONDEE

ROCKAWAY

BEACH AVE.

1

1 Mile

83

PHLEGER ESTATE

TO GET THERE... In Woodside, it can be reached by walking from Huddart County Park or from the southern Skyline Boulevard parking lot for Purisima Creek Open Space Preserve.

This 1,257-acre unit of the Golden Gate National Recreation Area is a mixture of second-growth redwoods, oak, bay, big-leaf maple, and madrone.

With the only redwood forest in the GGNRA, this steep, east-sloping unit ties together many public lands to form an unbroken greenbelt from Sweeney Ridge to the north all the way through the San Francisco watershed property to Huddart, Wunderlich, and Edgewood County Parks. It is also one of the last remaining Santa Cruz Mountains links in the Bay Area Ridge Trail, allowing it to parallel Skyline Boulevard up on the ridge.

This property can be reached from adjacent Huddart County Park. From the Zwierleim Picnic Area take Zwierleim Trail, turn left (North) on Richard's Road Trail, right (East) on the trail to Woodside, and left (North) on the Miramontes Trail in the Phleger Estate.

There is an existing trail system through this estate built long ago by equestrian clubs. Look for metal trail markers depicting an Indian on a

84

horseback placed by equestrians in the 1930's. Plans call for expanding this trail system, emphasizing low-intensity use by equestrians and walkers. Parking will be improved and interpretive stations may be added. A main access will be from Skyline Boulevard. It is even possible that spawning steelhead trout can be reintroduced into West Union Creek.

The Phleger Estate was clearcut in the 1860's and '70's. Redwood lumber was shipped out of Redwood City for the building of San Francisco. This property was the site of the old Whipple Lumber Mill and the former town of Union Creek.

National park rangers lead regularly scheduled walks. For more information, call the Golden Gate National Recreation Area at (415)556-8642 or (415)556-8371.

SPECIAL SECTION

Watch Out For Ticks

Ticks are small blood-sucking arachnids that wait on leaves and branches for victims to pass by. Once on board they excavate a hole in the skin and then excrete a powerful cement surrounding their mouthparts which makes them hard to remove.

You are most likely to pick up these unwanted hitchhikers by brushing against shrubs or branches. Fortunately, Lyme disease is not common in this area.

BEFORE AN OUTING: *Wear snug-fitting clothes and apply insect repellent containing DEET, especially at the cuffs, neck, and waist.*
AFTER AN OUTING: *Inspect your body thoroughly soon after your outing. If you find a tick grab it with tweezers as close to the skin surface as possible and pull outward with steady, even pressure. Then disinfect the bite with isopropyl alcohol and wash hands with soap and water.*

Henry Cowell Redwoods State Park

This redwood-forested park is divided into 2 sizable and unconnected units in the mountains near Felton.

SOUTHERN UNIT

TO GET THERE... The main entrance to the southern unit of this park is just south of Felton on Highway 9. The Rincon parking lot is 3.3 miles south of the main entrance on Highway 9. The campground entrance is on Graham Hill Road.

Most visitors are unaware that the popular Redwood Grove and picnic area just south of Felton is only a small part of this park. The great bulk of the southern unit of the park can be reached by well-developed hiking trails from several roadside pullouts on Highway 9, from the park campground on Graham Hill Road, and from the picnic area near park headquarters (the day use entrance). This unit covers 1,737 acres and has about 20 miles of hiking trails.

If you think this park is all redwoods you will be surprised to find an amazing ecological variety, including oak, Ponderosa pine, chaparral, and knobcone pine habitat. Keep in mind, especially during the rainy season, that none of the trails that cross the San Lorenzo River have bridges.

The Redwood Grove Nature Trail Loop (near the picnic area) is the easiest and the most popular trail in the park. It is less than 1 mile and is more of a stroll than a hike, though it winds through one of the finest old-growth redwood groves south of San Francisco, and is especially pleasant on weekdays when the crowds are gone. Most of the redwoods in the rest of the park are second-growth.

Nearby is a 260-site picnic area, each with a picnic table, barbeque pit, and shared water supply.

This is a hilly park, and the vegetation corresponds to the area's geography. Lower areas are forested with redwood and riparian vegeta-

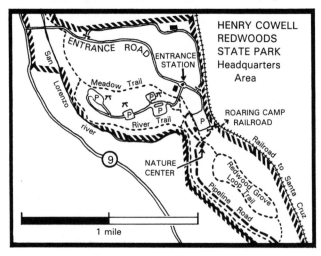

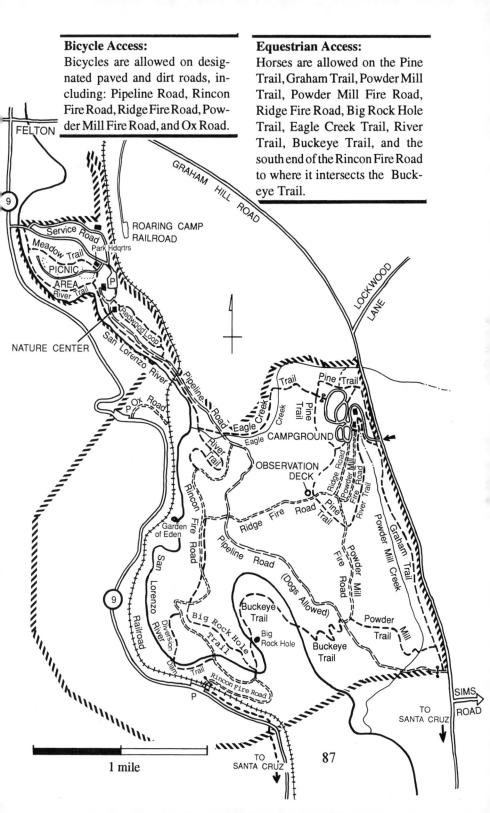

Bicycle Access:
Bicycles are allowed on designated paved and dirt roads, including: Pipeline Road, Rincon Fire Road, Ridge Fire Road, Powder Mill Fire Road, and Ox Road.

Equestrian Access:
Horses are allowed on the Pine Trail, Graham Trail, Powder Mill Trail, Powder Mill Fire Road, Ridge Fire Road, Big Rock Hole Trail, Eagle Creek Trail, River Trail, Buckeye Trail, and the south end of the Rincon Fire Road to where it intersects the Buckeye Trail.

87

tion in places, and ridges and hilltops are covered with oak, madrone, digger pine, manzanita, and other chaparral plants. The distribution of plants is also related to the availability of sunlight. Chaparral plants prefer the sunny ridgetops, while the understory plants of the redwood groves are satisfied with only indirect light and with occasional shafts of sunlight that penetrate the dense forest canopy.

A cross section of the park's ecology can be viewed on a short outing from the picnic area to the observation deck on the Ridge Fire Road Trail, which climbs from the redwood-forested streambeds to the chaparral ridgetops where a view of Santa Cruz and Monterey Bay are possible on clear days. The route is steep in places, though it is only slightly more than 3 miles and is easily completed in 2 hours by most hikers. The observation deck, on the water tank at the highest point of the trail, is a good place to relax and eat lunch.

To explore the southern part of this unit of Henry Cowell Redwoods State Park, take Highway 9 south of Felton to the parking lot at the Rincon Road Trailhead. The dirt road trail descends to the river, which is impassable during the rainy season because there are no bridges. It then makes a steep ascent up the other side. The Cathedral Redwoods is a beautiful picnic stop.

For a fun side trip on warm days during the dry season, follow the San Lorenzo River downstream from the Rincon Fire Road to the Big Rock Hole, which is one of the best swimming holes in the Santa Cruz Mountains. It has deep water, diving opportunities, and a sandy beach.

From the Rincon Fire Road access, hikers, bicyclists, and equestrians can take the Rincon Connector Trail south into Pogonip Open Space Preserve and on to the University of California at Santa Cruz, and Wilder Ranch State Park. Dogs are not allowed.

The only trail where your leashed canine friend may accompany you

Big Rock Hole, in Henry Cowell Redwoods State Park, is the best swimming hole in the Santa Cruz Mountains. Visit during the warm days of summer and early fall when the San Lorenzo River is more like a creek. The water next to the big rock is deep enough for swimming and diving, and the sandy riverbank beach is ideal for relaxing after taking a dip. To get there, park at the Rincon Fire Road trailhead and walk downhill to the river. Then walk downstream on the riverbed to the swimming hole.

The Roaring Camp & Big Trees Railroad, adjacent to Henry Cowell Redwoods State Park, offers a ride through the redwoods on the steepest narrow-guage railroad grade in North America. You can also take a train from here to the Santa Cruz Beach and Boardwalk. For more information call (831)335-4484.

is the 3-mile long paved Pipeline Road through the park.

There is a 112-unit year-around campground available on Graham Hill Road, complete with tables, fire rings, flush toilets, and hot showers. For reservations, call the park office at (831) 335-4598.

FALL CREEK UNIT
(Henry Cowell Redwoods State Park)
TO GET THERE... From Highway 9 in Felton, the main parking lot is less than a mile northwest on Felton-Empire Road.

The Fall Creek unit is a steep, forested, and completely magnificent 2,335-acre canyon, tucked into the rugged mountains northwest of Felton. Though this land is technically part of Henry Cowell Redwoods State Park, it is physically separated and has a very different character. It has a

Spring-fed Fall Creek flows cold and pure all year.

The lime kilns look like ancient Mayan ruins.

Bicycle Access:
Bicycles are not permitted.

Equestrian Access:
Horses are allowed on all trails except where otherwise indicated on map.

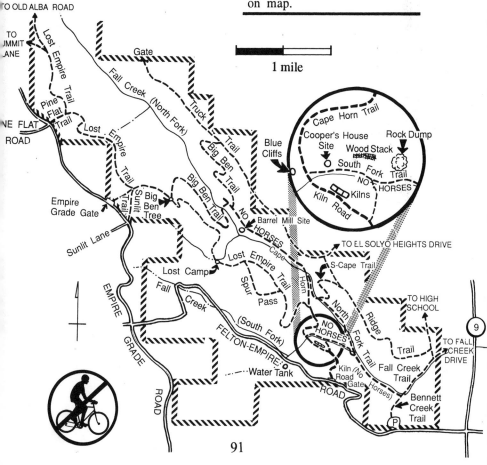

much wilder feel, with no picnic tables, campgrounds, visitors centers, or other amenities found in the southern unit of the park.

For an ideal 3.5-mile loop from the Felton-Empire Road parking lot, walk downhill to the creek and then upstream. Where the north and south forks of Fall Creek meet, follow the South Fork Trail upstream to the lime kiln area in a beautiful grove of maples, which becomes a brilliant blaze of color in autumn. Then continue north on the Cape Horn Trail and follow the North Fork Trail downstream along Fall Creek and back to the Bennett Creek Trail. This loop can be extended with a side trip upstream to the scattered remains of the waterpowered barrel mill, which was built in 1812.

For a 9.3-mile outing go north from the line kiln area on the Cape Horn Trail, charge uphill on the Lost Empire Trail and then turn right on the Big Ben Trail and then south along the North Fork Trail.

The lime kiln area is where the IXL Lime Company built 3 lime kilns in 1870, which were fired with split redwood logs, some of which are still stacked across the creek from the kilns. When heated to about 1700 degrees, limestone loses its carbon dioxide to become a calcium oxide powder called lime, which is used to make cement and to neutralize acid soil, among other uses. By 1880 this was one of the state's most important lime producers. Above these deteriorated kilns a steep and eroded trail rises to Blue Cliff, an old limestone quarry.

Limestone was broken into pieces about the size of a man's head and were then stacked to form arches 4-5 feet high around the kiln entrances. The limestone was stacked to the top of the kiln. Two men, working 12-hour shifts, stoked the fire for 3 or 4 days by feeding redwood firewood into the arched entrances. After waiting 2 days for the lime to cool, workers packed it into barrels, each weighing 250 pounds. Horse-drawn wagons carried the lime to the Felton train depot.

Most of this deep and shady canyon is occupied by second-growth redwoods, along with bay, big-leaf maple, and Douglas fir. The forest floor is carpeted with sorrel, wild ginger, several species of fern, and Solomon's seal. Chaparral grows on some of the high and dry south-facing ridges.

Fall Creek, issuing from countless springs, is one of the park's most wonderful features. It bounces wild and cold all summer, splashing over granite boulders which make it reminiscent of High Sierra streams. The granite was transported from hundreds of miles to the south by movement on the San Andreas Fault. The limestone was formed from the shells of countless sea creatures and then uplifted from the ocean by the collision of the tectonic plates. This beautiful canyon has more delightful qualities than I can mention here and is one of my favorite places in the Santa Cruz Mountains.

Bicycles and dogs are not allowed here. For more information, call park headquarters at (831)335-4598 (www.parks.ca.gov).

Are There Bears In The Santa Cruz Mountains?

When the Portola expedition came to the Bay Area in 1769, the grizzly bear, not man, dominated the landscape. "He was horrible, fierce, large, and fat" wrote Father Pedro Font.

The size, strength, and ferocity of the grizzlies humbled the native humans and probably kept the smaller black bears away from the coastal areas of California. There is no written record of black bears in this range during the eighteenth and nineteenth centuries. The niche occupied by grizzly bears was vacated in November 1885 when rancher Orrin Blodgett shot a 642-pound bear near Bonny Doon Mountain. It was the last grizzly ever reported in the Santa Cruz Mountains.

In July 1979 a large black bear created a media sensation by wandering into a residential area south of Saratoga. California State Fish and Game Department employees, sheriff's deputies, and animal control officers took more than a week to bait and trap the "Saratoga Bear", which was transported and released into a remote part of Los Padres National Forest.

In January 1980 another bruin was seen in the same Saratoga neighborhood. Fish and game wardens confirmed that tracks found there were made by a bear, but no attempt was made to capture this animal. Sergeant Leo Tombley, spokesman for the Santa Clara County sheriff's office, said the bear "is not causing any harm or damage and is in its natural habitat, out in the woods where it belongs." It was commonly assumed at the time that these bears were fugitives from captivity. That's one explanation, but there is another possibility. Could it be there is a small population of wild black bears in the Santa Cruz Mountains?

To find the answer to that question I asked rangers in various Santa Cruz Mountains parks if they have heard of any bear sightings. Some of them said that visitors have reported seeing bears, though none of the rangers had seen any. What appeared to be bear scat, scratch marks on trees, and bear tracks were reported. These reports center on Big Basin, Portola, Castle Rock, and Wilder Ranch State Parks. If there are bears in the Santa Cruz Mountains, they must be wary of humans and dwell in remote areas.

With increased restrictions on bear hunting in California the bruin population has been proliferating in recent years. As their population grows these wide-ranging creatures are spreading out in search of new habitat. What they are discovering is that their grizzly bear enemies are no longer around to keep them away from the Santa Cruz Mountains and other coastal environments. This range has a mild climate, with no need to hibernate, and plenty of natural animal and plant food sources. It is a bear niche waiting to be filled.

Hidden Villa Ranch

TO GET THERE ... take Highway 280 to the El Monte/Moody Road exit at Foothill College in Los Altos. The entrance is on Moody Road 2. 5 miles from Highway 280. Look for the "AYH" signs

This 1, 600-acre farm and wildland preserve is open to the public from Tuesday through Sunday from 9 a.m. until sundown. It is owned and maintained by the private nonprofit Trust for Hidden Villa.

An excellent trail system is maintained for use by equestrians and walkers, forming several easy to moderate loop routes through oak woodlands, chaparral, and grasslands. Bicycles are not allowed.

For more ambitious outings take the Ridge Trail into the Duveneck Windmill Pasture Area of Rancho San Antonio Open Space Preserve, or take the Black Mountain Trail 3 .5 miles and 2,300 feet up to the summit of Black Mountain in adjacent Monte Bello Open Space Preserve.

(Continues on page 84)

Equestrian Access:
Horses are allowed on Creek Trail, Pipeline Trail, Grapeview Trail, Ridge Trail, and Black Mountain Trail.

Bicycle Access:
Bicycles are not permitted

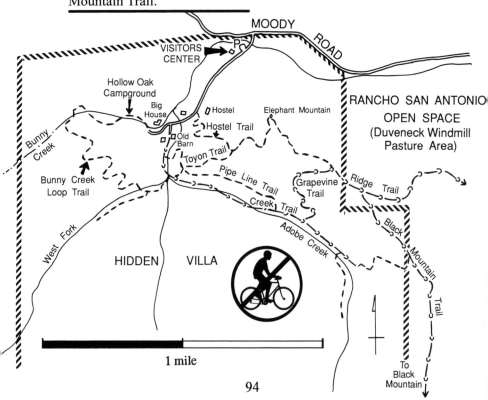

94

The white barn was built in the 1880's.

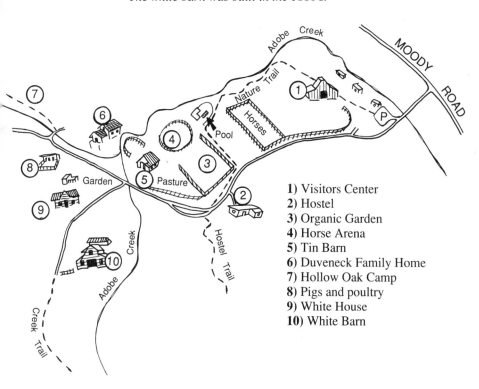

1) Visitors Center
2) Hostel
3) Organic Garden
4) Horse Arena
5) Tin Barn
6) Duveneck Family Home
7) Hollow Oak Camp
8) Pigs and poultry
9) White House
10) White Barn

The Creek Trail follows Adobe Creek through a shady wooded canyon that makes a refreshing contrast to the exposed farm area on hot days.

The White House and White Barn are the oldest buildings on the property, constructed in the 1880's. Frank and Josephine Duveneck founded Hidden Villa in 1925 and added most of the other buildings, including the Duveneck family home, which was completed in 1930. You will also find a Visitors Center, Youth Hostel, organic garden, horse arena, tin barn for sheep and cows, Hollow Oak Camp, and pig and poultry facilities. This is an old fashioned working farm with lots of antique agricultural equipment on display.

The Hidden Villa Hostel is open from September 1 through May. It has group, family, and couples cabins, a large living room, and kitchen. Established in 1937, it is the oldest youth hostel west of the Hudson River. For more information call (650)949-8648.

Hidden Villa also has a summer camp program for kids from ages 7 through 16 years. Hiking, swimming, games, and farm chores are designed to foster multicultural understanding and environmental awareness. For more information, call (650)949-8641

Contributions are always needed to maintain the area and to keep all the programs growing. Send your tax deductible donations to: Hidden Villa, 26870 Moody Road, Los Altos Hills, CA 94022 .

For more information, call (650)949-8650.

Huddart County Park

TO GET THERE ... take Woodside Road 3.5 miles west from Highway 280 and turn north on Kings Mountain Road.

This is one of San Mateo County's most popular parks, and its many recreational facilities often make it more crowded than most trail users like. Fortunately, however, you can leave the parking lots and picnic areas behind and explore about 24 miles of trails. The park covers 973 acres of oak woodlands, chaparral, Douglas fir and second-growth redwood forests.

This is a steep park, with trails to match. Easy walkers may want to take the .75 mile nature trail near the park entrance station. A more challenging route follows West Union Creek via Richard's Road Trail to near the Toyon Group Campground, and then returns by way of the Service Road. A more ambitious loop around the park, climbing the 2,000 foot Skyline Ridge may be accomplished by continuing uphill on the Richard's Road Trail, turn left on the Skyline Trail, and left (downhill) on the Chinquapin Trail.

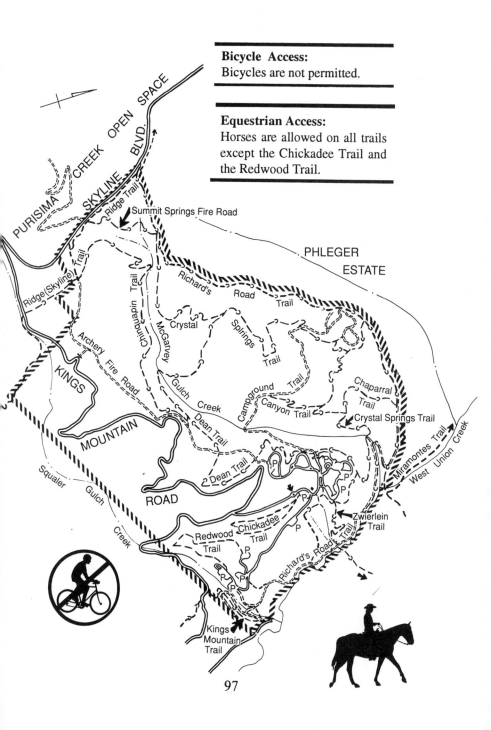

1 mile

Bicycle Access:
Bicycles are not permitted.

Equestrian Access:
Horses are allowed on all trails except the Chickadee Trail and the Redwood Trail.

PURISIMA CREEK OPEN SPACE

SKYLINE BLVD.

Ridge Trail

Summit Springs Fire Road

PHLEGER ESTATE

Ridge (Skyline) Trail

Richard's Road Trail

Chinquapin Trail

Crystal

Springs Trail

McGarvey Gulch

Archery Fire Road

KINGS

Crystal Canyon Trail

Campground Trail

Chaparral Trail

Crystal Springs Trail

Creek

Dean Trail

MOUNTAIN

Miramontes Trail

West Union Creek

Squaler Gulch Creek

ROAD

Dean Trail

P

P

P

P

P

Zwierlein Trail

Redwood Trail

Chickadee Trail

P

P

P

P

P

Richard's Road Trail

Kings Mountain Trail

97

This route offers a cross section of the Santa Cruz Mountains ecology. Oak woodlands cover the park's lower elevations, with chaparral on dry ridgetops and redwood groves tucked into streambed furrows. Tanoak, madrone, bay, Douglas fir, and several species of oak also contribute to this plant kingdom hodgepodge. The park's animal inhabitants include blacktail deer, squirrels, racoons, foxes, bobcats, woodrats, several species of lizards and snakes, and an abundant variety of birds.

You can visit the historic Woodside Store at the intersection of Kings Mountain Road and Tripp Road. Built in 1853, the store is open Tuesdays, Thursdays, Saturdays, and Sundays from noon to 5 p.m. For information, call (650)574-6441.

The redwood groves you see are second-growth descendants of an ancient forest of giants that was logged in the 1850's and 60's to supply the Bay Area's booming cities with lumber. You can still see massive stump remnants of the original forest and trace the "skid road" depressions up the hillsides, created by oxen dragging logs to the nearby sawmills.

This park has more than the usual recreational opportunities. A children's playground, picnicking and barbecuing facilities, and an archery range are provided, and an overnight campground is open in summer on a first-come, first-serve basis. Bicycles are not allowed.

The Phleger unit of the Golden Gate National Recreation Area can be reached from Huddart by taking the Richard's Road Trail to the Miramontes Trail.

There is an entry fee. For group picnic site reservations call (650)363-4021. For other information, call (650)851-0326 or (650)851-1210.

Jasper Ridge Biological Preserve

HOW TO GET THERE . . . there are two entrances. To reach the Searsville Lake entrance take Sand Hill Road west from Highway 280. To reach the Escobar Gate entrance take Alpine Road west from Highway 280, turn right on Westridge Drive, and right on Escobar Road.

This 1,300-acre preserve is only accessible by docent escort. Guided walks are regularly scheduled and independent group tours may be arranged from October to June. Docent walks observe wildflowers, birds, geology, lichens, trees, grasses, research projects or general interest. To schedule a tour, call Stanford University at (650)327-2277.

Jasper Ridge is famous for its spectacular springtime displays of wildflowers and remnants of native California grasslands. Operated by Stanford University, this preserve boasts examples of most of the plant communities found in the Santa Cruz Mountains.

The ridge's serpentine soils, lacking essential nutrients needed by most plants, allow native grasses to resist the invasion of alien annuals. Of the 16 grasses found on the serpentine, 12 are natives, including purple needle grass, pin bluegrass, and big squirreltail. This serpentine community has been the object of much scientific study of ecology and population biology. Check the website at: (http://jasper1.stanford.edu/home/).

La Honda Creek Open Space Preserve

TO GET THERE... From Skyline Boulevard take Bear Gulch Road .6 miles west and turn left on Allen Road. The preserve entrance is at a locked gate on Allen Road 1.1 miles from Bear Gulch Road.

PLEASE NOTE: Because Allen Road is private, you must have a permit to enter this part of the preserve. To obtain one, and the combination to the locked gate, contact the Midpeninsula Regional Open Space District at (650)691-1200.

The best thing about this preserve is the wonderful variety of scenery revealed by even a short and leisurely walk.

The gentle grassland slopes provide unobstructed mountain and ocean views to the south and west. Oak-madrone woodlands occupy the higher and drier zones, mixing easily with Douglas fir, and then blending quickly with second-growth redwoods in the moist and shady canyon bottoms.

Even a 2 to 4 mile ramble will take you through all courses of this ecological smorgasbord, which combines to form bountiful wildlife habitat. Throughout the preserve you will hear a perpetual medley of bird songs: the rat-a-tat tapping of woodpeckers among the oaks, the strident caw of steller jays in the redwood groves, and the piercing call of redtailed hawks circling high above the grasslands. Scat and tracks of deer, bobcats, coyotes, and other mammals attest to this area's value to wildlife.

Springtime brings an exceptional number and variety of wildflowers. Pink filaree flowers carpet the grassy slopes, mixed with blue-eyed grass, checkerbloom, buttercup, lupine, poppies, and wild cucumber. I am particularly impressed by the dense clusters of Douglas iris where grasslands and oak woods meet.

The trail system in this preserve consists of old ranch roads, in various states of disrepair. Some are in good condition, others are faint traces

100

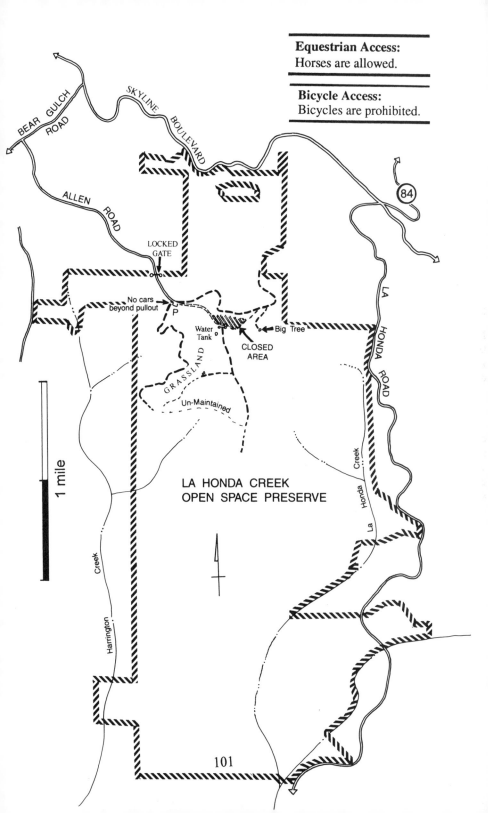

Equestrian Access:
Horses are allowed.

Bicycle Access:
Bicycles are prohibited.

BEAR GULCH ROAD

SKYLINE BOULEVARD

ALLEN ROAD

84

LOCKED GATE

No cars beyond pullout

P

Water Tank

Big Tree

CLOSED AREA

GRASSLAND

Un-Maintained

LA HONDA ROAD

La Honda Creek

1 mile

LA HONDA CREEK
OPEN SPACE PRESERVE

Harrington Creek

101

across the landscape; and others are nearly impassable because of dense brush. The gentle grasslands near the Allen Road parking lot, cropped by grazing horses, are easily crossed without trails. The ridgetop ranch road trail goes south from the residence about .75 miles to a fine vista above a steep dropoff.

There is one large old-growth redwood that somehow survived. To find the "Big Tree" take the path beyond the closed area to where it merges with a dirt road. Continue east on the dirt road and look on the right side for a faint unmarked path which leads to a dirt road. Then go downhill to the giant tree.

Adventurous hikers will work their way down the dropoff and along clandestine dirt road trails in the southern part of the preserve which, as of this writing, is still leased for ranching and not yet open to public use. This part of the preserve, which will be accessible by way of La Honda Road, is an exceptionally scenic land of high grassy hills and wooded valleys. There is a ready-made network of trails that can be fashioned from old ranch roads. As of this writing, a master plan for this area is being developed which will greatly increase recreational opportunities.

This preserve will be more than doubled when the 3,800-acre Driscoll Ranch, which was purchased by Peninsula Open Space Trust, is added to the preserve.

The private residence and all buildings in the immediate vicinity are closed to the public.

This preserve is open from dawn to dusk. For more information call (650)691-1200 (www.openspace.org).

Loch Lomond Recreation Area

TO GET THERE... From Highway 17 take Mount Herman Road exit at Scotts Valley and drive west to Graham Hill Road near Felton. Turn left (east) on Graham Hill Road and turn left (north) on East Zayante Road and Lompico Road. Turn left on West Drive and follow the signs to the recreation area.

Tucked into the forested Newell Creek watershed north of Felton, Loch Lomond is a beautiful setting for picnicking, walking, boating, and fishing. Be aware, however, that the area may be closed during drought years.

This reservoir, the water supply for the city of Santa Cruz, has a boat launch ramp for private boats. Sailboats and gas-powered boats are not allowed. The recreation area also has beautifully maintained picnic areas with clean restrooms and barbeques. You can rent row boats, paddle boats, and electric motor boats near the launch ramp.

Fishing is popular along the shore, especially for rainbow trout, bluegill, sunfish, and largemouth bass. Swimming is prohibited.

The Loch Trail, along the shore of Loch Lomond, offers one of the least known and most scenic walks in the Bay Area. It can be combined

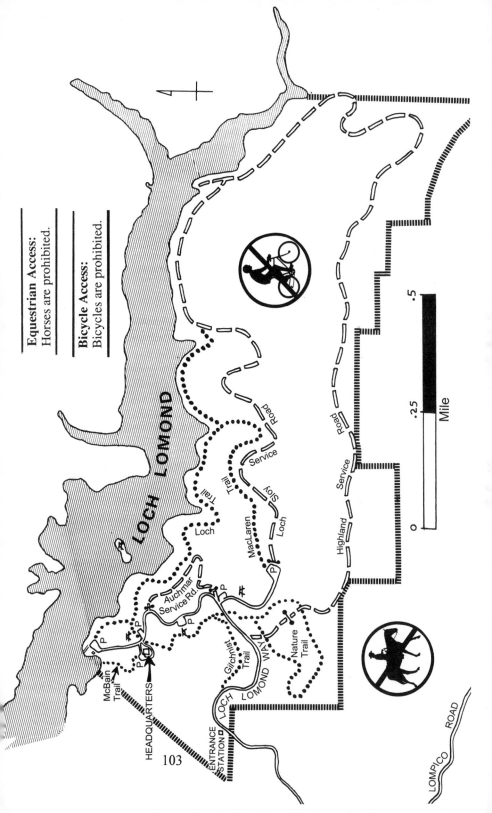

Equestrian Access:
Horses are prohibited.

Bicycle Access:
Bicycles are prohibited.

LOCH LOMOND

Loch Service Road

MacLaren Trail

Loch Trail

Sloy Loch

Highland Service Road

Auchmar Service Rd.

Gilchrist Trail

LOCH LOMOND WAY

Nature Trail

McBain Trail

HEADQUARTERS

ENTRANCE STATION

LOMPICO ROAD

103

Mile

0   .25   .5

with the Highland Service Road for a rugged 5-mile loop. Surrounded by beautiful forested mountains, Loch Lomond would be comparable to Crystal Springs Reservoir near San Mateo except for two significant differences: (1) There is no freeway anywhere near Loch Lomond. This place is amazingly quiet; (2) The city of Santa Cruz recognizes that quiet non-polluting forms of recreation are perfectly compatible with its responsiblity to provide high quality drinking water.

For a much shorter loop of less than 2 miles, combine the Loch Lomond Trail with the MacLaren Trail. It passes second-growth redwoods, tanbark oak, and madrone.

This area was logged in the nineteenth and early twentieth centuries and was purchased by the San Lorenzo Valley Water District in 1947. In 1959 the city of Santa Cruz bought the land and built the earthen dam that holds the 8,700-acre reservoir we enjoy today.

Under the supervision of the Water Department of the City of Santa Cruz, Loch Lomond is open March 1 through September 15. There is an entrance fee. For more information, call the Santa Cruz Water Department at (8310 335-7424 (www.ci.santacruz.ca.us).

Long Ridge Open Space Preserve

TO GET THERE... Park at the Grizzly Flat turnout on Skyline Boulevard, 5 miles south of Page Mill Road, and 3 miles north of Saratoga Gap (Skyline Boulevard and Highway 9). The turnout is identified by a gate and wooden fence, and is near a "Palo Alto City Limit" sign. There are also a few parking spaces at the southern access along Skyline Boulevard about 1.6 miles north of Saratoga Gap.

Spectacular ridgetop views, grassy and oak-studded ridges, shady wooded canyons, and a delightful pond combine to make Long Ridge one of the most beautiful places in the Santa Cruz Mountains. Most of the trails in this preserve are old ranch roads, which may account for its popularity with mountain bikers. The narrow trails are also open to bicycles.

The southern part of this 1,217-acre preserve includes Hickory Oak Ridge, which is crowned by stately groves of black and canyon oak, madrone, and Douglas fir, and there are sweeping views of Butano Ridge, the Pescadero Creek watershed, and the ocean on clear days. On the high point of this ridge are rocks believed to have been the site of Ohlone Indian solstice ceremonies. On exceptionally clear days you can see as far as the Farallon Islands.

A beautiful pond lies on the boundary between the preserve and land owned by the private Jikoji Zen Buddhist retreat. Western pond turtles are often seen here. Be careful not to stray onto private land. The Peters Creek Trail follows the creek downstream from the pond and forms part of an ideal loop route.

From the Grizzly Flat parking lot take the Bay Area Ridge Trail downhill to the creek and then turn south on the Peters Creek Trail and on to the pond. Then head uphill and follow the Long Ridge Road and Long Ridge Trail to complete the 4.3-mile loop. In the valley north of the pond along the Peters Creek Trail is an abandoned apple orchard that offers a welcome treat in the fall.

There is a more vigorous, 8.6-mile, hiking or bicycling loop through Long Ridge Open Space Preserve and adjoining Upper Stevens Creek

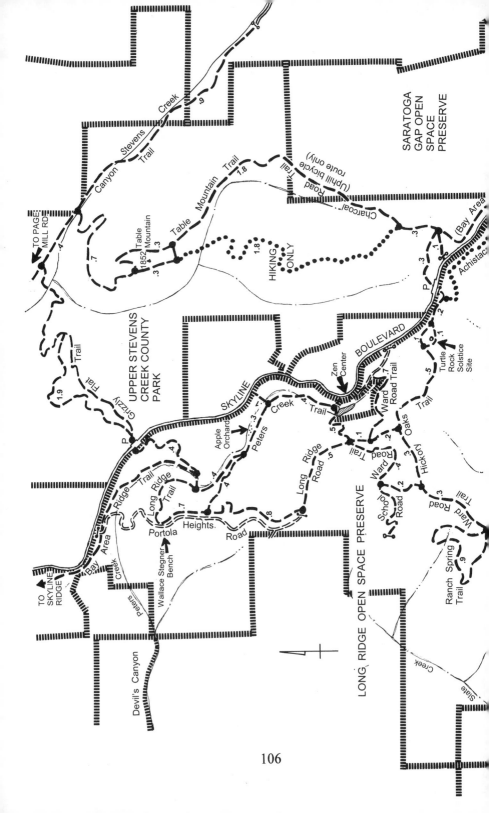

SARATOGA GAP OPEN SPACE PRESERVE

Stevens Creek

Canyon Trail

9

TO PAGE MILL RD.

.4

.7

Table Mountain 1852

.3

.3

Table Mountain Trail

1.8

Charcoal Road Trail (Uphill bicycle route only)

1.8

HIKING ONLY

.3

P.

.3

(Bay Area)

.1

.2

Achistaca

UPPER STEVENS CREEK COUNTY PARK

Grizzly Flat Trail

1.9

Trail

SKYLINE

Zen Center

BOULEVARD

Turtle Rock Solstice Site

.1

.7

.5

.1

Creek Trail

.4

Ward Road Trail

.7

P.

Apple Orchard

.3

Peters Creek Trail

.5

.1

.5

Oaks Trail

Hickory

.3

.4

.3

Ridge Trail

.4

Long Ridge Road

Long Ridge Trail

Portola Heights Road

.7

.4

.4

.8

.5

Ward Road

School Road

.2

.4

Ward Road Trail

.3

Wallace Stegner Bench

Bay Area

Peters Creek

TO SKYLINE RIDGE

LONG RIDGE OPEN SPACE PRESERVE

Ranch Spring Trail

.9

Devil's Canyon

State Creek

106

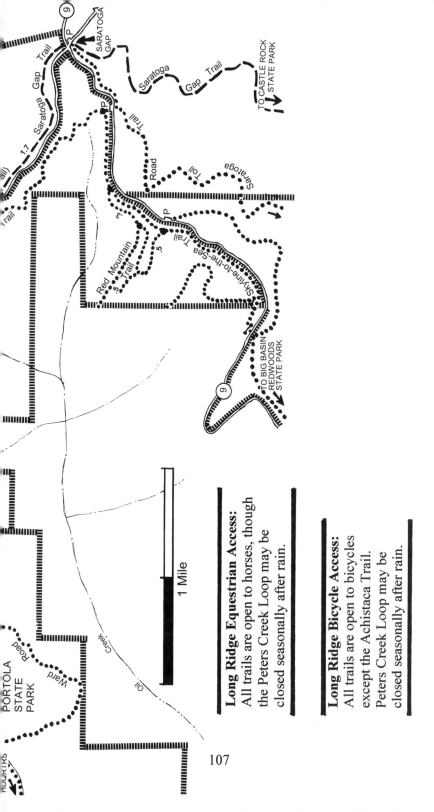

Long Ridge Equestrian Access:
All trails are open to horses, though the Peters Creek Loop may be closed seasonally after rain.

Long Ridge Bicycle Access:
All trails are open to bicycles except the Achistaca Trail. Peters Creek Loop may be closed seasonally after rain.

1 Mile

PORTOLA STATE PARK

Ward

Red

Creek

Oil

TO CASTLE ROCK STATE PARK

TO BIG BASIN REDWOODS STATE PARK

SARATOGA GAP

Saratoga Gap Trail

Saratoga Gap Trail

1.7

Road

Trail

Saratoga

Trail

Red Mountain Trail

Skyline-to-the-Sea Trail

.5

.5

.3

9

9

107

County Park beginning at the Grizzly Flat parking lot. It has lots of elevation range, ecological and scenic variety, and some great views. Walkers can do this loop either clockwise or counterclockwise. Bicyclists need to go clockwise because the Table Mountain Trail in Upper Stevens Creek County Park only allows uphill bicycle use.

Take the Grizzly Flat Trail to Stevens Creek and go south on the Canyon Trail. Then head uphill on the Table Mountain Trail and Charcoal Road to Skyline Boulevard. Hikers can take a narrow trail alternative. Cross the road and go uphill on the Hickory Oaks Trail and north on the Long Ridge Road to the turnoff to the pond. From the pond, go north on the Peters Creek Trail uphill on the Ridge Trail and back to the parking area.

By leaving a car in Portola State Park, which is downhill and to the west, you can enjoy a wonderfull 7.8-mile one-way ramble, with gravity doing much of the work. Just follow Ward Road as it drops about 800 feet from the sunny oakwood ridgetop to the shady redwood valley. Because bicyclists and horses are not allowed on the Portola State Park segment of this route, this is a hikers-only adventure.

The 1.7-mile long Achistaca Trail connects the Hickory Oaks Trail to Highway 9 and the Skyline-to-the-Sea Trail to the south. This route parallels Skyline Boulevard through a woodland of canyon live oak, Douglas fir, grassland, and chaparral. No dogs or bicylcles are allowed.

Long Ridge is ideal wildlife habitat, with tracks often visible in the mud after rain. Flocks of wild turkey are sometimes seen.

For more information, contact the Midpeninsula Regional Open Space District at (650)691-1200 (www.openspace.org).

SPECIAL SECTION

An Ohlone Legend of the Winter Solstice

At the highest point on Long Ridge are 2 rocks. One is vertical and has a notch at the top; the other is low and rounded, with a deep crack. According to legend passed down by Ohlone descendants and others, this was a gathering place for shamans from the bay side of the Santa Cruz Mountains to conduct sacred rituals on the winter solstice.

These rocks represent elements of an ancient creation story that tells of how the souls of all beings were brought from the ocean by Turtle. At sunset on the winter solstice the sun descended into the notch of the vertical rock and projected light onto the rounded rock behind it that represents Turtle's shell. At that instant Turtle's shell cracked open, and the souls of the people and other animals were set free.

Only on or near the winter solstice (the shortest day of the year),which is usually on December 21, does the sun set far enough south to settle into the notch of the vertical rock as described above.

Los Trancos Open Space Preserve

TO GET THERE... take Page Mill Road 5 miles west from Highway 280. The parking lot is uphill from Foothill Park and about 1 mile east of Skyline Boulevard.

This 274-acre preserve, with about 5 miles of trails, offers several easy trail loops through grasslands, chaparral, and oak woods, with sweeping views of the bay, Mount Diablo, and San Francisco. Los Trancos straddles a revealing part of the 600 mile long San Andreas Fault, and displays many features that evidence fault activity. The 1.5-mile San Andreas Fault Trail passes Los Trancos Creek, which follows an old line of broken rock within the San Andreas fault zone. Posts mark the location of known fault fractures.

Sag ponds, pressure ridges, and terraces in the park were created by the buckling of the rock under pressure from fault movement. Near the parking lot you will find conglomerate rocks that were sheared from Loma Prieta, a mountain 25 miles to the south, and were transported here by the

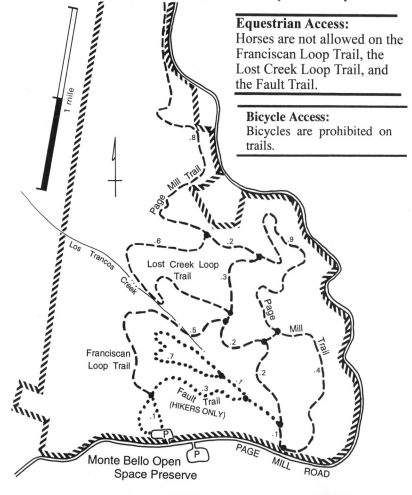

Equestrian Access:
Horses are not allowed on the Franciscan Loop Trail, the Lost Creek Loop Trail, and the Fault Trail.

Bicycle Access:
Bicycles are prohibited on trails.

gradual movement of land along the fault. The earth's crust is divided into massive plates of rock floating on the earth's mantle— and this is where 2 of them scrape together. East of here is the North American Plate, and to the west is the Pacific Plate. Naturalist tours are sometimes conducted from the parking lot on Sundays. For more information, call the Midpeninsula Regional Open Space District at (650)691-1200.

A brochure to the self-guided San Andreas Fault trail is available at the trailhead.

This is a brilliant wildflower garden in April when iridescent fields of blue-eyed grass, poppies, buttercups, and many others form a flowery carpet. Madrone and bay trees are common here, as are black, blue, canyon live, and coast live oaks.

Los Trancos can be used as a starting point for exploring other open space preserves to the south, and you can even travel about 8 miles from here to Saratoga Gap, where the Skyline-to-the-Sea Trail begins. See the Monte Bello Open Space Preserve chapter for details.

SPECIAL SECTION

A Short Guide to Earthquake Faults

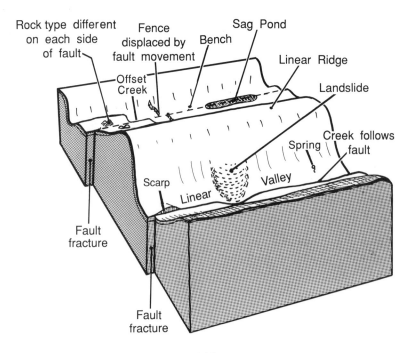

Earthquakes are a constructive force. They are responsible for most of the geography of California, including the Santa Cruz Mountains.

These mountains straddle the San Andreas Fault, which is the boundary between 2 vast continental plates. As the Pacific Plate (on the west side) and the North American Plate (on the east side) attempt to move in different directions, presure builds up which is released suddenly in the form of earthquakes. The collision between these plates pushed the range up from below the sea and wrinkled the land into parallel northwest-tending ridges.

Earthquakes cause characteristic distortions of the landscape which you can learn to recognize. When the fault slips in an earthquake, rock is pulverized and is then carried away by water erosion to form long, narrow valleys such as the one holding San Andreas Lake and the Crystal Springs Reservoir.

To walk on the San Andreas and associated faults is a rare privilege because California is one of the few places in the world where 2 continental plates come together on land.

This fence, at Los Trancos Open Space Preserve, was offset by movement on the San Andreas Fault.

Fissures appeared in Forest of Nisene Marks State Park, near the epicenter of the October 17, 1989 Loma Prieta Earthquake.

This sag pond, at Monte Bello Open Space Preserve, was formed where a bend in the San Andreas Fault made a sagging gap that filled with water.

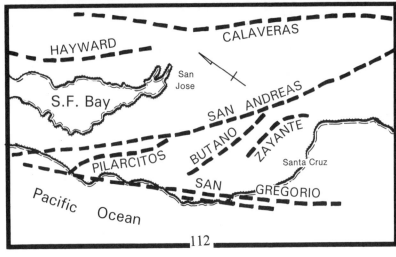

McNee Ranch State Park

TO GET THERE... Take Highway 1 north of Montara and park at the Martini Creek parking lot (8.1 miles north of Highway 92). Walk carefully along the Highway .2 miles and cross to a white metal gate where a dirt road trail enters the park. There is also parking and trail access farther north across Highway 1 from Gray Whale State Beach.

McNee Ranch sweeps down the steep slopes of Montara mountain to just above the vertical cliffs of Devil's Slide. Striking views of the ocean and mountains are seen from the dirt roads that make up the trail system. The hills are covered mainly with coastal scrub and coastal chaparral.

Be aware that strong and chilly Pacific winds lash these exposed slopes, and dense fog often covers them, especially in summer. Be prepared for changing conditions even on calm sunny days. The weather is often ideal in September and October.

McNee Ranch shares an eastern boundary with San Pedro Valley County Park and the San Francisco Fish and Game Refuge. By arranging a car shuttle with a friend you can travel by trail one way 4.5 miles from the trailhead on Highway 1 to the parking lot at San Pedro Valley County Park. This is a vigorous route, with an elevation gain of more than 1,500 feet and a lot of commanding views along the way. Add 2.2 miles for a side trip to the granite summit of the North Peak of Montara Mountain, which, on a clear day, affords one of the best views in the Bay Area.

A round-trip from Highway 1, via the Old Pedro Mountain Trail and the North Peak Access Road, to the Montara Mountain North Peak requires a steep 3.1-mile ascent followed by an equal and opposite descent. From the summit you will take in a 360 degree panorama of the Pacific Ocean, Farallon Islands, Point Reyes, Mount Tamalpais, San Francisco, San Bruno Mountain, San Francisco Bay, Mount Diablo, East Bay Area cities, San Francisco Fish & Game lands, including part of the rarely seen Pilarcitos Reservoir, and part of the San Mateo County coast.

The Old Pedro Mountain Road trail was built for automobile use in 1915 when it was known as Coastside Boulevard. This route was used by

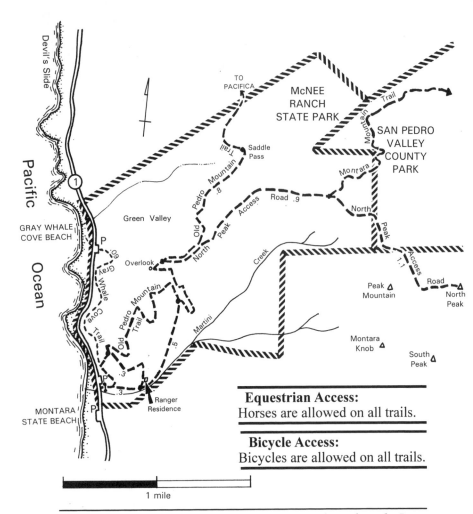

Devil's Slide

Pacific Ocean

1

TO PACIFICA

McNEE RANCH STATE PARK

Saddle Pass

Pedro Mountain Trail

Trail

Montara Mountain Trail

SAN PEDRO VALLEY COUNTY PARK

Montara

North Peak

Green Valley

Old

North Peak Access Road .9

GRAY WHALE COVE BEACH

P

.60

Creek

Peak Δ Mountain

North Peak

Access Road

North Peak

Gray Whale Cove Trail

Overlook

Old Pedro Mountain Trail

.5

Martini

Montara Knob Δ

South Peak Δ

.3

.3

P

P

Ranger Residence

MONTARA STATE BEACH

Equestrian Access:
Horses are allowed on all trails.

Bicycle Access:
Bicycles are allowed on all trails.

1 mile

Just south of McNee Ranch State Park you can stay the night at the Point Montara Lighthouse Hostel. For information call (650) 728-7177.

coastside bootleggers to deliver their merchandise to San Francisco during prohibition in the 1920's.

The expedition of Spanish explorer Gaspar de Portola camped on the bank of Martini Creek on October 30, 1769, just prior to their discovery of San Francisco Bay. Without the persistent effort of hundreds of dedicated volunteers, and years of struggle against Caltrans, this park would now be bisected by a highway. Dogs on leash are allowed.

Open from dawn to dusk, this park has none of the facilities you might expect at a state park. For more information, call the San Mateo County Coast District of the California State Parks Department at (650) 726-8820.

Monte Bello Open Space Preserve

TO GET THERE... The main parking lot is on Page Mill Road about 7 miles west from Highway 280 and 1.4 miles east of Skyline Boulevard.

Monte Bello is a large and varied land of deep wooded canyons, windswept grassy ridges, the San Andreas Fault, and a well-maintained system of trails for equestrians, hikers, and bicyclists.

From the parking area on Page Mill Road take the 3-mile Stevens Creek Nature Trail/Canyon Trail loop, which descends into a wooded canyon and then climbs past gnarled old oaks and through an abandoned walnut orchard. This loop passes a marshy sag pond filled with cattails and other aquatic plants. This pond lies right on a bend in the San Andreas Fault, and was formed when the land dropped between fault fractures. This loop can be expanded by .6 miles by substituting the White Oak Trail for the more heavily used Stevens Creek Nature Trail.

For a close look at the San Andreas Fault, combine the Stevens Creek Nature Trail and Canyon Trail in Monte Bello with the Fault Trail in Los Trancos OSP on the other side of Page Mill Road. Before starting this 5-mile loop, pick up a Fault Trail brochure at Los Trancos so you can read the numbered posts along the way.

The Canyon Trail, actually an old ranch road, is one of the area's most popular off-road bicycle routes. From Page Mill Road it plunges south-

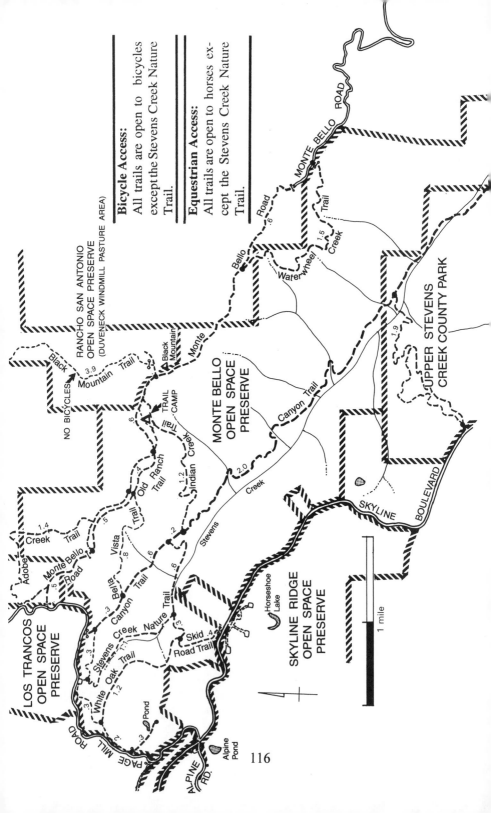

Bicycle Access:
All trails are open to bicycles except the Stevens Creek Nature Trail.

Equestrian Access:
All trails are open to horses except the Stevens Creek Nature Trail.

RANCHO SAN ANTONIO
OPEN SPACE PRESERVE
(DUVENECK WINDMILL PASTURE AREA)

MONTE BELLO
OPEN SPACE PRESERVE

LOS TRANCOS
OPEN SPACE
PRESERVE

SKYLINE RIDGE
OPEN SPACE
PRESERVE

UPPER STEVENS
CREEK COUNTY PARK

MONTE BELLO ROAD

Bello Road

Waterwheel

Creek Trail
1.5

.6

1.9

Canyon Trail

2.0

Stevens Creek

SKYLINE

BOULEVARD

Horseshoe Lake

Black Mountain Trail
3.9

NO BICYCLES

Black Mountain

Monte Bello Trail
.6

TRAIL CAMP

Old Ranch Trail
.4

Indian Creek Trail
1.2

.2

Creek Adobe
1.4

Monte Bello Road
.5

Trail
.5

Vista Trail
.8

Bella Canyon Trail
.6

.6

.3

Stevens Creek Nature Trail
.3

White Oak Trail
1.3

.3

Skid Road Trail
.4

1.2

.3

Pond

.2

.3

Alpine Pond

Alpine Pond

PAGE MILL ROAD

ALPINE RD.

1 mile

116

ward for about 8 miles through the wooded, shady canyon of Stevens Creek and on to Saratoga Gap (Highway 9/Skyline Boulevard intersection) via the Table Mountain Trail, Charcoal road, and Skyline Trail in Upper Stevens Creek County Park and Saratoga Gap Open Space Preserve. From there you can trek another 28 miles to the ocean by way of the Skyline-to-the-Sea Trail. By using 2 cars and a friend you can leave one vehicle at Saratoga Gap and then car shuttle back to the starting point.

This 2,758-acre preserve is the hub of a lot of other trail possibilities. Los Trancos Open Space Preserve is just across page Mill Road; and the Duveneck Windmill Pasture Area and Hidden Villa Ranch are reached by trail via the Black Mountain Trail. Other routes make connections with Upper Stevens Creek County Park and Long Ridge, Russian Ridge, Skyline Ridge, and Coal Creek Open Space Preserves.

From the Page Mill Road parking lot it is a 2-mile, 600-foot ascent via the broad Indian Creek Trail to the scenic summit of Black Mountain. With little shade along the way, this is not an easy walk at midday when it's hot. From Black Mountain there is a 3-mile downhill east-bound trail to the Duveneck Windmill Pasture Area unit of Rancho San Antonio Open Space Preserve and on to Hidden Villa Ranch. This is another good car shuttle opportunity. Or you can loop back to the Page Mill Road starting point via

Just west of Black Mountain is the Black Mountain Backpack Camp. With 6 spacious campsites perched atop the ridge, this is the only campground on Midpeninsula Regional Open Space District property. This is also the first campsite for backpackers traveling from the Santa Clara Valley to the coast. From the Page Mill Road parking lot the trailcamp can be reached by taking the Bella Vista Trail or the Indian Creek Trail 1.5 miles with an ascent of almost 500 feet. A pump provides washing water, but MPROSD advises you to bring your own drinking water. Campfires are prohibited. To obtain a camping permit, call (650) 691-1200.

the Bella Vista Trail for a 5.2-mile loop. You can even turn this into an easy 2-day trip by camping at the Black Mountain Backpack Camp.

There is limited public access to the south end of the preserve at the uphill end of Monte Bello Road, via Stevens Canyon Road from Cupertino. The Waterwheel Creek Trail passes through a mixture of woodland and grassy slopes on Monte Bello Ridge, with a good view into the Stevens creek watershed and the San Andreas Fault zone. The terraces on the hillsides are remnants of old vinyards. Docent tours for 5 to 25 people can be scheduled with MPROSD. You may want to stop at one of several wineries on Monte Bello road on your way back.

For additional information call the Midpeninsula Regional Open Space District at (650) 691-1200 (www.openspace.org).

SPECIAL SECTION
Where To Walk Your Dog

Mipeninsula Regional Open Space Preserves: Leashed dogs are allowed on all trails at Coal Creek, Foothills, Fremont Older, Pulgas Ridge, St. Joseph's Hill, and Thornewood Open Space Preserves. Dogs are allowed on most trails in Windy Hill Open Space Preserve, except for the Razorback Ridge and Sausal Pond Trails, and parts of the Lost and Eagle Trails. In Sierra Azul Open Space Preserve, dogs are only allowed on trails in the western part of the preserve, accessible from Kennedy Road and Lexington Reservoir. Pulgas Ridge has a 16-acre off-leash area.
State Parks: Dogs are prohibited on park trails. They are allowed on leash at parking lots, picnic areas, campsites, and on paved roads, including the Pipeline Road in Henry Cowell Redwoods State Park.
State Demonstration Forest: Dogs are allowed on leash on all trails in the Soquel Demonstration State Forest.
State Beaches: Dogs on leashes are allowed on most beaches. Dogs are not allowed at Ano Nuevo State Reserve.
Santa Clara County Parks: Leashed dogs are allowed on some or all trails in most parks, including Almaden Quicksilver, Mount Madonna, and Uvas Canyon. In Santa Teresa County Park, dogs are not allowed on the Joice, Bernal Hill, Vista Loop, and Stile Ranch Trails. For more detailed information, call (408) 358-3741.
San Mateo County Parks: Dogs are not permitted on trails.
Golden Gate National Recreation Area: Dogs are allowed on leash.
City Parks: Dogs are allowed on leash on trails at Foothills Park and Arastradero Preserve Monday through Friday except holidays.
Pogonip Open Space Preserve: Dogs are allowed on leash.
Private: Dogs are not allowed on trails at Hidden Villa Ranch, Jasper Ridge Biological Preserve, and Filoli Estate.

Mount Madonna County Park

TO GET THERE... From Highway 101 take Hecker Pass Highway (Route 152) 10 miles west from Gilroy. From Highway 1 take Highway 152 east.

This 3,219-acre park straddles a steep ridge near the southern end of the Santa Cruz Mountains. In addition to 20 miles of trails, it also has family, RV, and group campgrounds, including 117 drive-in and walk-in campsites available on a first-come, first-served basis. Picnic tables, a visitors center, archery range, and a pen for exotic white deer are nearby.

The trails are popular with hikers and equestrians, though some are for hikers only. Dogs on leashes not more than 6 feet long are allowed on trails. Bicycles are not allowed on any trails.

The well-maintained system of trails, many of which are old ranch roads, covers a surprisingly wide range of scenery, including second-growth redwood forest, chaparral, grassland, and oak woods. There are several excellent loops that offer a sample of all of these environments. Some trails are quite steep in places.

The Blackhawk, Iron Springs, and Merry-Go-Round Loop Trails combine to form an ideal 4.3-mile loop with an elevation range of about 800 feet. This loop can be started from either the ridgetop area or the Sprig Lake parking lot. It can be extended by including side trails to the deer pen and the stone ruins of cattle baron Henry Miller's nineteenth century house. The fallow deer are descended from a pair donated by William Randolph Hearst in 1932.

The Mount Madonna ridgetop, within view of Monterey Bay, is covered with second-growth redwoods, which are sustained by a moist shroud of fog that frequently settles on the ridge at night. Summer campers who nestle into their sleeping bags under a redwood tree, thinking there is no

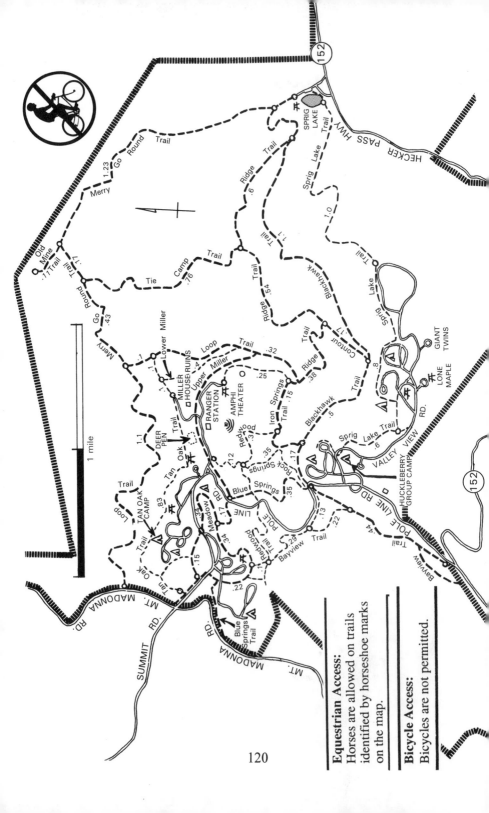

152

SPRIG LAKE

HECKER PASS HWY.

Merry Go Round Trail 1.23

Go Round Trail .17

Old Mine Trail .17

Ridge Trail .6

Sprig Lake Trail 1.0

Tie Camp Trail .76

Ridge Trail .54

Blackhawk Trail 1.1

Spring Lake Trail

Merry Go Round .43

Lower Miller .1

.1

.1

Loop Trail .32

Ridge Trail .25

Iron Springs Trail .38

Ridge Trail .15

Blackhawk Trail .5

Contour Trail .17

GIANT TWINS

LONE MAPLE

MILLER HOUSE RUINS

Upper Miller

RANGER STATION

AMPHI THEATER

Redwood Trail .3

DEER PEN Trail 1.1

Tan Oak Camp 12

Rock Springs .35

Blue Springs .35

Sprig Lake Trail .6

VALLEY VIEW RD.

HUCKLEBERRY GROUP CAMP

POLE LINE RD.

TAN OAK CAMP Trail .83

Loop Trail

Meadow RD. .35

17 RD.

Tan Oak .15

Redwood Trail .34

Bayview Trail .29

POLE LINE Trail .13

.44

.22

Bayview Trail

MT. MADONNA RD.

SUMMIT RD.

MT. MADONNA RD.

Blue Springs Trail .22

1 mile

152

Equestrian Access:
Horses are allowed on trails
identified by horseshoe marks
on the map.

Bicycle Access:
Bicycles are not permitted.

The fallow deer live in a pen on the ridge.

need for a tent at that time of year, may be awakened before dawn, by water drops condensed from fog that cascades off the tree's needles.

Sprig lake, a small seasonal reservoir along Hecker Pass Highway is open April through June for fishing by children ages 5 through 12.

For more information, call park headquarters at (408) 842-2341.

SPECIAL SECTION
Sudden Oak Death Syndrome

The majestic oaks of the Santa Cruz Mountains are threatened by a mysterious oval-shaped fungus called Phytophthora ramorum. The deadly infestation was first detected in Marin County in 1995, and was then found in tanoak and coast live oak in the Santa Cruz Mountains. It seems to be fatal in every oak tree infected..

The leaves of infected oaks turn yellow and brown. Cankers appear in the trunk that ooze dark red to black sap. Quickly all the leaves turn brown and the tree dies.

Sudden Oak Death Syndrome (SOD) is found in 7 species other than oak, including rhododendron, huckleberry, madrone, buckeye, big leaf maple, and bay. These plants host the fungus, but are not necessarily killed by it. How the microbe jumps from these species to oak trees is still a mystery. Perhaps it is carried on the feet of migrating animals. It could also be carried on the feet of hikers, the hooves of horses, and the tires of bicycles after passing through muddy ground.

Scientists at the University of California, Berkeley, and elsewhere, are researching ways to combat SOD. A compound is being tested which relieves the symptoms when injected into the trunk. Trail users can help by washing dirt and mud off of shoes, bicycle tires and horse hooves after an outing and by not transporting firewood from one woodland to another.

Pescadero Creek County Park

TO GET THERE... From Skyline Boulevard take Alpine Road west and turn south (downhill) on Camp Pomponio Road to the Tarwater Trail parking lot. From Pescadero Road, at San Mateo County Memorial Park, take Wurr Road south to a parking lot at the east end of the Old Haul Road Trail. This park can also be accessed from Portola State Park and Sam McDonald County Park.

This 6,486-acre forested park is on the watershed of one of the Santa Cruz Mountains' major creeks. There are more than 40 miles of trails, many of which form loop routes for hikers and equestrians. Bicycles are limited to designated dirt road trails. There are also 2 trailcamps which make this park a great place for backpacking. From Sam McDonald County Park, Tarwater Flat Trailcamp is 5 miles, and Shaw Flat Trailcamp is 4 miles. You can get a camping permit at San Mateo County Memorial Park.

From the Old Haul Road Trail you can ascend Butano Ridge Trail and then take the 1.5-mile Basin Trail easement through private land to the north end of Big Basin Redwoods State Park. From there you can descend the Basin Trail to connect with the Skyline-to-the-Sea Trail. Backpackers can stay at the Lane Trail Camp just inside Big Basin. Bicycles are prohibited.

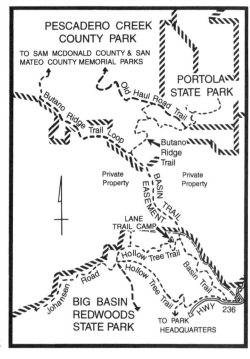

From the Camp Pomponio Road parking lot , the Tarwater Trailcamp is only about 2.8 miles downhill. The Shaw Flat Trailcamp is most easily reached from the parking lot at the Old Haul Road trailhead on Wurr Road. With metal fire cylinders, these are some of the only trailcamps in the Santa Cruz Mountains that allow camp fires. The camp sites are set deep in the shady redwood valley, separated from each other by dense huckleberry patches. Though these camps are near Pescadero Creek, climbing down the steep embankment to get water is no easy task.

There are many trail options. Here are a few:

Old Haul Road Trail (5.7 miles): The main route through the park, it connects San Mateo County Memorial Park to the west with Portola State Park to the east. This old logging road has an easy grade and connects with other trails to form numerous loop opportunities.

Pomponio Trail (5.3 miles): Traverses the park north of the creek and connects with many other trails.

Tarwater Loop Trail (5.45 miles): From the trailhead on Camp Pomponio Road, this pleasant and ecologically diverse route combines grasslands, oakwoods, redwoods, and Pescadero creek. The elevation range is 640 feet. This loop can be expanded to 6 miles by adding the Coyote Ridge and Upper Coyote Ridge Trails in Portola State Park. You can also expand this loop by adding the Pomponio Trail, Bear Ridge Trail, and Canyon Trail. There are an exceptional number of old-growth redwoods along the Canyon Trail. You will see tar seeping out of the creekbed where the Canyon Trail crosses Tarwater Creek.

Butano Ridge Loop (15-18 miles): From the Camp Pomponio Road parking lot you can make an enormous and strenuous loop across Pescadero Creek and up to the top of Butano Ridge via the Butano Ridge Trail loop. Depending on which route you take you can hike 15-18 miles with a 1,600 foot elevation range. Don't expect a lot of great views from the top of the ridge. The dense forest obstructs the views.

This is my favorite park for creek walking. Pick a warm day between May and October. Wear shorts and tennis shoes or water shoes without socks, and be sure to use a walking stick for maintaining equilibrium on the uneven creekbed. Be ready for occasional pools deep enough for swimming.

Pescadero Creek County Park was heavily logged early in the twentieth century and today has few old-growth redwoods. Evidence of logging is still visible. Rusting logging cables can be found wrapped around redwood trunks and notches for loggers' springboards can still be seen on old redwood stumps. This land was acquired by San Mateo County for the purpose of damming Pescadero Creek to form a large reservoir to provide water for the urbanization of the San Mateo County coast in the 1960's. When a higher level of environmental consciousness prevailed, and the development schemes were abandoned, this land became a park.

For more information call (650) 363-4021 (www.eparks.net).

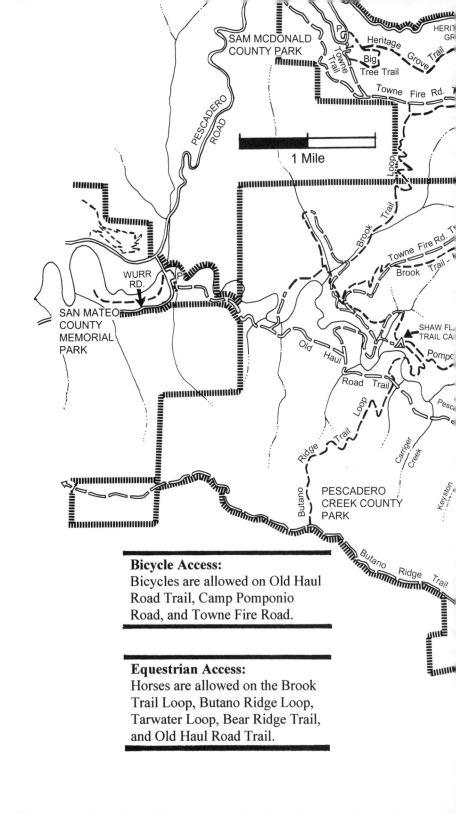

SAM MCDONALD
COUNTY PARK

HERIT
GR

Heritage
Grove Trail

Big
Tree Trail

Towne
Trail

Towne Fire Rd.

1 Mile

Loop

Brook Trail

Towne Fire Rd. T

Brook Trail

WURR
RD.

P

SAN MATEO
COUNTY
MEMORIAL
PARK

SHAW FL
TRAIL CA

Pompo

Old Haul

Pesca

Road Trail

Loop

Carriger Creek

Ridge Trail

Butano

PESCADERO
CREEK COUNTY
PARK

Keystor

Butano Ridge Trail

Bicycle Access:
Bicycles are allowed on Old Haul
Road Trail, Camp Pomponio
Road, and Towne Fire Road.

Equestrian Access:
Horses are allowed on the Brook
Trail Loop, Butano Ridge Loop,
Tarwater Loop, Bear Ridge Trail,
and Old Haul Road Trail.

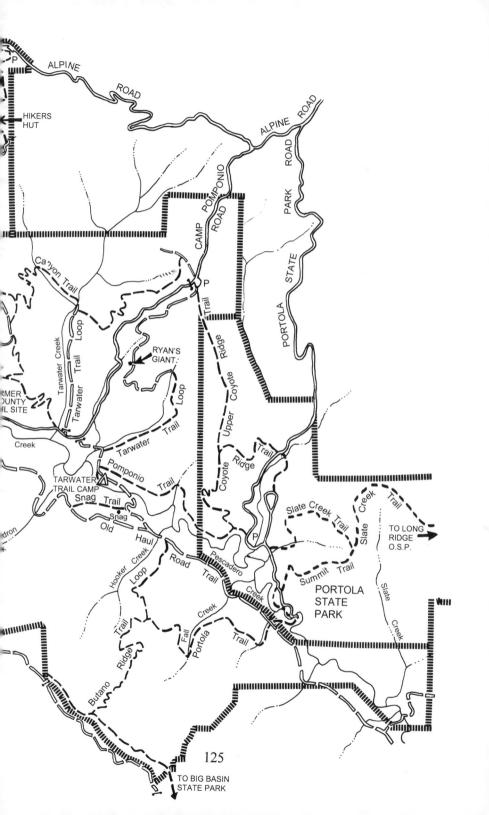

125

The Great Logging Boom

California was a sleepy place, with little population growth, until gold was discovered in the Sierra foothills in 1848. The resulting gold rush and population explosion triggered a construction frenzy in San Francisco and a nearly insatiable demand for lumber. The mountains south of San Francisco were the closest large source of redwood.

Beginning in the 1850's a rush for redwood lumber spread from the eastern slopes of the Santa Cruz Mountains in the Woodside vicinity to nearly all parts of the range where the trees grew. The free-for-all rush for "red gold" (redwood lumber and shingles) was in many ways similar to the gold rush of the Sierra foothills. By the 1920's there were hardly any unprotected large redwood trees left to cut, and the focus of the redwood lumber industry moved north to the more remote, but larger forests of Mendocino, Humboldt, and Del Norte Counties. Second-growth logging continues today on a much smaller scale in the Santa Cruz Mountains.

Evidence of the 70-year logging boom is still seen throughout the second-growth redwood forests of Pescadero Creek County Park, Purisima Creek Open Space Preserve, Forest of Nisene Marks State Park, Wunderlich County Park, and others. Look for notches in large redwood stumps used to hold springboards. Loggers would stand on these boards in order to be above the thickest part of the tree, using their axes or 2-handled whipsaws to fell these great trees. Before chainsaws it could take days of hard labor to fell one tree. Look for steel cables used to fasten logs.

Amid the rotting remains of sawmills you can find boilers used to power the saws (see above). Steam donkey engines would drag logs using a steel cable on a spool. Able to pull up to 100 tons, these machines were in use up to the 1920's. Many of the roads and trails in the Santa Cruz Mounatins began as logging roads.

Pescadero Marsh Preserve

TO GET THERE ... take Highway 1 to Pescadero Road, just west of the town of Pescadero. There are parking accesses on Highway 1 at Pescadero State Beach and on Pescadero Road.

Pescadero Creek and Butano Creek flow together to form the largest coastal marsh between Monterey Bay and the Golden Gate. The short trails that run along the 640 acres of wetlands, provide bountiful opportunities for seeing such birds as least and spotted sandpipers, godwits, great egrets, herons, and migrating waterfowl. Several short trails offer birding opportunities among the preserve's cattails, tules, and willows. Great blue herons nest in the eucalyptus trees on the hill.

Late fall through early spring is the best time to see many of the more than 160 species of birds sighted here. For more information, call (650)879-2170.

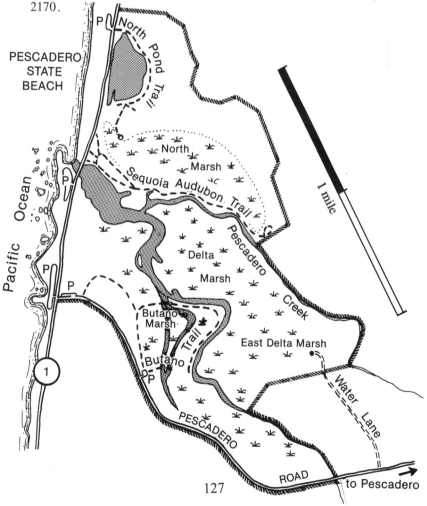

There are 2 places to start exploring the marsh. One is at the main Pescadero State Beach parking lot opposite North Pond. There is a day use parking fee. Cross Highway 1 and follow the North Pond Trail past the pond and up to a rise between the pond and Pescadero Marsh. Continue south to the Sequoia Audubon Trail, which parallels Pescadero Creek.

To explore the south side of the marsh take Pescadero Road east from Highway 1 and pull into a small parking lot on the north side of the road. Follow the West Butano Trail to a steel Bridge and on to a levee that separates Pescadero Creek from Butano Creek. This is a good place to enjoy the marsh and to see birds. Farther on, the trail peters out in the brush. Return back to the parking lot the way you came.

Picchetti Ranch Open Space Preserve

TO GET THERE... From Highway 280 take Foothill/Grant Road exit in Cupertino. Go southwest on Foothill Blvd. and Stevens Canyon Road 3.5 miles and turn west (right) on Monte Bello Road.

This 372-acre preserve offers 4 miles of trails through an easy blend of natural and agrarian qualities.

From the winery, head south on the Zinfandel Trail and then uphill on the Orchard Loop Trail or the Bear Meadow Trail to the oak-wooded ridge with views of the Stevens Creek Reservoir and the Santa Clara Valley. The 1.9-mile long Zinfandel Trail connects this preserve with the trails of Stevens Creek County Park and on to Fremont Older Open Space Preserve. This narrow path, for foot traffic only, wanders through a pleasant oak-bay woodland, with abundant bright red toyon berries, adding a festive look to the forest in fall and winter.

Near the winery are abandoned orchards of apricots, plums, walnuts, and pears. Apricots may be picked and eaten in early summer. The small pond along the Zinfandel Trail is a gathering place for waterfowl in winter.

This preserve is named for the Italian immigrants Vincenzo and Secondo Picchetti, who built the original homestead house in 1882. The large ranch house was built in 1886, and the brick winery was added in 1896. It operated under the Picchetti Brothers label until 1963. After 20 years of disrepair, these buildings, which are listed in the National Register of Historic Places, have been restored by the Midpeninsula Regional Open Space District and Picchetti Winery, which leases the buildings.

The Picchetti Winery is open daily from 11 am to 5 pm for wine tasting and sometimes live music. For information, call (408) 741-1310.

Though geographically separate, this preserve is administered as part of Monte Bello Open Space Preserve. For more information, call the Midpeninsula Regional Open Space District at (650) 691-1200.

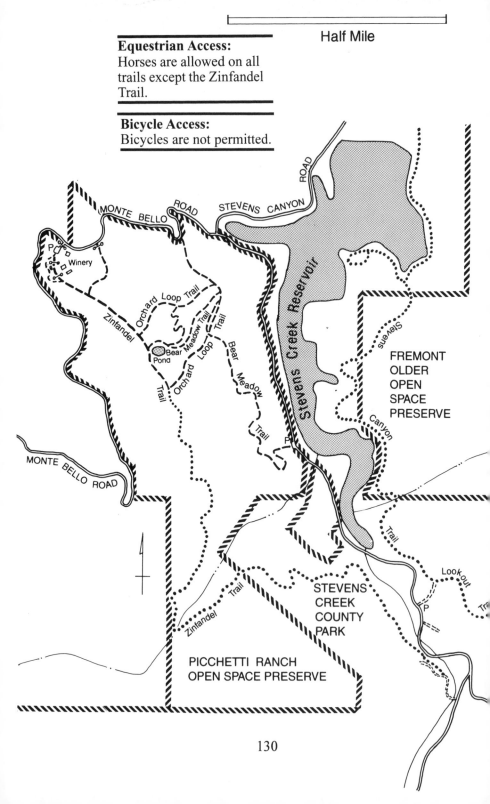

Half Mile

Equestrian Access:
Horses are allowed on all trails except the Zinfandel Trail.

Bicycle Access:
Bicycles are not permitted.

MONTE BELLO ROAD

STEVENS CANYON ROAD

Winery

Orchard Loop Trail

Zinfandel Trail

Bear Meadow Trail

Orchard Loop Trail

Bear Pond

Bear Meadow Trail

MONTE BELLO ROAD

Stevens Creek Reservoir

Stevens Canyon Trail

FREMONT OLDER OPEN SPACE PRESERVE

Zinfandel Trail

STEVENS CREEK COUNTY PARK

Lookout Trail

PICCHETTI RANCH OPEN SPACE PRESERVE

Pogonip Open Space Preserve

TO GET THERE... The north access is from the Rincon Road parking lot on Highway 9 in Henry Cowell State Park. From the University of California, Santa Cruz campus, there are 2 entrances. (1) From McLaughlin Drive take Chinquapin Road north to Crown College. Continue north past the gate on the Chinquapin Road Trail, turn right on the Fuel Break Road Trail, which becomes the U-Con Trail when it enters Pogonip. (2) You can also park at Stevenson College and walk a short distance down Coolidge Drive to the scenic pullout with trail access into Pogonip.

The city of Santa Cruz owns this 640-acre preserve located between the University of California and Henry Cowell Redwoods State Park. It is open from sunrise until 7 p.m. from April 1 through October 31 and from sunrise until 4 p.m. from November 1 through March 31. This is mainly a place for foot travel. Horses and bicycles are prohibited except on the U-Con Trail, which connects with the University of California.

Pogonip has a good variety of habitat, including oak forests, second-growth redwood, grasslands, chaparral, and a sycamore grove along the San Lorenzo River. Some of the trails are steep, but the entire elevation range in the preserve is only 450 feet.

For a scenic 3.5-mile loop that includes a variety of habitats from woodland to meadow, enter at the Lookout and head north on the Spring Trail, and combine Rincon Trail, Fern Trail, and Ohlone Trail into a loop. To extend the loop by half a mile follow the Brayshaw Trail to an old abandoned clubhouse. Leashed dogs are allowed on the Brayshaw, Fern, Limekiln, Lower Meadow, Ohlone, Rincon, Spring, and Spring Box Trails.

In 1849 Albion Jordan and Isaac Davis purchased 160 acres of this land to produce lime, used for making cement, from the area's plentiful limestone. Their lime kilns are still found on the Rincon Road Trail.

In 1865 Henry Cowell purchased Jordan's interests in the company. In 1888 Cowell bought out Davis' interests. Competition from other lime producers forced the closure of the company in 1946. The city of Santa Cruz purchased the property from the Cowell Foundation in 1989.

In 1911 Fred Swanton built a golf course and stately clubhouse, which is now closed.

For more information, call the city of Santa Cruz Parks and Recreation Department at (831) 420-5270.

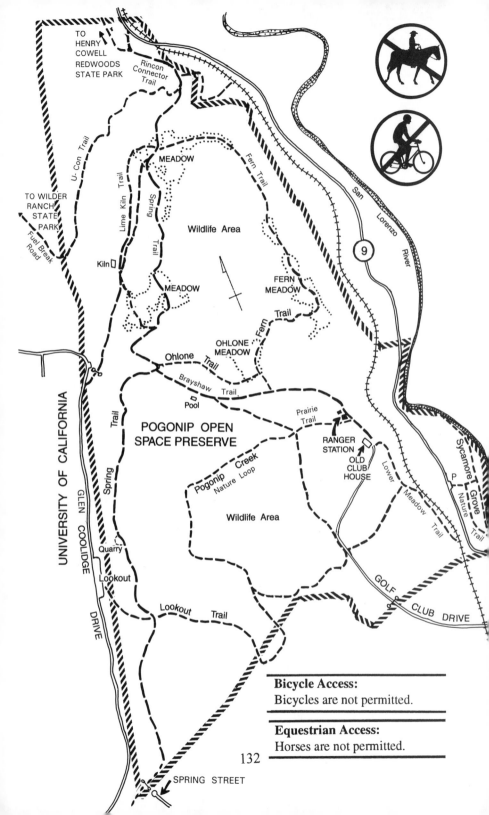

TO
HENRY
COWELL
REDWOODS
STATE PARK

Rincon
Connector
Trail

U-Con Trail

TO WILDER
RANCH
STATE
PARK

Fuel Break Road

Lime Kiln Trail

Spring Trail

MEADOW

Kiln

MEADOW

Wildlife Area

Fern Trail

FERN
MEADOW

Fern Trail

San Lorenzo River

9

OHLONE
MEADOW

Ohlone Trail

Brayshaw Trail

Pool

POGONIP OPEN
SPACE PRESERVE

Prairie Trail

RANGER
STATION

OLD
CLUB
HOUSE

UNIVERSITY OF CALIFORNIA

GLEN COOLIDGE DRIVE

Spring Trail

Pogonip Creek
Nature Loop

Wildlife Area

Lower Meadow Trail

P

Sycamore Grove Nature Trail

Quarry

Lookout

Lookout Trail

GOLF CLUB DRIVE

132

SPRING STREET

Bicycle Access:
Bicycles are not permitted.

Equestrian Access:
Horses are not permitted.

Portola State Park

TO GET THERE... Take Alpine Road west from Skyline Boulevard and turn south on Portola State Park Road

Since 1945 Bay Area hikers have been exploring this redwood forested park along Pescadero Creek. Its 2,800 acres offer more than 18 miles of trails through mostly second-growth redwood groves, though a few stands of big trees somehow survived. The park offers excellent opportunities for picnicking, car camping, and trail camping.

The park's self-guided Sequoia Nature Trail loop, which can be started just behind park headquarters, is a good place to start. Though it's less than a mile long, the Sequoia Trail can be connected with the Iverson Trail for a more extensive outing.

The Iverson Trail meanders along Pescadero Creek, which contains water all year and has a summer wading pool near the visitors center. The Old Haul Road is a 6-mile public trail (actually a fire road) connecting Portola State Park with San Mateo County Memorial Park. The trail travels through Pescadero Creek County Park. It can be reached from the Iverson Trail where it intersects a fire road southeast of Iverson Creek, at the site of the Iverson Cabin, built in 1860. Bicycles are permitted on the Old Haul Road. See the Pescadero Creek County Park chapter for more details.

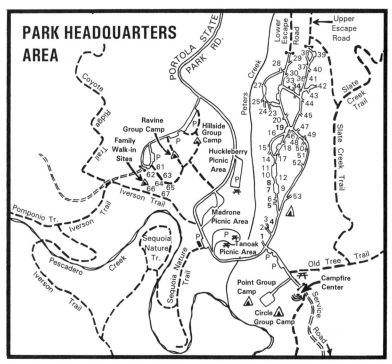

The Summit and Slate Creek Trails can be formed to combine an enjoyable hike of about 2.7 miles. You can add a .5-mile round-trip excursion to the Old Tree, which is 12 feet in diameter and 297 feet tall. An extra 2.5 miles can be added by including the Coyote Ridge Ridge Trail.

Equestrian Access:
Horses are not permitted.

Bicycle Access:
Bicycles are only allowed on State Park Road.

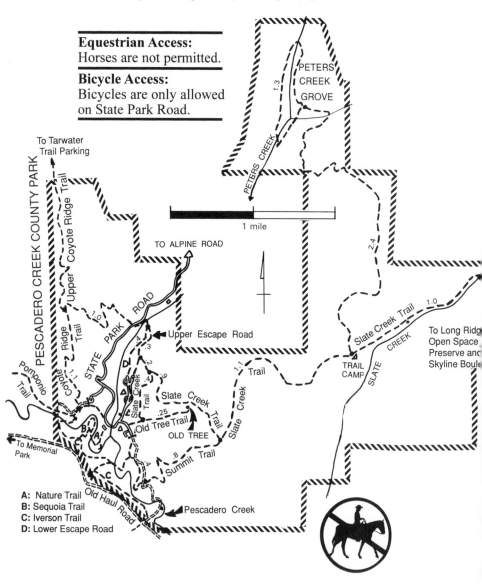

To Tarwater
Trail Parking

PESCADERO CREEK COUNTY PARK

Upper Coyote Ridge Trail

Coyote Ridge Trail

Pomponio Trail

To Memorial Park

TO ALPINE ROAD

STATE PARK ROAD

Upper Escape Road

Slate Creek Trail

Old Tree Trail

OLD TREE

Summit Trail

Old Haul Road

A: Nature Trail
B: Sequoia Trail
C: Iverson Trail
D: Lower Escape Road

Pescadero Creek

PETERS CREEK GROVE

PETERS CREEK

1 mile

Slate Creek Trail

Trail

SLATE CREEK

TRAIL CAMP

To Long Ridge Open Space Preserve and Skyline Boule

134

The Summit Trail links with the Slate Creek Trail, which goes to Slate Creek, Page Mill Site, and to the magnificent Peters Creek Grove. Before reaching the Page Mill Site there is a trailcamp about 3 miles from the trailhead at the intersection of Slate Creek Trail and Bear Creek Trail. The Slate Creek Trailcamp has 6 campsites limited to 6 people each. No campfires are allowed. Call park headquarters for reservations.

The trail beyond the Page Mill Site intersects unpaved Ward Road, which climbs through Long Ridge Open Space Preserve to the east to Skyline Boulevard, a distance of about 8 miles and an elevation gain of about 800 feet.

For an outing with lots of views and exceptional ecological variety, combine the Coyote Ridge Trail, and the Upper Coyote Ridge Trail in Portola State Park with the Tarwater Loop Trail and the Pomponio Trail in Pescadero Creek County Park. This loop covers 7.2 miles and an elevation range of 600 feet.

Acquired by the Save the Redwoods League, the 50-acre Peters Creek Grove is a beautiful old-growth redwood grove in a remote canyon. No one knows why the loggers spared these ancient trees. Beautiful Peters Creek and a lush carpet of redwood sorrel and ferns add to the charm of this "Shangri-La", which is isolated from the outside world by a strenuous 13-mile, round-trip hike, and an elevation range of nearly 800 feet. The trail is narrow, and steep in places, but you will be amply rewarded by one of the most unspoiled places in the Bay Area.

To hike there, take the Summit Trail and the Slate Creek Trail to the

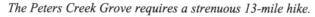

The Peters Creek Grove requires a strenuous 13-mile hike.

Slate Creek Trailcamp. Then take the Bear Creek Trail north, over an oak-forested ridge, and into the Peters Creek canyon.

The park has 53 drive-up and 7 walk-in campsites, 4 group camps, 3 for 50 people and 1 for 25 people. Showers and flush toilets are available. Campsites may be reserved by calling California Campground Reservation System at (800) 444-7275 or on the internet at www.reserveamerica.com

Nearby Pescadero Creek County Park has accessible trailcamps.

For more information, call park headquarters at (650) 948-9098.

SPECIAL SECTION

Banana Slugs

One of the most easily observed denizens of the Santa Cruz Mountains is a bright yellow mollusk which is the largest land slug in North America and one of the largest in the world.

Banana slugs glide through shady forests and along creek beds, eating almost anything organic, including leaves, animal droppings, and fungus. They have even been observed eating soap. They don't, however, eat redwood trees. Breaking off pieces of food with a rasping tongue that is covered with thousands of minute teeth, these slugs can eat several times their body weight each day.

You might wonder how such a slow, brightly colored, unarmed, and utterly vulnerable-looking creature can survive in the wild. Looks are deceiving, because the banana slug has one very effective defense: slime. This slippery substance is essential for moisture retention and for traction and lubrication when moving; but it is also loaded with caustic and bitter-tasting chemicals that make it unappetizing to predators.

If you see 2 banana slugs intertwined, especially during the rainy season, you are probably witnessing a very exotic form of mating. These ceatures are hermaphrodites, which means that each individual is both male and female. Two slugs fertilize each other during a 12-30 hour period and each leaves pregnant. Eggs are typically laid in the fall and hatch in the spring.

These slugs live about 6 years. On warm days during the dry season they constrict their bodies to a fraction of their crawling length and retreat into shady places, creek beds, and under logs to reduce dehydration. They thrive in areas of summer fog drip.

On the right side of the slug is a breathing hole called a pneumostome. Two sensory tentacles each contain a tiny eye.

Portola Valley Trails
COAL MINE RIDGE

TO GET THERE... Take Alpine Road south from Highway 280. Park on the north side of Alpine Road near the Willowbrook Drive intersection.

Portola Valley is an affluent community with a wonderful trail system that combines residential and wildland areas. Just east of the San Andreas Fault, this land is a pleasant patchwork of woodlands and grassy meadows. It is particularly enticing in late winter and early spring when the grasses are green and the wildflowers are in bloom. The land is forested mostly with oak, madrone, and bay.

For a moderate 3.7-mile loop, combine the Old Spanish Trail, Coal Mine Trail, and Toyon Trail. You will enjoy views of Mount Diablo, Mount Tamalpais, and especially nearby Windy Hill. The map reveals many opportunities to expand this loop. The San Andreas Fault runs through the Corte Madera Creek valley along Alpine Road. A straight fracture zone depression aligned with this fault can be seen between the Toyon Trail and the Coal Mine and Old Spanish Trails.

Just south of the intersection of Alpine Road and Willowbrook Drive is a trail entrance to Windy Hill Open Space Preserve.

These wooded 250 acres in the eastern foothills of the Santa Cruz Mountains are owned by the Portola Valley Ranch Homeowner's Association. Remember that the ridge is private land; so be sure to stay on the trails. Dogs on leash are allowed on some trails. Bicycles are prohibited.

For information call the Portola Valley town hall at (650) 851-1700 (www.portolavalley.net).

LARRY LANE TRAIL

This 1.75-mile trail begins at the intersection of Portola Road and Hayfield Road in Portola Valley. This is an easy ramble through a wooded residential area to a grassy meadow where hay was once grown. You will ascend 500 feet, passing expensive homes and woodlands of oak, madrone, and bay. Named for a local equestrian, this trail is for hikers and horses. Bicycles are prohibited. There are rest benches along the way. This route goes through private property, so stay on the trail.

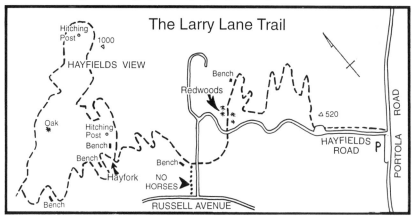

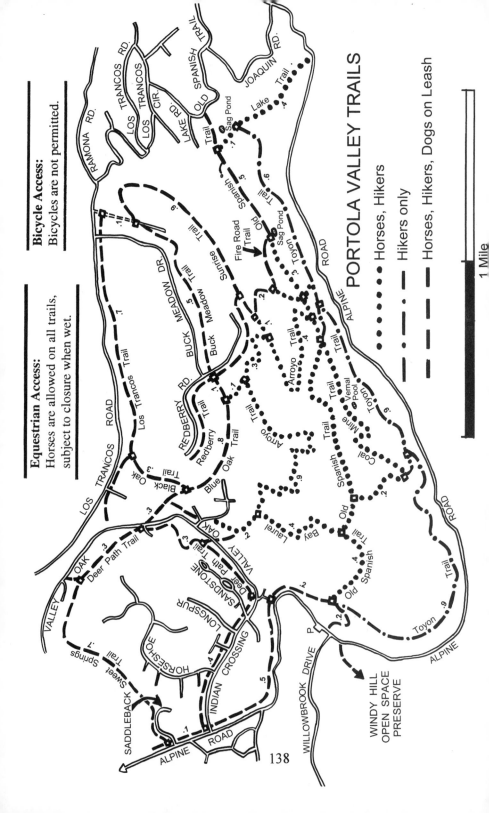

PORTOLA VALLEY TRAILS

Equestrian Access:
Horses are allowed on all trails, subject to closure when wet.

Bicycle Access:
Bicycles are not permitted.

• • • • • • • Horses, Hikers

— · — · — Hikers only

— — — Horses, Hikers, Dogs on Leash

1 Mile

138

Pulgas Ridge Open Space Preserve

TO GET THERE... from Interstate 280 take Edgewood Road east, turn left on Crestview Road, and left on Edmonds Road. Begin at the parking lot near the Redwood Center on Edmonds Road and take the Cordilleras Trail or the Blue Oak Trail.

This 366-acre preserve covers a ridge and 2 wooded valleys in the dry eastern foothills of the Santa Cruz Mountains. On the site of the

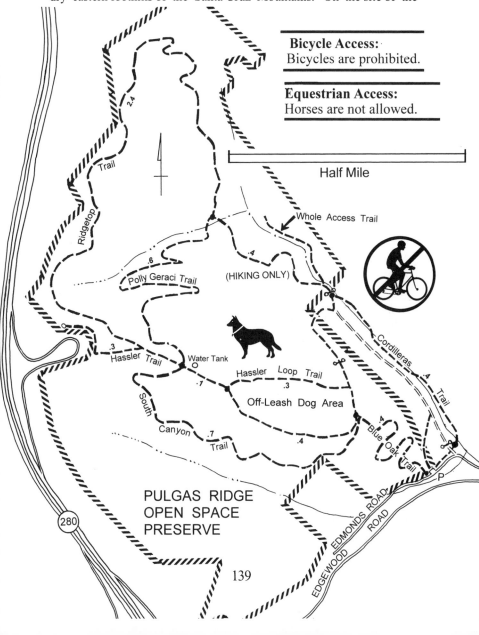

Bicycle Access: Bicycles are prohibited.

Equestrian Access: Horses are not allowed.

Half Mile

2.4

Trail

Ridgetop

Whole Access Trail

.6

Polly Geraci Trail

.4

(HIKING ONLY)

Cordilleras

.3

Hassler Trail

Water Tank

Hassler Loop Trail

.1

.3

Off-Leash Dog Area

Trail

South

Canyon

.7

.4

Blue Oak Trail

Trail

P

PULGAS RIDGE
OPEN SPACE
PRESERVE

280

EDMONDS ROAD

ROAD

EDGEWOOD

139

former Hassler Health Home, a tuberculosis sanitarium which operated here from 1926 to 1972 the land is now in the process of reverting to a more natural condition. Relics of its former use still abound, though, with abandoned fire hydrants and steps that go nowhere. The preserve is named for the ridge on which it lies. The Pulgas Water Tunnel bisects the northern part of the preserve. Pulgas means "fleas" in Spanish.

The hills are covered mainly with a combination of oak groves, chaparral, and grasslands. There are also ornamental trees and shrubs, especially around the site of the sanitarium, which have adapted to our summer drought cycle. Be aware that poison oak grows in abundance in places.

From the parking area on Edmonds Road, walk uphill through an oak forest on the Blue Oak Trail to the site of the sanitarium. This 16-acre area is the only place on MPROSD lands where dogs are allowed to roam off-leash. Then follow the Hassler Trail, Polly Geraci Trail, and Cordilleras Trail to complete a 2.4-mile hiking loop back to your car. This route can be expanded to 3.8 miles by taking the ridgetop Trail.

Leashed dogs may accompany you on all 6 miles of trails. The northern part of the Cordilleras Trail is whole access.

For more information, contact the Midpeninsula Regional Open Space District at (650) 691-1200 (www.openspace.org).

Purisima Creek Redwoods
Open Space Preserve

TO GET THERE... The main entrance is on Skyline Boulevard, 4.5 miles south of Highway 92. There is a smaller parking area at the uphill end of Purisima Creek Trail about 2 miles farther south on Skyline Boulevard. From Highway 1, just south of Half Moon Bay, the preserve's western access may be reached by taking Higgins-Purisima Road 4.5 miles to an entrance gate by a small bridge. There are a few places to park along Tunitas Creek Road at the Grabtown Gulch Trailhead. This is the closest parking to the Irish Ridge part of the preserve.

Climbing 1,600 feet of steep terrain just east of Skyline Boulevard, this preserve has the northernmost major redwood forest in the Santa Cruz Mountains. This 2,633-acre has lots of ridgetop views of the Pacific and the local mountains. Be prepared for a workout on about 21 miles of trails, some of which are steep.

Purisima Canyon is a major east-west drainage, with a perennial Creek. Though the area was logged intensively between the 1850's and 1920, supporting 7 sawmills for awhile, the second-growth forest now rises tall, and stumps up to 16 feet in diameter remind us of the great trees that were

141

Equestrian Access:
Horses are allowed on all trails except the Soda Gulch Trail and the footpath from the northern Skyline Boulevard parking lot.

Bicylce Access:
Bicycles are allowed on all trails except the Soda Gulch Trail and the footpath from the northern Skyline Boulevard parking lot. The Whittemore Gulch Trail may be closed during the rainy season.

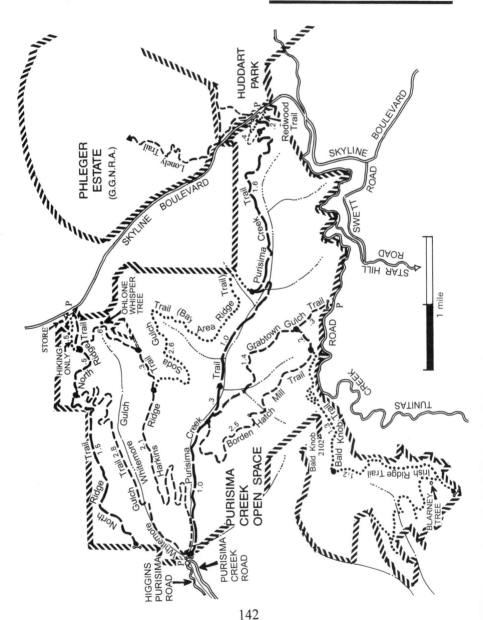

cut. There are still a few majestic stands of large, old-growth redwoods in the park, though you won't find many along the park's main trails. Though this preserve is known for its redwoods, it also has chaparral, Douglas fir, and scattered groves of oak.

A special trail for the physically handicapped begins off Skyline Boulevard at the southern access north of Kings Mountain Road. This is also a good access to the Phleger Estate unit of the Golden Gate National Recreation Area.

The Soda Gulch Trail connects the Harkins Fire Trail with the Purisima Creek Trail. Passing mostly through second-growth redwoods, it is a fairly gentle route that is open to foot travel only. These 3 trails form a strenuous 10.6-mile loop from the Purisima Creek Road entrance on Skyline Boulevard.

The Purisima Creek Trail is an old logging road that connects Skyline Boulevard with Higgins-Purisima Road. This route is 4.1 miles one way, with an elevation range of 1,600 feet.

My favorite hike is a one-way trek of 5.8 miles that requires 2 cars. Meet a friend at the main parking lot on Skyline Boulevard. Leave 1 car there and drive to the southern Skyline Boulevard access. Then combine the Purisima Creek Trail with the Soda Gulch Trail, and go uphill on the Harkins Ridge Trail to the North Ridge Trail and on to the parking lot.

For a spectacular, though physically-demanding 7.3-mile loop through Whittemore Gulch, begin at Skyline Boulevard and combine the Whittemore Gulch Trail and the Harkins Ridge Trail. This route combines great views with ecological variety, and requires an elevation range of about 1,400 feet. The Harkins Ridge Trail is steep in places. Be sure to carry water.

This route can be extended to 10.1 miles by charging uphill on the Purisima Creek Trail instead of the Harkins Ridge Trail and then looping back to the parking lot via the Soda Gulch Trail and the upper end of the Harkins Ridge Trail.

From the Tunitas Creek Road entrance, take the Grabtown Gulch Trail, the Purisima Creek Trail, and the Borden Hatch Mill Trail to form a 5 mile loop. From the upper part of the Borden Hatch Mill Trail you can travel 1.3 miles one way to enjoy views of the ocean from near the summit of Bald Knob. From there, the Irish Ridge Trail continues another 1.2 miles with great views and a giant redwood.

This preserve provides an essential link in the proposed "City-to-the-Sea" Trail, which begins at Edgewood County park in Redwood City, follows the Crystal Springs Trail to Huddart Park, climbs to Skyline, and then continues down through Purisima Canyon to Higgins-Purisima Road. All the trails needed for this crossing of the Santa Cruz Mountains already exist except for the last last link to the ocean. It is ideal for equestrians as well as walkers.

Being on the coast side of Skyline, be prepared for windy and foggy weather. For more information, call the Midpeninsula Regional Open Space District at (650) 691-1200 (www.openspace.org).

Even in the most heavily logged areas of these mountains, such as Purisima Canyon, a few old-growth redwood ancients survived the timber-cutting juggernaut that rolled through here in the late nineteenth century.

Most survivors are scarred by fire or deformed; or just too big to be cut up into pieces small enough to be hauled out of a steep canyon.

This fire-scarred tree, on Irish Ridge, in Purisima Creek Open Space Preserve, is one of these lone survivors. It is known as "The Blarney Tree".

According to Patrick Colgan, an Irish native who lives in La Honda, kissing this tree is just as effective as kissing the Blarney Stone in County Cork, Ireland. Patrick should know. He is an authority on Blarney. He claims to have an m.s. in b.s.

144

The Fog Forest

The mountains of the eastern side of the Santa Cruz Mountains look dry and dusty, in a kind of hibernation, during the long summer drought season. But this is not the case in the Purisima Creek watershed, especially near the Skyline Boulevard area. Even during the driest part of summer luxuriant gardens of moss, and other green and growing plants fill the lush forest.

Many times I have walked this preserve, especially in the early morning, when the fog drifts heavily through the groves, condensing on the needles of redwood and Douglas fir trees and dripping to the ground as steady as a winter rain. This phenomena is called "fog drip" and it contributes a large share of this area's precipitation, in many places the equivalent of 20 or more inches of rain each year.

Warm air can hold more water vapor than cool air. Fog forms when an air mass cools and the water vapor condenses into water droplets that are small and light enough to stay suspended in the air.

Along the northern California coast are currents that draw deep and cold water to the ocean surface. When the moist marine winds approach the coast they are suddenly cooled by contact with this cold upwelling water and the moisture in the air condenses into fog.

You will notice that the fog is thickest at night and early morning, often burning off by mid day. This is because the temperature is lowest at

145

night, causing the water vapor to precipate into fog. As the temperature rises during the day, the air is able to absorb this fog.

When the Central Valley bakes during the summer months the hot inland air rises and sucks cool marine air in from the coast. This heavy moist air mass then sweeps over low areas such as San Francisco, but it usually can't quite make it over the Skyline Ridge area, stalling atop the ridge and delivering this vitalizing fog bath.

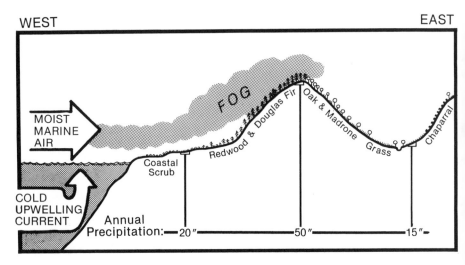

As moist marine air sweeps inland from the ocean it is forced upward by the Santa Cruz Mountains. As the air rises, it is cooled, causing water vapor to condense into fog and rain. This is why verdant forests thrive on the western slopes of the range.

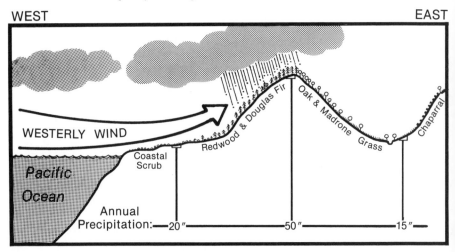

Quail Hollow Ranch County Park

TO GET THERE... from Highway 9 (north of Felton) take Glen Arbor Road and Quail Hollow Road west. The ranch is on the north side of quail Hollow Road.

There are few places in the Santa Cruz Mountains that manage to cram as much history, geology, and botany into such a small area as at Quail Hollow Ranch.

Be aware that this park is only open weekends and holidays, 10 a.m. to 4 p.m. from May to October. Call for current information.

Owned by Santa Cruz County, this 300-acre park features a beautiful forest of ponderosa pines, a tree that is common in the Sierra, but a rare relic of a cooler and moister time in the coastal ranges. This stately tree can be easily identified by needles about 10 inches long grouped in bunches of 3.

Notice that this tree grows in the granitic sandy soils that are characteristic of this park. They were formed as an inland marine sand deposit 10-25 million years ago when this area was below the ocean near the rapidly uplifting California coast. Called the "Santa Margarita Formation", it lies on top of an impermeable layer of shale, forming the Santa Margarita Aquifer, which is an important source of groundwater for the San Lorenzo Valley.

This unusual geology makes this habitat for 2 endangered species: the silver-leaved manzanita, and the Ben Lomond wallflower.

You will notice that some of the ponderosa pines are riddled with thousands of small holes made by colonies of acorn woodpeckers to store the acorns they have gathered in the fall for later consumption. These lively birds, easily identified by their black and white markings and red head patch, live in colonies that defend an established territory and collectively share the feeding and raising of young. One popular "granary tree" is the ponderosa next to the ranch house.

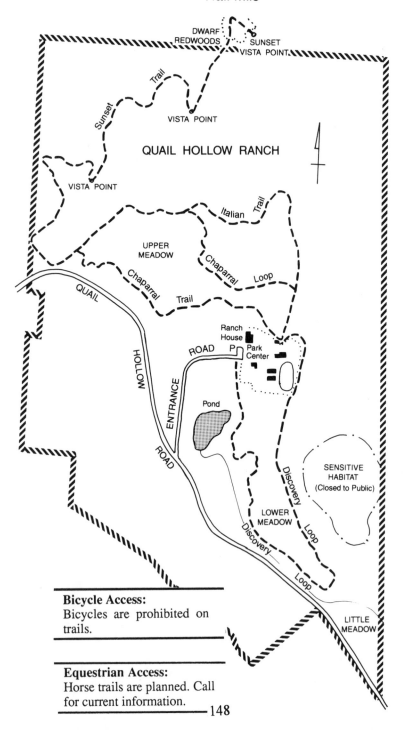

Half Mile

DWARF REDWOODS

SUNSET VISTA POINT

Sunset Trail

VISTA POINT

QUAIL HOLLOW RANCH

VISTA POINT

Italian Trail

UPPER MEADOW

Chaparral Loop

Chaparral Trail

QUAIL HOLLOW ROAD

ENTRANCE ROAD

Ranch House

P Park Center

Pond

SENSITIVE HABITAT
(Closed to Public)

Discovery Loop

LOWER MEADOW

Discovery Loop

LITTLE MEADOW

Bicycle Access:
Bicycles are prohibited on trails.

Equestrian Access:
Horse trails are planned. Call for current information.

148

Other biotic communities in this ranch include second-growth red-woods, including mature dwarf redwoods that grow only 18-20 feet high in areas of shallow rocky soil; oak groves, chaparral, riperian vegetation, and a pleasant little pond which is home to sunfish and largemouth bass, and a feeding place for blue herons, kingfishers, and other birds.

The **Discovery Loop** is a nearly level .8-mile route which includes a visit to the pond. The **Chaparral Loop** is 1 mile with a moderate ascent and can be lengthened by adding the **Italian Trail**. The **Sunset Trail** makes a climb, steep in places, for a scenic overlook and a stand of dwarf red-woods. Because of the fragile ecology, visitors are encouraged to stay on the trails.

Joe Kenville and his family lived in the ranch house from the 1880's until it was sold to Emil Grunig in 1910. From 1937 until 1957 Lawrence Lane, the publisher of Sunset Magazine, owned the property and featured it in his magazine as an example of western ranch living. The laboratory Lane put in for magazine related experiments can still be seen in the main ranch house. The land was ranched by several other owners until Santa Cruz County purchased it in 1985.

For more information and to be placed on the calendar of events mailing list, call (408) 335-9348 (www.scparks.com).

Rancho Canada del Oro Open Space Preserve

TO GET THERE... From Highway 101 southbound from San Jose take Bernal Road west, Santa Teresa Boulevard south, and Bailey Avenue west. Go south on McKean Road to the entrance to Calero County Park. As of this writing, the only access to the preserve is through Calero County Park.

See Map in the Calero County Park chapter.

This spectacular 2,428-acre property is a recent acquisition of the Santa Clara County Open Space Authority. As of this writing the only access is by traveling by foot or horseback about 4 miles through Calero County park to its boundary with Rancho Cañado del Oro. There is sepa-rate access being planned. .

If you like Calero County Park, then here is a place to get a second helping. The scenery here is as rugged as it gets in the Santa Cruz Mounains. You will trek through mountains covered with oak, chaparral, and grassland, with frequent views of nearby Loma Prieta and Mount Umunhum, the highest peaks in the range.

The only 2 trails now open are the Bald Peaks Trail and the Longwall Canyon Trail. You will notice other intersecting dirt roads that will form additional trails in the future. Combined with Calero County Park, the 2 units form 4,849 acres of public land. Because of excellent trails, a large equestian staging area, and horse rental in Calero Park, and no bicycles

allowed in either property, this is probably the best equestian opportunity in the Santa Cruz Mountains.

For more information, go to the Santa Clara County Open Space Authority website at: www.openspaceauthority.org.

Rancho San Antonio Open Space Preserve & County Park

TO GET THERE... To reach the main entrance from Highway 280 take Foothill Boulevard south and turn west (right) on Cristo Rey Drive. Parking is in Rancho San Antonio County Park. To reach the Rhus Ridge entrance from Highway 280, take Moody Road west, past Foothill College, turn left on Rhus Ridge Road, and park at the small parking lot near the tennis courts.

With easy access to the Mountain View, Los Altos, and Cupertino vicinity, this is the most popular of the open space preserves. It's a perfect destination for walking, running, horseback riding, and picnicking. Bicycles are not allowed west of Deer Hollow Farm. A well-established system of trails roam 23 miles throughout the 3,635 acres of this preserve. The county park is only 167 acres.

Historic Deer Hollow Farm is one of the preserve's most popular features and is used for a variety of environmental education programs by the city of Mountain View. For more information, call (650)903-6430. For summer camp information call (650)903-6331. It is especially popular with children. These old nineteenth-century farm buildings were built by the Grant Brothers, who purchased the land in 1860 for cattle ranching. It is only about a mile from the parking lot via an easy and nearly level Lower Meadow Trail. The farm is open Tuesdays through Sundays 8 am-4 pm.

Rancho San Antonio was the name of this area when it was part of a Mexican land grant in the early nineteenth century.

150

This preserve is in the foothills on the east side of the range. With an elevation ranging from 400 to over 2,000 feet, this area is characterized by chaparral and grasslands, and by oak woodlands composed of several species of oak, bay, madrone, and buckeye. Wildflowers.are abundant in spring. Reptiles are common here, including the prehistoric-looking Coast Horned Lizard, which is identified by a flattened body, a row of horns at the back of the head, and spiny scales at the edge of its belly.

The High Meadow Trail and Wildcat Canyon Trail can be combined to form a pleasant 5.6-mile loop. The rounded grassy slopes of the High Meadow Trail provides sweeping views of the Santa Clara Valley and the Peninsula cities to the east and north and 2,800-foot Black Mountain to the west. By adding the Upper High Meadow Trail, this loop can be extended to 7.5 miles.

Being a very popular preserve, it may be hard to find solitude. But it can be found, along with a feeling of rugged remoteness, in the western part of the preserve. For an exceptional one-way 5.4-mile outing, arrange with a friend to leave a car at the Rhus Ridge Road entrance and begin your outing at Rancho San Antonio County park. Take the trail to Deer Hollow Farm and continue on the Rogue Valley Trail. Turn right at the pond and climb the Chamise Trail uphill, passing an old quarry and some great views of the preserve, and Santa Clara Valley, and on to the Duveneck Windmill Pasture Area. Then continue downhill to your awaiting car.

From the Rhus Ridge Road entrance take the steep .9-mile Rhus Ridge Trail to the grasslands of the Duveneck Windmill Pasture Area, with a beautiful panorama of the hills and mountains to the south and west, including Black Mountain. Where the trail forks in 3 directions you can take the middle route, which heads east through the oak-studded grasslands and connects with the rest of Rancho San Antonio Open Space Preserve.

A vigorous and spectacular 3.9-mile trail climbs 2,380 feet to the summit of Black Mountain, in adjacent Monte Bello Open Space Preserve. By arranging a car shuttle, you can horseback or hike about 7 scenic and inspiring miles up Black Mountain, and north on Monte Bello Ridge to the Page Mill Road parking lot. A trailcamp near Black Mountain allows the trip to be broken into 2 days and allows the rare opportunity to camp in the grasslands east of Skyline. Fire is prohibited and reservations are required. See the Monte Bello Open Space Preserve chapter for more information.

The Duveneck Windmill Pasture Area, named for a windmill which once stood here, was once part of the adjacent Hidden Villa Ranch. Frank and Josephine Duveneck owned this land between 1923 and 1977, when they gave it to the public as a preserve. From near the Pasture you can take a trail into adjacent Hidden Villa Ranch, famous for its Youth Hostel and environmental education programs. Bicycles are not allowed on Hidden Villa trails. See the Hidden Villa Ranch chapter for more information.

For more information, call the Midpeninsula Regional Open Space District at (650)691-1200 (www.openspace.org).

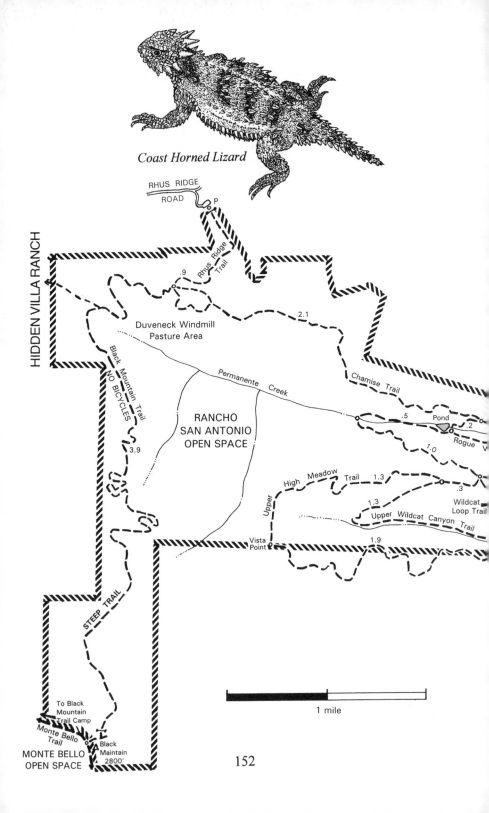

Coast Horned Lizard

RHUS RIDGE ROAD

P

HIDDEN VILLA RANCH

Rhus Ridge Trail

.9

2.1

Duveneck Windmill Pasture Area

Black Mountain Trail
NO BICYCLES

3.9

Permanente Creek

Chamise Trail

RANCHO SAN ANTONIO OPEN SPACE

.5   Pond   .2

Rogue V

1.0

Upper High Meadow Trail   1.3

1.3

.3

Wildcat Loop Trail

Upper Wildcat Canyon Trail

Vista Point

1.9

STEEP TRAIL

To Black Mountain Trail Camp

Monte Bello Trail

MONTE BELLO OPEN SPACE

Black Maintain 2800'

1 mile

152

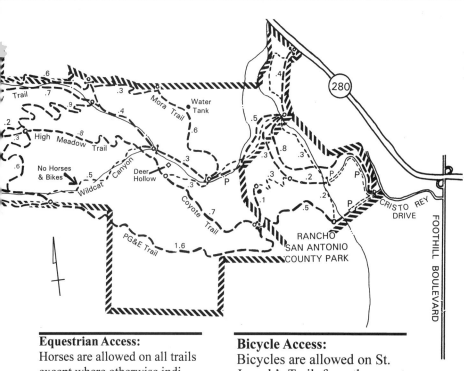

Equestrian Access:
Horses are allowed on all trails except where otherwise indicated on map. Coyote Trail may be closed when wet.

Bicycle Access:
Bicycles are allowed on St. Joseph's Trail from the county park to Deer Hollow Farm and Lower Meadow Trail.

The Ridge Trail

The Bay Area Ridge Trail (BART) is an ambitious 400-mile long 9 county loop around the Bay Area. Though most of the route tends toward the wild and mountainous areas, it will also span 3 bridges across the bay and pass through the city of San Francisco and cross the Santa Clara Valley.

Much of the route is already in place through existing public lands. The real challenge has been to find ways to connect these lands together into a continuous trail.

The Santa Cruz Mountains portion of the Ridge Trail enters San Mateo on the coast and ascends Sweeney Ridge. The proposed route passes through the San Francisco Fish and Game Refuge (Watershed) and follows the Skyline Ridge southward. When finished it will link nearly all the trails in the range together into one vast trail network.

The longest trail gap in the Santa Cruz Mountains is through the 23,000 acre San Francisco Fish and Game Refuge, which is owned by the San Francisco Water Department. The SFWD has been reluctant to allow the Ridge Trail to follow a 9.2-mile dirt service road that connects Sweeney Ridge to the north with Highway 92 at the Skylawn cemetary to the south.

The entire route will be open to walkers, with alternate routes wherever feasable, for offroad bicycles and horses. The trail passes through many existing parks and preserves which are discussed in more detail in other parts of this book. For more detailed maps refer to the appropriate chapters.

For more information call the Bay Area Ridge Trail Council at (415) 543-4291 (www.ridgetrail.org).

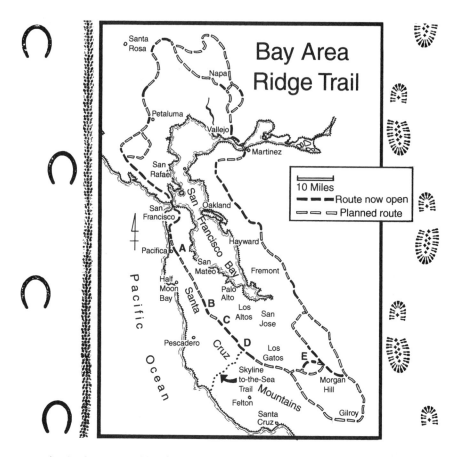

Bay Area Ridge Trail

10 Miles
▬ ▬ ▬ Route now open
☐ ☐ ☐ Planned route

A: On Sweeney Ridge from Sneath Lane to Skyline College: **6.5 miles.**
B: From Bear Gulch Road at Wunderlich County Park take the Skyline Trail through the California Water Service Company land to Huddart County Park. Then cross Skyline Blvd. to Purisima Creek Open Space Preserve and follow the Purisima Creek, Soda Gulch, and Harkins Fire Trails. This stretch of the Ridge Trail is about **12 miles.**
C: Windy Hill Open Space Preserve: **3.5 miles.**
D: A continuous stretch of the Ridge Trail passes through Russian Ridge Open Space Preserve, Skyline Ridge Open Space Preserve, Long Ridge Open Space Preserve, Upper Stevens Creek County Park, Saratoga Gap Open Space Preserve, Castle Rock State Park, and Sanborn Skyline County Park for a total distance of **18.6 miles.**
E: Santa Teresa County Park, Stile Ranch Trail, and Los Alamitos/Calero Creek Trail: **6.2 miles.**

　　Please note: This mileage is for hiking routes. Alternate routes are required for portions of the Ridge Trail for other trail users.

155

Russian Ridge Open Space Preserve

TO GET THERE... From Highway 280 take Page Mill Road uphill and west to where it intersects Skyline Boulevard. The main parking lot is just west of this intersection on Alpine Road. You can also take Skyline Boulevard 19.8 miles south from Highway 92. Another access is at the vista point turnoff on Skyline a little over a mile to the north. The north access is on Rapley Ranch Road just west of Skyline Boulevard.

This 1,822-acre preserve sprawls across grassy ridges and wooded valleys which can be explored by walkers, equestrians, and bicyclists.

Take the Ridge Trail uphill from the Alpine Road parking lot and along the spine of the ridge. This route offers an overview of the entire preserve, visiting Borel Hill, the highest named point in San Mateo County, which unfolds a 360 degree panoramic display of Mount Tamalpais and San Francisco to the north; the bay and Mount Diablo to the east; Mount Umunhum and Monterey Bay to the south; and the ocean and Butano Ridge to the west.

A wonderful 4.5-mile loop can be enjoyed by combining the Ridge Trail, The Hawk Ridge Trail, and the Ancient Oaks Trail. Splendid wind-swept ridgetop vistas and some exceptionally large and gnarled old canyon live oaks await you. The map reveals alternative routes to expand this loop.

This is one of the best places in the Santa Cruz Mountains to see wildflowers. The flowers bloom well into May, when the grasslands at lower elevations are brown. The ridgetop glistens with johny jumpups and with lots of big showy mule ear sunflowers. You will see lots of birds of prey, especially over the grassy hills, where they feed on abundant

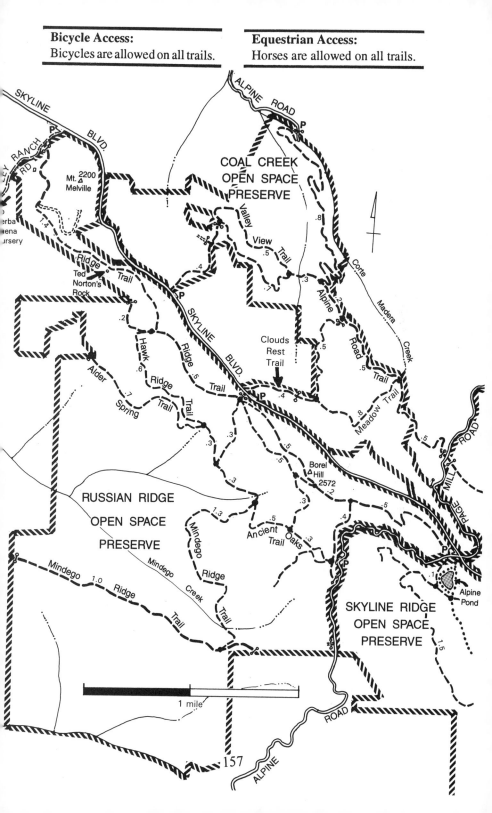

SKYLINE

BLVD.

ALPINE ROAD

P

RANCH RD.

P

Mt. Melville 2200

erba ena rsery

COAL CREEK OPEN SPACE PRESERVE

Valley

View Trail

.8

.5

Corte

.4

.3

Alpine

.7

.2

Madera Creek

Ridge Trail

Ted Norton's Rock

.2

Hawk

.6

Ridge

Trail

Ridge

Trail

SKYLINE BLVD.

Clouds Rest Trail

.5

.5

Road Trail

Alder

.7

Spring

Ridge

Trail

.3

P

.4

.8

Meadow Trail

.5

MILL ROAD

.3

.3

.5

.5

.2

Borel Hill 2572

.3

.5

PAGE

RUSSIAN RIDGE OPEN SPACE PRESERVE

1.3

.5

Ancient Oaks Trail

.3

.4

.5

P

P

Mindego

Ridge

Trail

Mindego

1.0

Ridge

Trail

Mindego Creek Trail

SKYLINE RIDGE OPEN SPACE PRESERVE

.1

Alpine Pond

1.5

1 mile

ALPINE ROAD

ground squirrels and other rodents; so bring binoculars. This is also a good place for cross country skiing and other snow activities on those rare winter days when snow mantles the hills. With its smooth, rounded forms, Russian Ridge offers miles of skiing in the early morning before the snow melts.

Mindego Ridge Trail descends from the ridge to Mindego Creek as it passes through grasslands and oak woodlands. Mindego Hill, the large promontory just west of the preserve, is the remnant of an ancient submarine volcano formed under the ocean more than 135 million years ago.

Mount Melville, at the north end of the preserve, is easily ascended to a grove of stately oaks, affording a grand panorama of the Pacific to the west and San Francisco Bay to the east. From Rapley Ranch Road, the Ridge Trail meanders south past several pieces of environmental art, including Ted Norton's Rock. It is about 3.1 miles from one end of the preserve to the other.

For more information, call the Midpeninsula Regional Open Space District at (650)691-1200 (www.openspace.org).

This standing stone is the work of artist Sam Richardson, who placed it here in memory of Edward Norton (1959-1984). The inscription reads: "For me there is only traveling paths that have heart."

158

St. Joseph's Hill Open Space Preserve

TO GET THERE. . . from **Highway 17 take Alma Bridge Road at Lexington Reservoir, cross the dam and park at the first parking lot on the right. To enter the preserve, walk uphill on the dirt road across from the parking lot.**

There aren't enough miles of trails in this park to keep you going for long, unless you slow down and make frequent stops to enjoy the scenery. The ranch road trail to the 1,253-foot summit of Saint Joseph's Hill is just steep enough to get the blood pulsing, but not far enough for a serious workout.

On the way up you will find increasingly attractive views of Lexington Reservoir and the surrounding mountains. The trail passes through

Equestrian Access:	Bicycle Access:
Horses are allowed on all trails.	Bicycles are allowed on all trails.

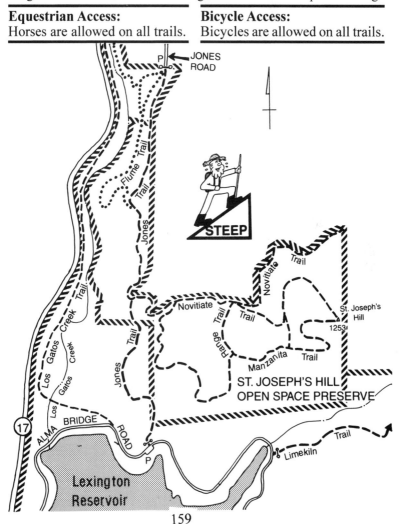

Lexington Reservoir from the trail up St. Joseph's Hill.

splendid groves of exceptionally large manzanita bushes. They seem to prefer to grow in the areas of serpentine, a rock easily identified by its smooth and waxy feel.

Part of the trail is bordered by a chain link fence which keeps visitors from wandering onto property owned by The California Province of the Society of Jesus. The entire preserve is only 170 acres, though it seems much bigger because of the grandiose views. An additional 97 acres are retained by the Jesuits to be undeveloped under an open space easement.

Near the summit the chaparral suddenly yields to a grassland area that the Jesuits once used as a vineyard. The top of Saint Joseph's Hill is a wonderful place for a picnic. A 360-degree panorama offers views of Mount Hamilton, the Diablo Range, and the Santa Clara Valley to the east; San Francisco Bay and the cities of the Peninsula to the north; and the ridges and peaks of the Santa Cruz Mountains and Lexington Reservoir to the west and south.

For more information contact the Midpeninsula Regional Open Space District at (650)691-1200 (www.openspace.org).

SPECIAL SECTION
Wild Pigs

In recent years wild pigs have been ravaging their way north through the Santa Cruz Mountains, "roto-tilling" the grassy slopes as they proliferate. Though you will rarely see these pigs, the evidence of their presence is easily observed.

Wild pigs usually come out at night, though they are sometimes seen during daylight. The males can weigh more than 300 pounds and stand about 3 feet tall. The females weigh a little less. Their color can range from brown to black. Their upper tusks, which are usually 3-5" long, are actually modified canines.

Wild boars were brought to California from Europe and released into the wild by hunters in 1925. They interbred with feral domestic pigs to form the hybrid that now inhabits large parts of California, including the Santa Cruz Mountains.

Much of pig behavior is explained by the fact that they have poor vision and a keen sense of smell. Wild pigs are more likely to smell you than to see you. They are most active at dawn and dusk, when they use their amazing noses to locate acorns, roots, tubers, fungi, snails, berries, eggs, salamanders, and lots of other edibles. Acorns are one of their staple foods in the fall. Their endless quest for food, both on and below the surface, causes not just a blight on the landscape, it also causes environmental damage by eroding the hillsides and by depriving native wildlife of food.

What makes wild pigs so hard to control is their prolific breeding ability. They can reproduce twice each year, producing 4-10 young at a time. Female piglets can breed when 6 months old. Compounding this problem is that predation has only a small impact on pig population. Piglets are sometimes taken by coyotes and mountain lions. Mature hogs are occasionally killed by lions, but it's a dangerous and uncommon way for a cougar to get a meal.

Humans are the only predator in the Santa Cruz Mountains capable of controlling wild pig numbers. That is why public agencies are contracting with professional hunters and trappers to do the job. The Midpeninsula Regional Open Space District is focusing its anti-porcine assault on the part of this range most heavily impacted: the Skyline Boulevard area, especially Long Ridge, Skyline Ridge, and Russian Ridge Open Space Preserves.

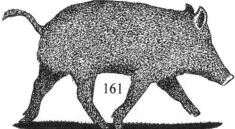

161

Sam Mcdonald County Park

TO GET THERE. . Take La Honda-Pescadero Road about 3 miles west of La Honda.

This is a beautiful 1,003-acre forest of mostly second-growth redwoods and an ideal destination for a picnic and a hike. The park is kept in a semi-primitive state by limiting automobile access only to the park office area off Pescadero Road.

The Forest Loop Trail is a good 3.1-mile hike northwest from the parking lot, and though not very long, this peaceful redwood garden of sorrel and ferns has plenty of scenic diversions and its share of challenging ups and downs. The continuation of the Forest Loop Trail beginning on the other side of the parking lot is equally rewarding. This part of the trail continues as a dirt road for about 2 miles southwest from Pescadero Road and passes some splendid first-growth redwoods, the most magnificent of which can be seen along the short footpath that crosses and then returns back to the dirt road.

You can travel by trail from Sam McDonald to Pescadero Creek County Park, San Mateo County Memorial Park, and Portola State Park. The route is about 6 miles from Sam McDonald park headquarters to San Mateo County Memorial Park, and a little more than 7 miles to Portola State Park. This route climbs past first and second-growth redwoods to grassy hilltop vistas and then descends into a forest of Douglas fir and second-growth redwoods. When you get to the top of the ridge, in the grassy meadow, head south on Brook Trail or Towne Fire Road to Pomponio Trail. Head west to San Mateo County Memorial Park and east to Portola State Park, or combine Brook Trail, Pomponio Trail, and Towne Fire Road together into a scenic 8-mile loop ramble.

For an exceptional 4.1 mile loop, begin at the ranger station and take the Big Tree Trail across the road and uphill to the Heritage Grove Trail, which continues 2.6 miles to the small but beautiful Heritage Grove of old-growth redwoods. From there head uphill to the Towne Fire Road and an optional stopoff at the Sierra Club's hikers hut. Then take the Towne Fire Road west and downhill back to where you began.

The hikers hut, atop a scenic ridge, is a cozy place to stay. For reservations, call the Loma Prieta chapter of the Sierra Club at (650)390-8411. Equestrians can stay at the Jack Brook Horse Camp between April 15 and November 15. Corrals, picnic tables, and barbeques are available. For reservations, call (650)879-0212.

Organized youth groups can reserve sites at 3 walk-in campgrounds: Modoc, Chinook, and Choctow Youth Group areas. They range in distance from .5 to 1 mile from the plarking lot.

Sam McDonald (1884-1957) was a popular Stanford University employee who owned the property until his death. He loved nature and willed that his forest be preserved in its natural state. Stanford owned the land until it became a county park in 1969.

162

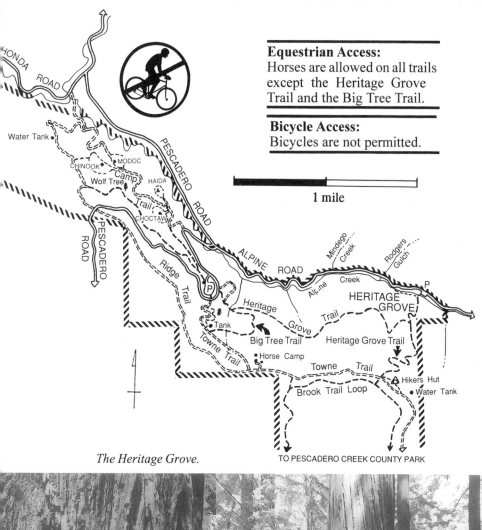

1 mile

HONDA ROAD

Water Tank

CHINOOK   MODOC

Camp

Wolf Tree   HAIDA

Trail

CHOCTAW

PESCADERO ROAD

PESCADERO ROAD

Ridge Trail

P

ALPINE ROAD

Mindego Creek

Rodgers Gulch

Alpine Creek

P

HERITAGE GROVE

Heritage   Grove   Trail

Tank

Big Tree Trail

Heritage Grove Trail

Towne Trail

Horse Camp

Towne   Trail

Hikers Hut

Water Tank

Brook Trail Loop

The Heritage Grove.

TO PESCADERO CREEK COUNTY PARK

For more information, and reservations for group camping, call park headquarters at (650)879-0212 or (650)363-4021.

THE HERITAGE GROVE

This 37-acre, old-growth redwood grove is part of Sam McDonald Park and can be reached by taking the Heritage Grove Trail from park headquarters or from the hikers' hut or by driving east to a parking lot on Alpine Road one mile from its intersection with Pescadero Road. This small, but magnificent grove, along Alpine Creek, was scheduled to be logged until a citizens group raised funds and purchased the land. The loggers' paint marks can still be seen on some of the trees they intended to remove. A short and easy trail takes you through the grove.

San Bruno Mountain County Park

TO GET THERE... From Bayshore Boulevard in Brisbane, turn west on Guadalupe Canyon Parkway to the park entrance and picnic area.

This 1,314-foot high promontory is a grassland island in an urban sea and is the only large open space in this densely settled and industrialized area. It's an ecological remnant of northern San Mateo County and a wonderful wildflower garden in spring. Actually, this "mountain" consists of 2 parallel ridges separated by the Guadalupe Valley.

Spring wildflowers here are exceptional both in abundance and diversity. Perhaps the best wildflower walk is the 3.1-mile Summit Loop Trail, which begins at the parking lot just south of Guadalupe Canyon Parkway and climbs 725 feet to the summit. This route is notable for striking vistas down the mountain and north to San Francisco. Along the

164

way the trail dips into a steep canyon along April Brook, a place known as "The Flower Garden" for its extraordinary springtime flowers.

You can drive up Radio Road to the summit parking lot near the antennas. For exceptional Bay Area windswept panoramas ramble west along the spine of the ridge for about 2.5 miles toward East Peak. The park has about 11 miles of trails.

Most of the mountain is covered with coastal chaparral vegetation and with annual grasses that make it green in the winter and spring and golden brown in summer. Most of the trees are in the canyons and on north-facing slopes. Coastal wood, bracken, and chain ferns dwell in moist and shady places.

Surrounded by dense urban development, this 4-mile-long mountain is an ecological island that supports a unique community of plants and animals. The mission blue butterfly, the San Bruno elfin butterfly, and several species of manzanita are unique to this area. Fourteen species of plants growing here are classified as rare and endangered.

Equestrian Access:
Horses are allowed on all trails except the disabled trail and the Bog Trail. Unload horses at the day camp area.

Bicycle Access:
Bicycles are only allowed on the Old Guadalupe Trail, the Saddle Loop Trail, Radio Road, and the Day Camp Access Trail.

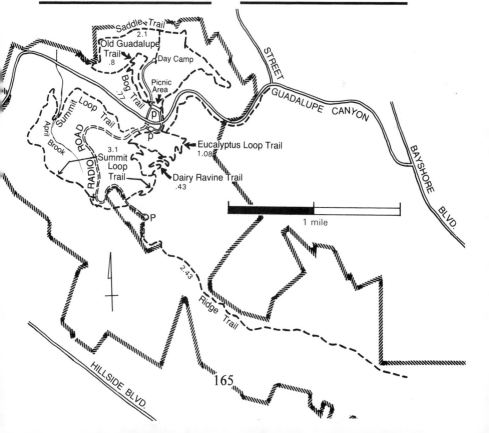

San Francisco Fish & Game Refuge

The 23,000-acre Crystal Springs Watershed is the largest unit of public land in the Santa Cruz Mountains. It is also one of the most restricted. For many years the San Francisco Water Department, which owns the property, has sealed off the vast majority of its land, allowing public access only on a few peripheral trails bordered by barbed wire fences. In a recent change in policy, there are now docent-led tours of the Fifield-Cahill Ridge Trail. To sign up for these tours go to www.sfwater.org; (650) 652-3203. There are special tours for hikers, equestrians, and mountain bikers. Toilets are at approximately 2-mile intervals. There is no drinking water available.

The entire Fifield-Cahill Ridge Trail is about 10 miles from Highway 92 to Sweeney Ridge. There is an additional 3.7 miles through the Sweeney Ridge unit of the Golden Gate National Recreation Area to parking on Sneath Lane. At this time most of the tours begin at the Quarry Gate on the north side of Highway 92 about half a mile west of the reservoir. Most walks are 3.5 to 8 miles. Other tours begin at Cemetery Gate at Skylawn Cemetery and at Portola Gate via the Sweeney Ridge Trail from the west terminus with Sneath Lane in San Bruno. Participants must stay with the tour. The northern part of this route is mostly chaparral. The southern part is forested with Douglas fir.

The Pulgas Water Temple, just west of Canada Road and just south of Crystal Springs Reservoir, is one of the wonders of the Watershed. Built during the depression, the temple affords a glimpse of Yosemite waters roaring through on their way to Crystal Springs Reservoir. The temple grounds, with its lawn and reflecting pond, is an ideal place for a picnic. The grounds can be reserved for group events. Inscribed on the temple from the book of Isaiah: "I give waters in the wilderness and rivers in the desert to give drink to my people."

CRYSTAL SPRINGS TRAIL

The Crystal Springs Trail, paralleling Canada Road, connects Huddart Park with Highway 92. From the parking lot at the north end of the trail, at Highway 92 just east of where it crosses the reservoir, the trail heads south 4 miles to the parking lot at the intersection of Edgewood Road and Canada Road. This section of the trail passes the historic Pulgas Water Temple. From the Edgewood/Canada parking lot you can go by trail 2.4 miles south to Huddart Park by way of Raymundo Road in Woodside. This trail is open to hikers, joggers, and equestrians.

EDGEWOOD TRAIL

This trail connects the Crystal Springs Trail, at the Edgewood/Canada parking lot, with Edgewood County Park and Preserve.

FILOLI ESTATE

See the separate chapter on the Filoli Estate.

RALSTON TRAIL

This paved bicycle, hiking, and jogging trail connects Belmont with the Crystal Springs Trail.

SAN ANDREAS TRAIL

This wide and relatively level trail begins at Skyline Boulevard near San Bruno Avenue to the north and runs 2.9 miles south to connect with Sawyer Camp Trail. It is popular with bicyclists, joggers, and hikers. Part of the trail is paved.

SAWYER CAMP TRAIL

The southern access to this trail is at the intersection of Skyline Boulevard and Crystal Springs Road. Southbound from Highway 280 take the Black Mountain Road exit. Northbound take the Bunker Hill Drive exit. The northern end is at Hillcrest Boulevard, which can be reached southbound on Highway 280 via the Larkspur Drive exit or northbound via the Millbrae Avenue exit.

This is the most popular trail in the Santa Cruz Mountains. With more than 200,000 visitors a year, this 6-mile paved road trail, now closed to motor vehicles, can be pretty crowded on weekends with walkers, joggers, bicyclists, skateboarders, rollerbladers, equestrians, and just about every other non-motorized form of transportation.

The trail passes along the east side of the Lower Crystal Springs Reservoir and San Andreas Lake. The easy access to Peninsula cities, combined with striking backdrops of water and mountains makes it easy to overlook the fact that the entire route is bordered by barbed wire to keep trail users from getting too close to the reservoirs. North of Crystal Springs Reservoir the trail straddles the San Andreas Fault and passes an enormous bay tree, called the Jepson Bay, one of the largest in the area.

It was named in 1923 for botanist Wilis Linn Jepson. There are picnic tables nearby.

The trail is named for a camp where Leander Sawyer trained performing horses for circuses in the 1870's. To reduce conflict among trail users, a 5 m.p.h. speed limit is set for bicycles on the first eighth of a mile of the trail at each end. The rest of the route has a 15 m.p.h. speed limit.

The trail is open from sunrise until sunset. Facilities include picnic tables, restrooms. and telephones. For more information, contact the San Mateo County Parks Department at (650) 363-4020.

SHEEP CAMP TRAIL

This trail begins at Crystal Springs Trail, along Canada Road, and gently climbs towards the east through grasslands and oak groves. It crosses Highway 280 and continues north and east to St. James Road in Belmont. This route is just over a mile long (one way), and connects with Waterdog Lake Trail in Belmont. There is also a Cross Country Running Course.

SNEATH LANE TRAIL

From Highway 280 in San Bruno, take Sneath Lane west all the way to the locked gate, where you can park. The paved road continues as a trail

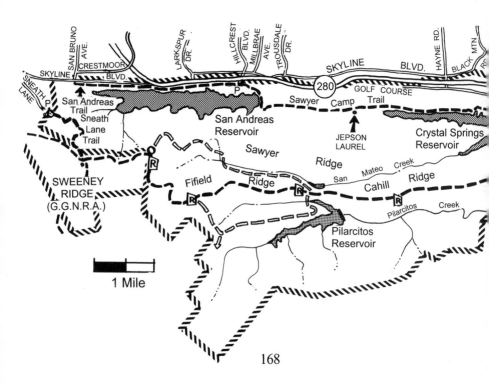

The Fifield-Cahill Ridge Trail

through the San Francisco Fish & Game Refuge, with barbed wire on both sides until it enters the Sweeney Ridge unit of the Golden Gate National Recreation Area. See the Golden Gate National Recreation Area chapter for more information about Sweeney Ridge.

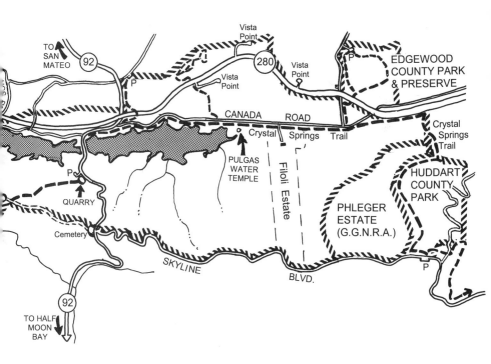

San Mateo County Memorial Park

TO GET THERE... It's southwest of Sam McDonald Park on Pescadero Road about 10 miles east of Highway 1.

Visitors to this park may swim in Pescadero Creek, camp, picnic amid old-growth redwoods, and walk about 10 miles of trails.

The Mount Ellen Summit Trail-Lower Nature Trail Loop around the summit of Mount Ellen is a scenic route involving a climb of about 400 feet and a distance of less than 2 miles.

The Pomponio Trail takes you on a 3.5-mile loop north of Pescadero Road as it climbs above the redwoods and into the Douglas fir, chaparral, and oak. This route offers great views of the Pescadero Creek Valley and the ocean.

If you're looking for something a bit more challenging than Memorial Park has to offer, head off for Portola State Park or Sam McDonald County Park, both about 6 miles away. For information on routes to these parks see the chapters on Pescadero Creek and Sam McDonald County Parks.

Sawmill owner Edwin Peterson bought a tract of old-growth redwoods at the present site of San Mateo County Memorial Park. He would have logged the area if it hadn't been for Roy W. Cloud, county superintendent of schools. When Cloud visited the nearby Wurr School in 1923 he was so impressed by the magnificent forest he presented a plan to save it to the county board of supervisors. The 310 acres were purchased for $70,000.

This park has some of the best picnicking and camping facilities in the Santa Cruz Mountains. There are 140 family campsites, available on a first-come, first-served basis. for more information, call (650)879-0212.

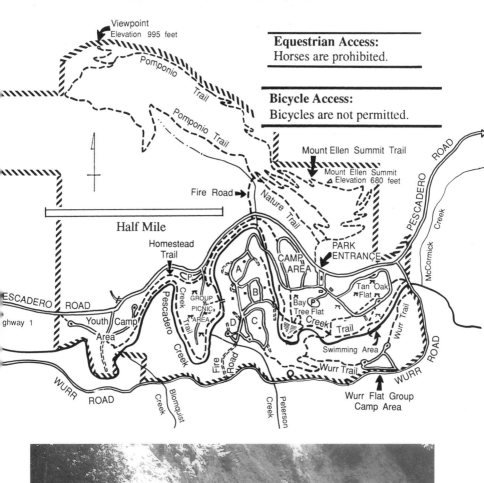

Viewpoint
Elevation 995 feet

Pomponio Trail

Pomponio Trail

Mount Ellen Summit Trail

Fire Road ➤

Nature Trail

Mount Ellen Summit
△ Elevation 680 feet

PESCADERO ROAD

Half Mile

Homestead Trail

PARK ENTRANCE

McCormick Creek

ESCADERO ROAD

ghway 1

Pescadero Creek Trail

CP

GROUP PICNIC AREA

A

B

D

C

CAMP AREA

Bay Tree Flat

P

Creek Trail

Tan Oak Flat

Wurr Trail

Swimming Area

WURR ROAD

Youth Camp Area

Wurr Trail

Wurr Trail

WURR ROAD

Blomquist Creek

Fire Road

Peterson Creek

Wurr Flat Group Camp Area

San Pedro Valley County Park

TO GET THERE. . .take Highway 1 to Pacifica, and head southeast on Linda Mar Boulevard to Oddstad Boulevard. Public parking and park access are next to Saint Peters Catholic Church.

This park covers 1,300 acres of coastal scrub and chaparral, with a few grassy places and riperian woodlands for diversity. You can get an easy look at it by taking the nearly level Weiler Ranch Trail along the Middle Fork of San Pedro Creek.

Keep an eye open for the Valley View Trail that switchbacks up the hillside from Weiler Ranch Trail, climbing about 600 feet to some nice views of the San Pedro Valley and winding around the hills for 1.6 miles and back to the dirt road.

The middle and south forks of San Pedro Creek flow year around and are among the few remaining spawning areas of steelhead trout in San Mateo County, especially from December to February. Views of Brooks Falls, which drops 175 feet in 3 tiers, may be enjoyed during the rainy season on the Brooks Falls Trail. Because of dense chaparral, you can't get close to the falls. By combining the Brooks Creek and Montara Mountain Trails you can form a moderate 2.4-mile loop with an elevation gain of about 450 feet.

The Montara Mountain Trail climbs 1,400 feet in 2.5 miles as it enters McNee Ranch State Park. It then intersects the service Road, where you can take a l-mile detour to enjoy great views from the top of Montara Mountain. On clear days the rugged 1,898-foot summit of the North Peak of Montara Mountain affords a grand panorama of the northern

Santa Cruz Mountains, including much of the off-limits San Francisco watershed land and the ocean.

The Hazelnut Trail and Weiler Ranch Trail can be combined to form a spectacularly scenic loop of about 4.3 miles and an elevation gain of about 800 feet. Hazelnuts and thimbleberries are abundant and delicious in late spring and early summer.

Common coastal scrub vegetation includes: monkeyflower, shrubby lupine, ceanothus, coastal sage scrub, and thimbleberry. This vegetation thrives in the coastal zone where steady ocean winds sweep the land and make life difficult for most trees. Along the park's small creeks you will notice dense stands of willows, which shelter a ground cover which in-

Equestrian Access:
Horses are allowed on all trails except the Brooks Creek Trail and Brooks Falls View Trail.

Bicycle Access:
Bicycles are only allowed on the Weiler Ranch Road Trail.

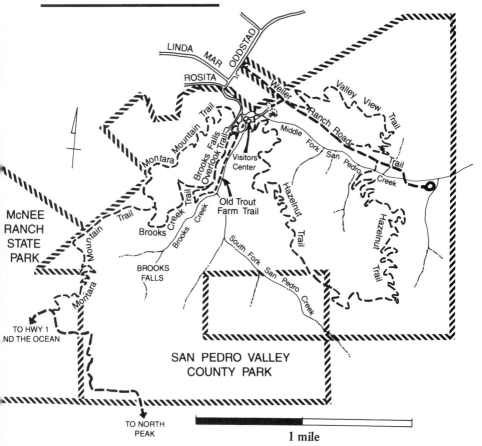

cludes poison hemlock, blackberry, horsetail, and bracken fern.

This park has a group picnic area and family picnic sites with barbecue pits. Reservations are required for all youth groups, regardless of size or activity. To reserve the group picnic area, call (650) 363-4021. For other park information, call (650)355-8289 (www.eparks.net).

SPECIAL SECTION
Off-Road Bicycling

Public land managers are being pulled in opposite directions by those who think there should be more trails open to mountain bikers and those who think there should be fewer trails they can use. Fortunately, many of the trails in the Santa Cruz Mountains were originally ranch, logging, and fire roads that are wide enough to accomodate bicycles without conflicting with the safety and enjoyment of people who prefer slower means of transportation.

Midpeninsula Regional Open Space District: *Bicycles are prohibited in Foothills, La Honda Creek, Los Trancos, Picchetti, Pulgas Ridge, Teague Hill, and Thornewood Preserves. Bicycles are allowed on only a few trails east of Deer Hollow Farm at Rancho San Antonio Open Space Preserve. All trails in the other preserves are open to bicycles except for a few that are marked otherwise at the trailhead.*

State Parks: *Bicycles are allowed on all dirt road trails unless otherwise posted.*

Soquel Demonstration State Forest: *Bicycles are allowed on all trails*

Santa Clara County Parks: *Mountain bikes are allowed on designated trails in Almaden Quicksilver, Stevens Creek, Upper Stevens Creek, and Santa Teresa County Parks.*

San Mateo County Parks: *Bicycles are permitted mainly on paved roads and a few dirt roads. These include:*

    Pescadero Creek County park: Camp Pomponio Road, Bridge Trail, and Old Haul Road.

    San Bruno Mountain County Park: Day Camp Access Trail, and Radio Road.

    Sawyer Camp Trail: The entire trail is open to bicycles.

    San Pedro Valley County Park: Weller Ranch Road.

Golden Gate National Recreation Area: *Bicycles are allowed on all paved and dirt road trails on Sweeney Ridge.*

City Parks: *Bicycles are not allowed on trails in Arastradero Preserve, Foothills Park, and the Portola Valley Trails.*

Private Land: *Bicycles are not allowed on trails in Filoli Estate, Hidden Villa Ranch, and Jasper Ridge Biological Preserve.*

Sanborn Skyline County Park

TO GET THERE... Take Highway 9 (Big Basin Way) west from Saratoga and turn south on Sanborn Road. The Lake Ranch area may be reached by taking Black Road 1.5 miles east from Skyline Boulevard. You can enter the uphill side of the park from the parking lot on Skyline Boulevard just south of the Castle Rock State Park entrance.

Sanborn Skyline County park covers more than 3,600 acres of mostly second-growth redwoods on the steep east side of Skyline Boulevard. It has more than 15 miles of scenic trails, excellent family and group picnicking facilities, a walk-in campground, and one of the Bay Area's best hostels. The trails are open to hikers, joggers, and equestrians.

Park headquarters are in an interesting sandstone and redwood house built in 1912. Nearby is a self-guided 1-mile nature trail. The Sanborn Trail charges uphill past the walk-in campground and climbs nearly 1,700 feet in about 2.4 miles one way to near Skyline Bouleveard at the summit of the ridge. This route offers beautiful views of the Santa Clara Valley and passes through several ecological zones. Second-growth redwoods predominate in the shady canyon bottom around park headquarters. Douglas fir, tanoak, and madrone become increasingly common in the higher and drier parts of the park near Skyline Boulevard.

Be sure to visit the natural history exhibit at the visitors center and the Youth Science Institute.

The Sanborn Trail may be used as an extension to the Skyline-to-the-

---

Indian Rock is a short walk from the Skyline Boulevard entrance.

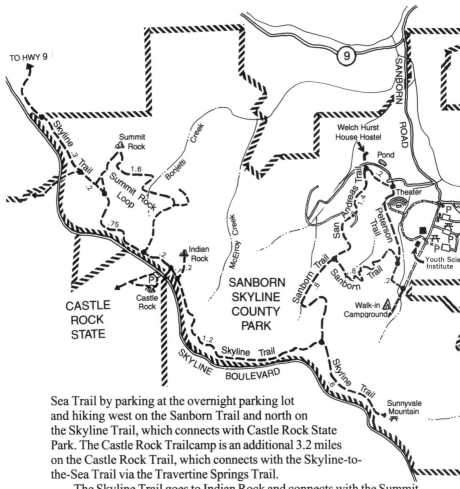

Sea Trail by parking at the overnight parking lot
and hiking west on the Sanborn Trail and north on
the Skyline Trail, which connects with Castle Rock State
Park. The Castle Rock Trailcamp is an additional 3.2 miles
on the Castle Rock Trail, which connects with the Skyline-to-
the-Sea Trail via the Travertine Springs Trail.

The Skyline Trail goes to Indian Rock and connects with the Summit
Rock Loop, which takes you to Summit Rock, a sandstone counterpart to
Castle Rock. Summit Rock, a popular destination for rock climbers, affords
spectacular views of the Santa Clara Valley and has some interesting shallow caves. From park headquarters the one-way distance to Indian Rock is
3.8 miles. Summit Rock is 1.25 miles farther one-way. These rocks are more
easily reached from the Skyline Boulevard entrance.

This park has one of the most unusual and interesting Hostels in the
state. Built of redwood logs, the hisoric Welch-Hurst house (1908) is about
as rustic as any place can be, and makes an ideal getaway from the city.
Thoughtfully renovated, the inside is comfortable and has many modern
conveniences. The log house is in a shady grove of redwoods, which also
has picnic tables, a barbeque, a wonderful old gazebo, and a duck pond.
The hostel is open all year from 5 p.m. to 9 a.m. For more information call

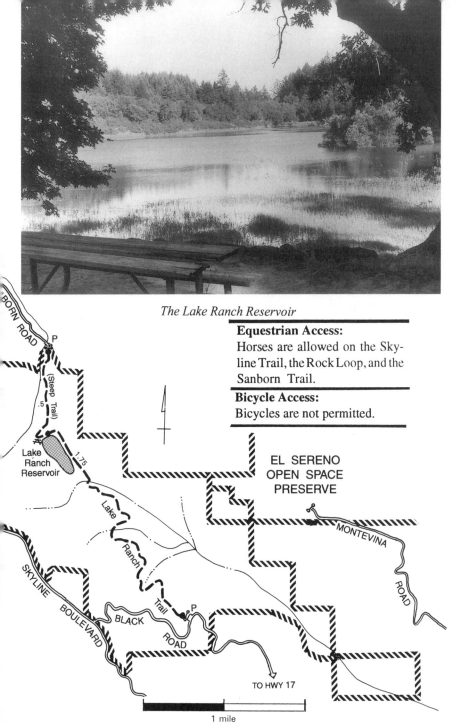

The Lake Ranch Reservoir

Equestrian Access:
Horses are allowed on the Sky-line Trail, the Rock Loop, and the Sanborn Trail.

Bicycle Access:
Bicycles are not permitted.

EL SERENO
OPEN SPACE
PRESERVE

BORN ROAD

P

(Steep Trail)

.5

Lake
Ranch
Reservoir

1.75

Lake

Ranch

Trail

SKYLINE

BOULEVARD

BLACK

ROAD

P

MONTEVINA

ROAD

TO HWY 17

1 mile

(408)741-0166 (www.sanbornparkhostel.org).

The Lake Ranch Reservoir is an easy 1.75-mile ramble on the Lake Ranch Trail from Black Road, or you can park at the end of Sanborn Road and make a steep .5-mile ascent to the reservoir from the north end of the same trail. You can stop at the shore for lunch with the newts, who consider this a favorite hangout. It is also a popular destination for bass fishing.

The terrain here is steep and the mountains are wooded with bay, Douglas fir, oak, maple, madrone, and redwood. Just east of the dirt road trail is the canyon abyss of the San Andreas Fault rift zone, where the North American Plate grinds past the Pacific Plate. The fault cuts a linear rift valley which runs along Lyndon Canyon and through Lake Ranch Reservoir.

This park has both RV and walk-in campsites. There are 33 tent campsites on the Sanborn Trail, available on a first-come, first-served basis from the last Saturday in March until October 15. Park at the overnight parking lot, register at the nearby park headquarters, and walk the short distance uphill to the campground. The RV campground is open all year and offers electric and water hookups and a dump station. Call (408) 358-3751 to make reservations.

Except for registered camping, the park is open from 8 a.m. until sundown. For more information, call (408)867-9959 (www.parkhere.org).

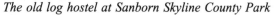

The old log hostel at Sanborn Skyline County Park

178

Santa Teresa County Park

TO GET THERE... The east side (Santa Clara Valley) entrance can be reached from Highway 85 or 101 by taking the Bernal Road exit and heading west. To reach the west entrance, from San Jose, take Almaden Expressway to its end. Then turn right onto Harry Road, left on McKean Road, and go 1.3 miles to Fortini Road. At the end of Fortini Road turn left on San Vicente Avenue. There is a 10-car parking lot on the right.

Above the south-bounding amorphous sprawl of San Jose, this gentle, grassy park is witness to the dramatic urbanization that has transformed this part of the Santa Clara Valley. Housing tracts and industry encroach on this park at this narrow part of the valley, making Santa Teresa an important wildland remnant and urban recreation area.

Santa Teresa County Park is 1,688 acres of low grassy hills capped by rock outcroppings which offer views of the Santa Clara Valley immediately below, and Mount Hamilton and the Diablo Range in the distance. The trails here are easy and relaxed; ideal for a liesurely ramble. Scattered stands of oak and bay punctuate the grassy hills, which turn brilliant green between January and May. In late spring and summer the hills turn brown and the weather can be hot.

This park has more than 14 miles of trails for hikers, equestrians, and bicyclists. Leashed dogs are allowed on all trails. It has group picnicking, a field archery range, and an eighteen-hole golf course. The Pueblo Group Area can be reserved for large gatherings by calling (408) 358-3751.

From the Pueblo Day Use Area you can enjoy a liesurely 3-mile loop by combining the Rocky Ridge, Coyote Peak, and Hidden Springs Trails. The ascent of Coyote Peak, the highest point in the park, will reward you with views of the entire park and surrounding area. You can add another 2 miles to this loop by continuing on the Coyote Peak Trail and then taking the Ohlone and Hidden Springs Trail.

The Stile Ranch Trail goes through IBM's Almaden Research Facility serpentine grassland and chaparral slopes which are great for viewing wildflowers in April. Look for an historic stone wall built by Chinese workers in the nineteenth century.

For more information call (408)225-0225 (www.parkhere.org).

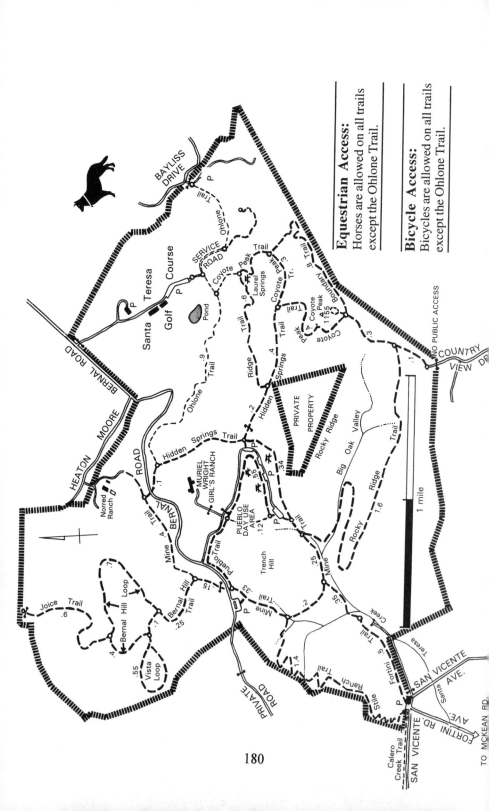

Equestrian Access:
Horses are allowed on all trails except the Ohlone Trail.

Bicycle Access:
Bicycles are allowed on all trails except the Ohlone Trail.

BAYLISS DRIVE

P

Ohlone Trail

SERVICE ROAD

P

Santa Teresa Golf Course

P

Pond

Coyote Peak Trail

Coyote Peak Trail

Laurel Springs

.6

Coyote Peak Tr.

.3

Boundary Trail

.8

Coyote Peak
1155

.4

Coyote Peak Trail

.3

NO PUBLIC ACCESS

COUNTRY VIEW DR.

BERNAL ROAD

HEATON MOORE ROAD

Ridge Trail

Ohlone Trail

.9

Hidden Springs Trail

.4

Hidden Springs Trail

.2

PRIVATE PROPERTY

Rocky Ridge

Big Oak Valley

Rocky Ridge Trail

.1

.3

1.6

1 mile

Hidden Springs Trail

Norred Ranch

MURIEL WRIGHT GIRL'S RANCH

.1

Mine Trail

.4

.55

.34

P

PUEBLO DAY USE AREA

.12

P

Pueblo Trail

Trench Hill

BERNAL ROAD

Joice Trail

.6

Bernal Hill Loop

.7

.4

Vista Loop

.55

Bernal Hill Trail

.25

.7

.15

.33

Mine Trail

.25

.35

Mine Trail

.2

Creek Trail

.1

Santa Teresa

Ranch Trail

1.4

Fortini Trail

Stile

SAN VICENTE AVE.

SAN VICENTE AVE.

P

Calero Creek Trail

SAN VICENTE RD.

FORTINI RD.

AVE.

TO McKEAN RD.

PRIVATE ROAD

Saratoga Gap Open Space Preserve

TO GET THERE... The trail through this preserve can be started at Saratoga Gap near the northeast corner of the intersection of Skyline Boulevard and Highway 9. This trail continues north through Upper Stevens Creek County Park and Monte Bello Open Space Preserve.

Saratoga Gap Open Space Preserve is at the northeast corner of Saratoga Gap. The trail through this 701 acre park parallels Skyline Boulevard, crossing grassy hills that explode with wildflowers in early spring. The route then enters 1,095-acre Upper Stevens Creek County Park and dips into the steep, shady canyon that contains the cool and perennial waters of Stevens Creek. You will find many impressive vistas along this trail and see beautiful stands of bay trees, madrone, and canyon live, coast live, and black oak. The Stevens Creek canyon is forested largely with Douglas fir and with big-leaf maple and alder along the creek. The banks of this bouncing, bubbling creek make an excellent picnic stop.

The trail climbs the other slope of the canyon, following a dirt road and rising to the oak and bay-studded grasslands of Monte Bello Ridge. Monte Bello Open Space Preserve contains 3,758 acres and can be reached from Saratoga Gap via the trail previously described or from Page Mill Road.

There are 3 parks that can be combined to form a grand and diverse adventure of nearly 8 miles from Saratoga Gap to Page Mill Road and Los Trancos Open Space Preserve. Unless you want to travel another 8 miles back, use 2 cars and at least I friend and leave a car at Page Mill Road to shuttle back to the trailhead. This route passes through Saratoga Gap Open Space Preserve, Upper Stevens Creek County Park, and Monte Bello Open Space Preserve. Just north of Page Mill Road is Los Trancos Open Space Preserve. This route explores grassy ridges, chaparral, oak woodlands, and forests of Douglas fir, and involves an elevation range of about 1,400 feet.

For more information, call the Midpeninsula Regional Open Space District at (650)691-1200 (www.openspace.org).

Sierra Azul Open Space Preserve

TO GET THERE... There are 3 areas of access to this preserve:
<u>LEXINGTON RESERVOIR AREA:</u> Take Highway 17 south of Los Gatos to the Lexington Reservoir. Turn off at Alma Bridge Road and continue about 1.6 miles to where the trail begins in Lexington County Park.
<u>KENNEDY ROAD AREA:</u> From Highway 17 in Los Gatos, head southeast on Saratoga-Los Gatos Road and turn left on Los Gatos Boulevard. Turn right on Kennedy Road and continue about 2.4 miles to the park entrance at its intersection with Top Of The Hill Road. The entrance trail begins just to the left of a private driveway.
<u>MOUNT UMUNHUM AREA:</u> From Highway 17 take Camden Road south, turn right on Hicks Road and continue 6.3 miles to where it intersects Mount Umunhum Road. The Woods Trail begins near the lower end of Mount Umunhum Road. There is another small parking area farther uphill at the locked gate.

In the rugged and dry part of the Santa Cruz Mountains east of Highway 17, the Sierra Azul (Spanish for "Blue Range") Open Space Preserve is a rugged land of steep ravines and breathtaking views. The diverse ecology includes large expanses of chaparral, oak and bay woodlands, serpentine grasslands, and riperian corridors. It is a place for hikers and mountain bikers who yearn for adventure. Be aware that this preserve can be hot during the dry season, and there are large areas with no shade.

Your canine friend can join you on the trails in the western part of the preserve.

For a grand cross section of the preserve, with no backtracking, meet a friend at the parking lot on Alma Bridge Road next to Lexington Reservoir. Then drive to the Woods Trail trailhead on Mount Umunhum Road. From there hike or bike west for 11.7 miles on the Woods Trail, the Limekiln Trail, and the Priest Rock Trail. This route involves an elevation range of nearly 2,000 feet and a complete range of the preserve's diverse ecology.

From the Lexington Reservoir entrance, you can enjoy a 5-mile loop by combining the Priest Rock Trail and the Limekiln Trail. This loop begins in the oak woods, and then ascends 700 feet into the nearly shadeless realm of chaparral. Unless you bring plenty of water during the warm months the only moisture you will find anywhere will be your own persperation. Look for views of Mount Hamilton, the Santa Clara Valley, San Francisco Bay, and the Skyline Ridge.

The Kennedy Trail climbs 1,600 feet from the trailhead on Kennedy Road to the ridgetop intersection with the Priest Rock Trail. Along the way you will pass steep and wooded canyons filled with oak, bay, and maple, and views of ever-increasing splendor reveal Mount Hamilton and the Diablo Range, San Jose, and the Santa Clara Valley. The scenery gets increasingly wild and remote as you climb higher on this chaparral-clad ridge. Poison oak is common, but easily avoided on the well-maintained dirt road trail. At the beginning of the trail is an abandoned apricot orchard that still bears fruit around late June and early July.

Mount Umunhum Road was built by the U.S. Air Force on a non-exclusive easement over private land. It climbs through the preserve and is blocked by a locked gate where there is room for a few cars to park. This road continues to the 3,486-foot summit of Mount Umunhum. However, you can't take the road to the summit because it goes through private property and because the former Almaden Air Force Station on Mount Umunhum is a toxic waste site that is closed to the public. There are plans to clean up the toxic mess and remove deteriorating buildings so the public can enjoy the view from the top of the mountain.

Mount Umunhum, one of the most prominent features of the Santa Cruz Mountains, means "resting place of the hummingbird" in the Ohlone Indian language and was considered to be one of their 4 sacred Bay Area peaks.

To visit Bald Mountain, drive 1.8 miles up Mount Umunhum Road

The Air Force built the 9-story concrete blockhouse atop Mount Umunhum in 1957. It was designed to withstand a nuclear blast.

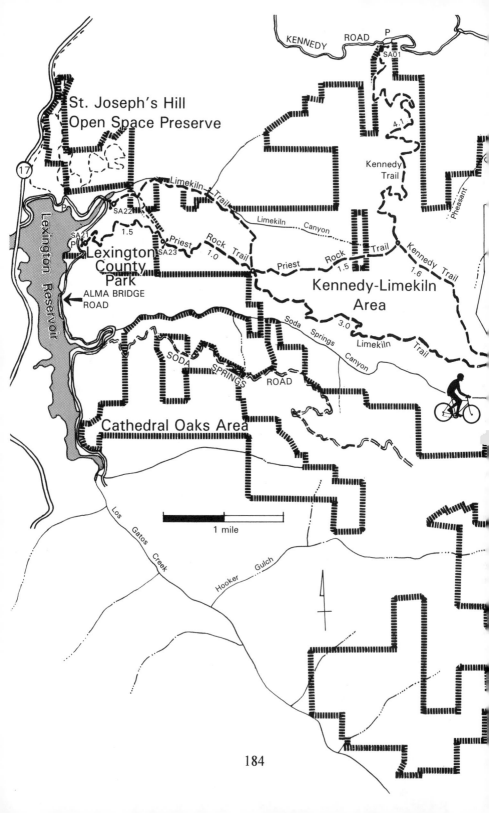

KENNEDY ROAD P
SA01

St. Joseph's Hill
Open Space Preserve

17

Lexington Reservoir

P
SA22
1.5
SA21
P
Lexington County Park
Priest
SA23
ALMA BRIDGE ROAD

Limekiln Trail

Rock Trail 1.0

Limekiln Canyon

Priest Rock Trail 1.5

4.1

Kennedy Trail

Pheasant

Kennedy Trail 1.6

Kennedy-Limekiln Area

SODA SPRINGS ROAD

Soda Springs Canyon 3.0

Limekiln Trail

Cathedral Oaks Area

1 mile

Los Gatos Creek

Hooker Gulch

184

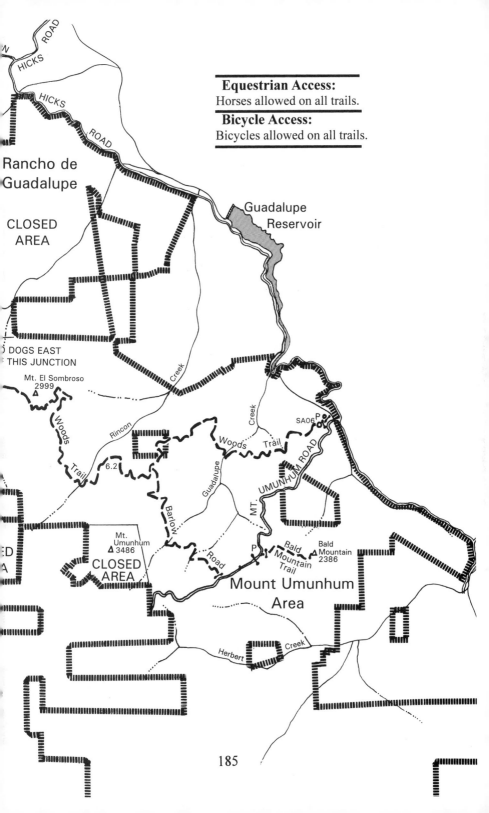

HICKS ROAD

HICKS ROAD

Rancho de
Guadalupe

CLOSED
AREA

Guadalupe
Reservoir

DOGS EAST
THIS JUNCTION

Mt. El Sombroso
2999

Woods
Trail

Rincon

6.2

Barlow

Creek

Creek

Woods   Trail

SA06   P

MT. UMUNHUM ROAD

Guadalupe

Mt.
Umunhum
3486

CLOSED
AREA

Road

P

Bald
Mountain
Trail

Bald
Mountain
2386

Mount Umunhum
Area

Herbert   Creek

185

and park near the stop sign at the locked gate. Then follow the dirt road that heads to the southeast and up the grassy hilltop. This 2,387-foot rounded summit is an easy .5 mile walk to a place that is perfect for picnicking and kite flying. Dramatic views of the Sierra Azul Range and the Santa Clara Valley are among the best reasons to visit.

The Woods Trail, beginning near the intersection of Mount Umunhum Road and Hicks Road, is a well-maintained dirt road through a bay/maple/oak/madrone woodland on the eastern flanks of Mount Umunhum. It climbs the ridge into the chaparral and on to the Kennedy Trail and the Limekiln Trail, which will take you to Kennedy Road and Lexington Reservoir. Be aware that there is limited trailhead parking. The 11.8 mile segment from Lexington Reservoir to Almaden Quicksilver County Park, via the Priest Rock, Limekiln, and Woods Trails is the official route of the Bay Area Ridge Trail.

At nearly 17,000 acres, and growing, this is the largest of the open space preserves. For more information, call the Midpeninsula Regional Open Space District at (650) 691-1200 (www.openspace.org).

Skyline Ridge Open Space Preserve

TO GET THERE... The main entrance is on Skyline Boulevard about a mile south of the intersection with Page Mill/Alpine Roads. There is one parking lot each for equestrians, handicapped, and all others. You can also access this preserve from the Russian Ridge Open Space Preserve parking lot on Alpine Road just west of its intersection with Skyline Boulevard. Take the trail through the tunnel under Alpine Road south from the parking lot.

Tranquil ponds, deep forested canyons, rounded mountain peaks with great views, and about 10 miles of trails make this 2,143-acre preserve an ideal destination for hikers, equestrians, and off-road bicyclists.

From the Russian Ridge Open Space parking lot you can easily visit Alpine Pond, which is actually a reservoir created in the 1950's. The half mile footpath around the pond, designed for the physically challenged, is the easiest trail in the preserve. Next to the pond is the David C. Daniels Nature Center, where you may enjoy docent-led activities and natural history exhibits weekends from April until mid-November. A floating pier is a good place to see birds, bass, and pond turtles. Just west of the pond, along the Old Page Mill Road trail, is a mortar rock with an impressive display of ancient Ohlone Indian acorn grinding holes.

Ranch buildings near Alpine Pond date back to the 1930's, when this was a retreat for Governor James "Sunny Jim" Rolph.

Horseshoe Lake is easy to reach from the main preserve access off of Skyline Boulevard. This 27-foot-deep springfed reservoir, named for its U-shape, is inhabited by bass and is a rest stop for migrating waterfowl. Fishing and boating are not allowed. There is an easy and exceptionally

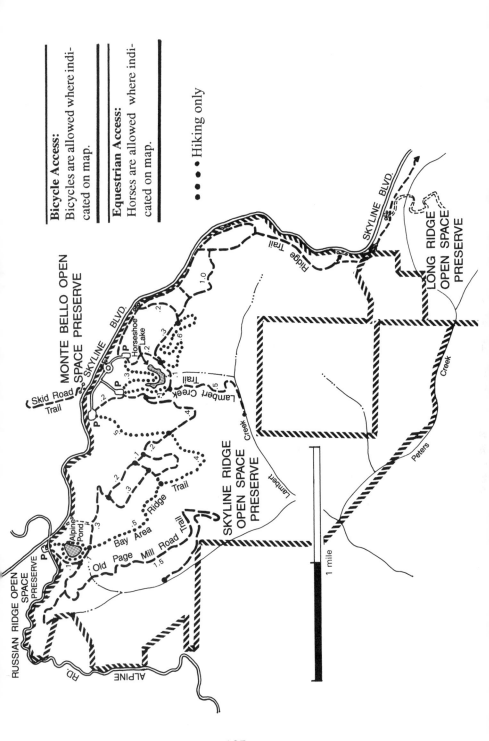

Bicycle Access:
Bicycles are allowed where indicated on map.

Equestrian Access:
Horses are allowed where indicated on map.

●●● Hiking only

MONTE BELLO OPEN SPACE PRESERVE

SKYLINE RIDGE OPEN SPACE PRESERVE

RUSSIAN RIDGE OPEN SPACE PRESERVE

LONG RIDGE OPEN SPACE PRESERVE

SKYLINE BLVD

Skid Road Trail

Horseshoe Lake

Lambert Creek Trail

Ridge Trail

Bay Area Ridge Trail

Old Page Mill Road Trail

Alpine Pond

Lambert Creek

Peters Creek

ALPINE RD.

1 mile

187

scenic 1.1 mile walking loop from the parking lot to and around Horseshoe Lake. This loop approaches the lake's south shore, swings north through a dense Douglas fir woodland to the equestrian parking lot, and then heads south and west through an oak grove with picnic tables that overlook the lake.

For a vigorous outing, head uphill from either pond, passing ancient oaks and steep grasslands that yield broad vistas of the deep Pescadero Creek watershed and Butano Ridge to the west, Monte Bello Ridge to the east, and Loma Prieta, the highest peak in the Santa Cruz Mountains, to the south. The highest point at Skyline Ridge is 2,493 feet. The Ridge Trail, for hikers only, offers the best views. Bicyclists travel the ranch road trails.

From the main general access parking lot you can take a 3.3-mile walking loop via the Ridge Trail to and around Alpine Pond and then back

This mortar stone, near Alpine Pond, was used centuries ago by Ohlone women to grind acorns into a flour. Acorn mush was the most important item in the Ohlone diet. The acorn harvest was so important to these people it marked the beginning and end of each year.

The Joy of Bay Nuts

Among all our native edible plants the nut of the bay tree is one of the most delicious and also one of the most overlooked. Roasted bay nuts will remind you of chocolate and coffee, but with their own unique taste. They can be used in any recipe that calls for chocolate or coffee, including cookies, icecream, pudding, kahlua, milkshakes,brownies, and my favorite, bay nut mousse. Here is how to do it:

1  Gather bay nuts under bay trees in the fall. November is the best month.

2 Soak nuts in a bucket of water for a few days until the outer skins are soft. Then remove the skins.

3 (OPTIONAL) Put nuts on a cookie sheet and roast at 150F for an hour to dry out the shells so they are easy to crack open with pliers.

4  Break shells with pliers to remove nuts, which will divide into 2 hemispheres.

5 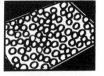 Put nuts on a cookie sheet and roast at about 400F for about 10 minutes. Then check every few minutes to make sure they don't turn black. Remove from oven when nuts are dark brown.

6  Grind nuts with a coffee grinder or flour mill; or put them in a plastic bag and smash with a hammer. A blender is then helpful to mix powder with liquid.

You are now ready to create an amazing treat. Let me know what you have discovered.

by way of the ranch road trails. You can add another mile on the way back by including the loop around Horseshoe lake. For bicyclists it's about 1.5 miles one-way on ranch road trails to Alpine Pond, and from there you can head into Russian Ridge Open Space Preserve.

The original Page Mill Road was built by William Page in 1868 to transport lumber from his mill in what is now Portola State Park to Palo Alto. Part of the western segment of this road, west from Skyline Boulevard, is now a one-way trail through Skyline Ridge Open Space Preserve. This route now ends at the southern preserve boundary, but eventually it may be a public trail all the way to Portola State Park.

This preserve is an important part of the Skyline open space corridor, and is a key link in the developing Bay Area Ridge Trail through San Mateo and Santa Clara Counties. There is now a section of the Ridge Trail that links Skyline Ridge to Long Ridge Open Space Preserve just to the south. The 752-acre Big Dipper Ranch will be added to this preserve.

For more information, call the Midpeninsula Regional Open Space District at (650) 691-1200 (www.openspace.com).

Skyline-to-the-Sea Trail

TO GET THERE... The trail begins at the intersection of Skyline Boulevard (Saratoga Gap) or at Highway 1 at Waddell Beach in Big Basin Redwoods State Park. It can be extended through Castle Rock State Park to the south and Monte Bello Open Space Preserve to the north.

WARNING: Overnight parking is not allowed at the Saratoga Gap parking lot; and there has been a problem with burglaries of cars parked along Highway 9. The safest parking is at Castle Rock State Park. Otherwise, arrange to be dropped off at the trailhead.

SKYLINE TO BIG BASIN

The Skyline-to-the-Sea Trail offers real backpacking opportunities from Saratoga Gap or Castle Rock State Park to Big Basin Redwoods State Park and on to the coast.

The total distance from Saratoga Gap to the ocean is about 28 miles. The trail passes through grasslands, chaparral, and forests of oak, madrone, Douglas fir, and redwoods. Impressive vistas are common along the route.

The trailhead at Saratoga Gap (where Skyline Boulevard intersects Highway 9) is on the south side of Highway 9 just west of Skyline. From the Castle Rock State Park trailcamp the trail crosses Skyline twice before reaching the trailhead at Saratoga Gap; or you can take the Travertine Springs Trail shortcut. The trail parallels Highway 9 for about 6.3 miles from Saratoga Gap to Waterman Gap Trailcamp. The distance to Waterman Gap from the Castle Rock trailhead is about 8.9 to 13.6 miles, depending on the route. The Travertine Springs Trail offers the most direct route.

The Skyline-to-the-Sea Trail, which was built by thousands of volunteers in 1969, closely parallels Highways 9 and 236 because this land was already owned by the state. Hikers and equestrians who prefer straying farther from the sound of traffic should try the Toll Road south of Highway 9. This abandoned logging road, built in 1871, connects with the main Skyline-to-the-Sea route west of Saratoga Gap and again west of the junction of Highways 9 and 236. The Toll Road is a longer route.

The trail continues for about 9.5 miles from Waterman Gap to Big Basin park headquarters. From China Grade Road the trail passes through chaparral and stands of knobcone pine and enters the shady redwood groves along Opal Creek. Just before the trail drops into Big Basin, you will be greeted by splendid views of the mountains to the southwest.

Due to a lack of water on parts of the trail during the dry season, hikers are advised to bring water. The Castle Rock Trailcamp has water, pit toilets, and fireplaces. The Waterman Gap Trailcamp has water, pit toilets, and does not permit ground fires. The Big Basin Jay Camp has water, flush toilets, fireplaces, and showers. For campsite information, call (800) 444-PARK; www.reserveamerica.com.

Castle Rock parking lot -- Castle Rock Trailcamp: **2.8 miles**.
Castle Rock Trailcamp -- Saratoga Gap: **4.5 miles**.
Castle Rock Trailcamp -- Waterman Gap Trailcamp (via Travertine Springs Trail): **7.1 miles**.
Saratoga Gap -- Waterman Gap Trailcamp: **6.3 miles**.
Waterman Gap Trailcamp -- Big Basin Jay Camp: **9.5 miles**.
Big Basin Jay Camp -- Camp Herbert: **7.5 miles**.
Camp Herbert Trailcamp -- Twin Redwoods Trailcamp: **1.5 miles**.
Twin Redwoods Trailcamp -- Alder Trailcamp: **.5 miles**.
Alder Trailcamp -- Trailhead: **.5 miles**.

HIKING/EQUESTRIAN TRAILS
• • • • • • • • • • • • • •

BICYCLES ALLOWED
━ ━ ━ ━ ━ ━ ━

▲ Car Camping

△ Trail Camping

Ⓗ Hostels

P Parking

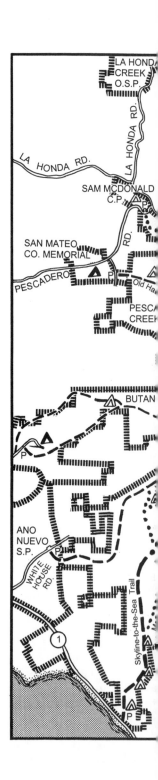

192

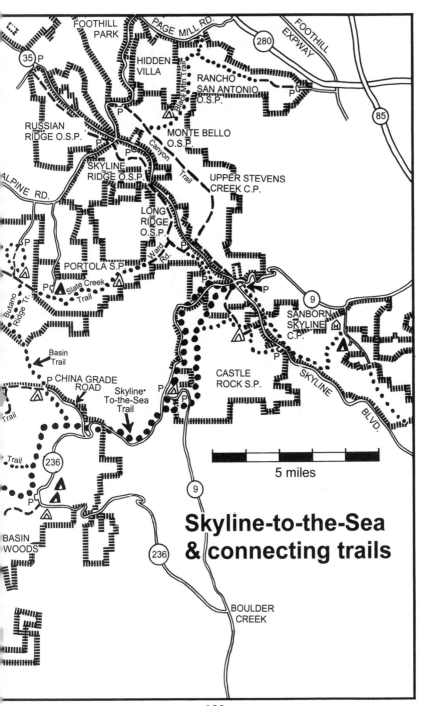

FOOTHILL
PARK

PAGE MILL RD.

FOOTHILL
EXPWAY

280

35 P

85

HIDDEN
VILLA

RANCHO
SAN ANTONIO
O.S.P.

RUSSIAN
RIDGE O.S.P.

MONTE BELLO
O.S.P.

Canyon Trail

SKYLINE
RIDGE O.S.P.

UPPER STEVENS
CREEK C.P.

ALPINE RD.

LONG
RIDGE
O.S.P.

P

Ward Rd.

PORTOLA S.P.

9

Butano Ridge Tr.

Slate Creek Trail

SANBORN
SKYLINE
C.P.

Basin
Trail

P CHINA GRADE
ROAD

Skyline
To-the-Sea
Trail

CASTLE
ROCK S.P.

SKYLINE BLVD.

Trail

236

5 miles

9

Skyline-to-the-Sea
& connecting trails

BASIN
WOODS

236

BOULDER
CREEK

BIG BASIN TO THE SEA

The Skyline-to-the-Sea Trail follows Waddell Creek through the 1,700-acre "Rancho Del Oso" part of the park and on to the coast. From the ridge west of park headquarters the trail follows Waddell Creek all the way to Highway 1. A short sidetrip up the Berry Creek Falls Trail will reward you with 2 of the great wonders of the Santa Cruz Mountains: Berry Creek and Silver Falls. The distance from park headquarters to the trailhead near Highway 1 is about 10.5 miles on the Skyline-to-the-Sea Trail, and 11 miles on the Howard King Trail, and about 12 miles on the Sunset Trail. The Skyline-to-the-Sea route has the easiest grade of the 3 options. Travelers on the Sunset Trail may want to make camp at Sunset Trailcamp, which is above the waterfalls about 5.5 miles from park headquarters.

There are 3 trailcamps in "Rancho Del Oso": Camp Herbert is about 7.5 miles from Big Basin park headquarters; Twin Redwoods is 1.5 miles downstream from Camp Herbert; and Alder Camp is less than half a mile downstream. Ground fires are prohibited and campers are encouraged to make reservations by calling Big Basin park headquarters at (831) 338-8861. There is a camping fee.

Rancho Del Oso is an important feeding area for birds, with more than 200 species sighted. Near the trail is the Eagle Tree, an impressive old-growth redwood which once hosted an eagle nest.

The Skyline-to-the-Sea Trail is the hub of a vast network of trails developing in the Santa Cruz mountains. It is possible to travel by trail from Los Trancos and Monte Bello Open Space Preserves on Page Mill Road to Saratoga Gap, where you can connect with the Skyline-to-the-Sea Trail. To hike across the range, park at Sanborn Skyline County Park and take the Sanborn and Skyline Trails to Castle Rock State Park and on to Saratoga Gap via the Castle Rock Trail. To cross the range from Rancho San Antonio Open Space Preserve, near Los Altos, ascend to the trailcamp near Black Mountain, and then head downhill to the Canyon Trail and south to Saratoga Gap. The Basin Trail connects Big Basin Redwoods State Park with Pescadero Creek, San Mateo County Memorial, and Sam McDonald County Parks and Portola State Park.

See the Big Basin and Castle Rock chapters for more detailed maps and additional information.

Castle Rock parking lot -- Castle Rock Trailcamp: **2.8 miles.**
Castle Rock Trailcamp -- Saratoga Gap: **4.5 miles.**
Castle Rock Trailcamp -- Waterman Gap Trailcamp (via Travertine Springs Trail): **7.1 miles.**
Saratoga Gap -- Waterman Gap Trailcamp: **6.3 miles.**
Waterman Gap Trailcamp -- Big Basin Jay Camp: **9.5 miles.**
Big Basin Jay Camp -- Camp Herbert: **7.5 miles.**
Camp Herbert Trailcamp -- Twin Redwoods Trailcamp: **1.5 miles.**
Twin Redwoods Trailcamp -- Alder Trailcamp: **.5 miles.**
Alder Trailcamp -- Trailhead: **.5 miles.**

The Skyline Trail

TO GET THERE... The trail can be entered from Skylonda, Wunderlich County Park, and Huddart County Park.

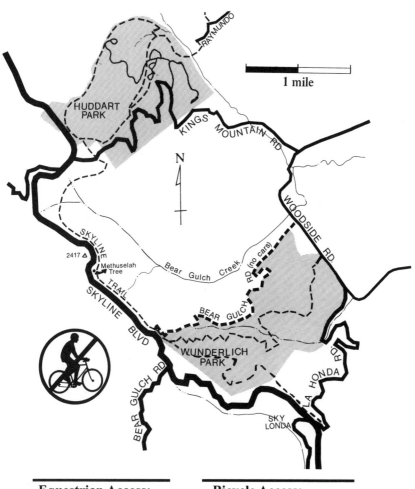

Equestrian Access:	**Bicycle Access:**
Horses are allowed.	Bicycles are prohibited.

Above the town of Woodside, the Skyline Trail parallels Skyline Boulevard for about 8.5 miles. The south end of the trail is at Skylonda, at the intersection of Skyline Boulevard and La Honda Road, and continues north through Wunderlich County Park, the California Water Company's Bear Gulch Watershed, and on through part of Huddart County Park .

The section from Wunderlich Park to Kings Mountain Road, near Huddart Park, is 4.7 miles. The trail crosses Kings Mountain Road .5

miles downhill from Skyline Boulevard. You can begin this walk at Wunderlich Park where the Bear Gulch Road forms the northern boundary of the park about 3 miles north of the La Honda/Skyline Boulevard intersection.

The Bear Gulch watershed is noteworthy for its trees. The largest of them is the "Methuselah" redwood, which is a short distance off the trail and just off Skyline Boulevard. It is 15 feet in diameter.

Several other old-growth redwoods also stand along the trail, though none are nearly that size. Exceptionally large Douglas fir trees are more common, as are madrone and bay. In the northern part of this watershed, near Kings Mountain Road, you will find exceptionally large stands of rather rare golden chinquapin, often referred to as an oak, but actually more closely related to chestnut trees. It is easily identified by the golden-yellow underside of its leaves and by its sharp spiny nut hulls.

The Skyline Trail is well maintained and has little elevation range. Dogs and bicycles are prohibited. It is a part of the 400-mile long Bay Area Ridge Trail. For more information, contact the San Mateo County Parks Department at (650)363-4020 (www.eparks.net).

The Methuselah Tree is 15 feet in diameter.

Soquel Demonstration State Forest

TO GET THERE. . . from Highway 17 take Summit Road and Highland Way east 9.8 miles and turn right at a small bridge leading to a parking lot at the east end of the forest. From Highway 1 at Aptos, take Freedom Boulevard, Corralitos Road, and Eureka Canyon Road to Highland Way.

Soquel Demonstration State Forest was acquired by the California Department of Forestry in 1990 and is the first state forest to be added to the system since 1949.

A demonstration forest is a parcel of timberland used primarily for research, education, recreation, and the demonstration of innovative timber harvesting and forestry techniques.

This 2,700-acre forest is not a park, but it is open to the public, for use by walkers and bicyclists and can also be accessed through The Forest of Nisene Marks State Park, which adjoins the property to the south. Horses are allowed in this property, but not in the adjacent state park. At the headwaters of the east fork of Soquel Creek, including portions of Amaya Creek and Fern Gulch Creek, this area is covered mainly with second-growth timber stands of mixed conifers and hardwoods, with dominant species being redwood, along with some areas of oak, madrone, chaparral, and a few small groves of old-growth redwoods.

All of the trails are multi-use and are either old logging roads or single track trails that tie these roads together to provide loop routes.

The picnic area at Badger Springs makes a good outing destination. This wide, flat area between Hihn's Mill Road and Soquel Creek displays a magnificent stand of big-leaf maple, mixed with oak, with picnic tables and sitting logs. November delivers a wonderful display of fall foliage as the maples turn bright shades of yellow and orange before shedding their leaves. Just across Hihn's Mill Road is a cold, pure, calcium-carbonate spring that tumbles down the rocky slope, forming small stalagtite-like formations. Also nearby are a few old-growth redwoods.

The Sulphur Springs, Corral, Tractor and Saw Pit Trails make steep ascents to the Ridge Trail, where you will find some pure stands of madrone and views into the Forest of Nisene Marks State Park.

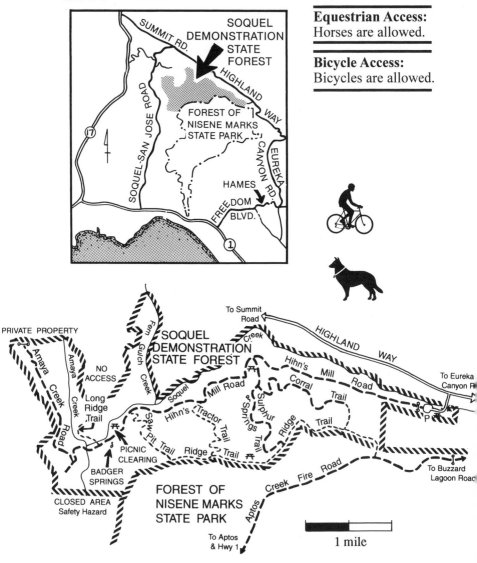

Equestrian Access:
Horses are allowed.

Bicycle Access:
Bicycles are allowed.

198

The San Andreas Fault passes through this land, as evidenced by natural springs and sag ponds. In some areas are fissures formed by the October 17, 1989 Loma Prieta earthquake which was centered only 2 miles away in The Forest of Nisene Marks State Park.

This forest is particularly popular with mountain bikers and equestrians. Dogs are allowed on leash. It is open from dawn until dusk.

For more information, call the State Departmnt of Forestry and Fire Protection at (831)475-8643 (www.fire.ca.gov).

Highland Gate to Sulpher Springs Trail: **2.3 miles**
Sulphur Springs to Badger Springs: **2.4 miles**
Badger Springs to nortwest boundary: **3.0 miles**
Sulphur Springs Trail/Corral Trail Loop: **3.7 miles**
Sulphur Springs Trail/Tractor Trail Loop: **5.0 miles**

SPECIAL SECTION

Acorn Woodpeckers

When you see a dead tree trunk or branch riddled with holes and stocked with acorns then you have made yourself a guest in the territory of a colony of woodpeckers.

These raucous birds fill the air with a shrill "JACK-A jack-a" and are easily identified in flight by flashes of black and white on their wings and a glimmering red crown.

This is one of the few species of colonial woodpeckers, with all members of the community tending the eggs and young and digging out nesting holes in trees.

The most interesting time to watch these birds is in September and October when they gather acorns for winter provisions and wedge them tightly into holes in trees, fence posts, and even telephone poles so that squirrels can't pry them out. With binoculars you can easily see woodpeckers position the acorns pointed-end first into holes, and then lodge them in securely with a few good whacks with their beaks.

Stevens Canyon Ranch Open Space Preserve

TO GET THERE... From Highway 280 take Foothill Boulevard south and continue on Stevens Canyon Road past its intersection with Redwood Gulch Road.

PLEASE NOTE: As of this writing this preserve is open by permit only. Call (650) 691-1200 (www.openspace.org) for details.

Tucked deep into the Stevens Creek Canyon east of Skyline Boulevard, this 240-acre preserve adjoins Upper Stevens Creek County Park and Saratoga Gap Open Space Preserve.

Several miles of dirt roads and footpaths will take you through groves of bay, oak, maple, and second-growth redwood. One ranch road climbs above the forest to a grassy meadow. A short path goes to a single giant old-growth redwood that somehow avoided the fate of all the other sizeable trees when loggers came through here in the late nineteenth century. As of this writing none of the trails are marked.

Near the swimming pool and orchard you will see acorn grinding holes in a large flat piece of sandstone, testimony to Ohlone habitation centuries ago. Beginning in 1881 the property was used for agriculture. There is a ranch house built over a sandstone wine cellar and several other buildings.Over the past several decades vinyards were replaced by pear and apple orchards, which still lend an agricultural quality to the property.

Stevens Creek County Park

TO GET THERE... From Highway 280 take Foothill Boulevard south. It becomes Stevens Canyon Road.

Stevens Creek begins in Monte Bello Open Space Preserve and tumbles down the steep east side of the Santa Cruz Mountains and on through Stevens Creek County Park.

This 777-acre park offers visitors a wide variety of activities, including picnicking, horseback riding, and archery. Boating and fishing are allowed in the Stevens Creek Reservoir.

Trails wander along tree-shaded streams and climb to scenic ridgetop vistas. You can explore the remnants of long-abandoned nineteenth century orchards and vineyards.

The climb to 1000-foot-high Lookout Point offers sweeping views of the Santa Clara Valley and nearby mountains. You can then continue on into Fremont Older Open Space Preserve.

The 2-mile Stevens Creek Trail climbs through oak woodlands, and cuts through chaparral as it contours the steep slopes above the reservoir. See the Fremont Older Open Space Preserve chapter for a description of a grand 7.5-mile loop and Picchetti Ranch Open Space chapters for more trail routes from this park.

This is the oldest of the Santa Clara County parks, established in 1927. It has excellent family and group picnic areas. The park is open from dawn until half an hour after sunset. For more information call (408) 867-3654 (www.parkhere.org).

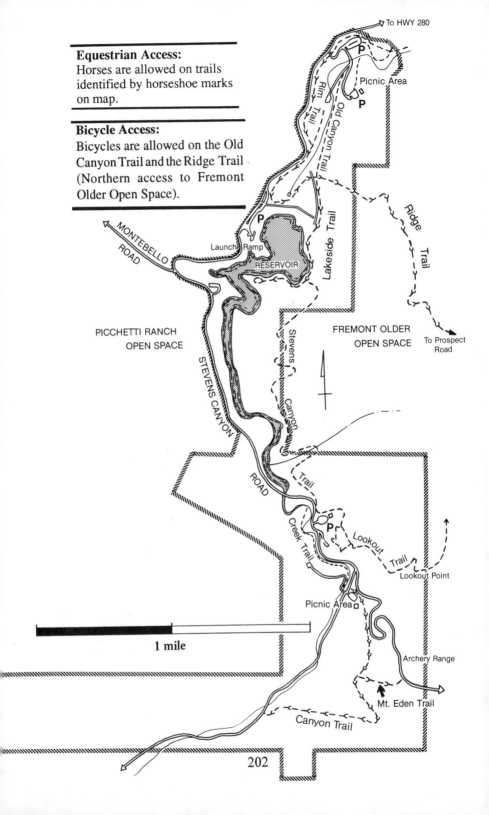

Equestrian Access:
Horses are allowed on trails identified by horseshoe marks on map.

Bicycle Access:
Bicycles are allowed on the Old Canyon Trail and the Ridge Trail (Northern access to Fremont Older Open Space).

To HWY 280

P

Picnic Area

P

Old Canyon Trail

Rim Trail

Ridge Trail

Lakeside Trail

P

MONTEBELLO ROAD

Launch Ramp

RESERVOIR

PICCHETTI RANCH OPEN SPACE

FREMONT OLDER OPEN SPACE

To Prospect Road

Stevens

STEVENS CANYON

Canyon

ROAD

Trail

Creek Trail

P

Lookout Trail

Lookout Point

1 mile

Picnic Area

Archery Range

Mt. Eden Trail

Canyon Trail

202

Teague Hill Open Space Preserve

TO GET THERE... It is just south of Huddart Park near Woodside. Parking access is at Huddart and Wunderlich County Parks. There is imited parking along Kings Mountain Road about .25 miles east of Skyline Boulevard.

This heavily-wooded preserve slopes eastward toward the Town of Woodside. It is forested with madrone, bay, maple, oak, and scattered stands of second-growth redwood.

There is no trail system here, but part of the Skyline Trail (Bay Area Ridge Trail), which connects Huddart and Wunderlich parks, passes through part of the preserve.

For current information, call the Midpeninsula Regional Open Space District at (650) 691-1200 (www.openspace.org).

Thornewood Open Space Preserve

TO GET THERE... from Highway 280 take Woodside Road (Highway 84) west and continue uphill on La Honda Road 1.5 miles from its intersection with Portola Road. From Skyline Boulevard take La Honda Road (Highway 84) southwest 1.9 miles. The preserve entrance is at a brick gate on the south side of the road. A parking lot is inside the preserve.

An easy .7-mile ramble through oak, chaparral and second-growth redwood will take you to a pleasant little pond called Schilling Lake. Here

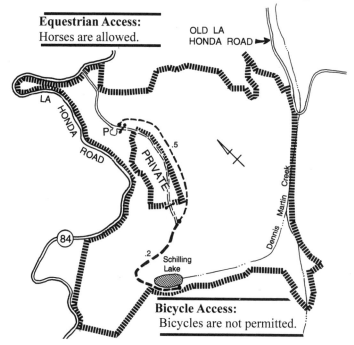

you are likely to enjoy the sounds of frogs and the sight of a mated pair of white swans. The pond is named for August Schilling, who bought part of the property from the Thornes. The property was named by Edna and Julian Thorne, who purchased it in 1908.

This 163-acre former estate was willed to the Sierra Club Foundation and was later given to the Midpeninsula Regional Open Space District. The impressive Thornewood mansion, built in the 1920's, is part of a 3.5-acre leased-out part of the preserve. The mansion is occasionally open for docent-led tours.

Dogs on leash are allowed in the preserve. Bicycles are prohibited.

For more information, contact the Midpeninsula Regional Open Space District at (650) 691-1200 (www.openspace.org).

University of California, Santa Cruz

TO GET THERE... From Highway 1 in Santa Cruz take Bay Drive north to the University campus.

The 8 colleges of this university, with more than 15,000 students, are nestled into 2,000 gently sloped and wooded acres of the Santa Cruz Mountains just above Santa Cruz.

An extensive dirt road, bikepath, and footpath trail system allows students and visitors to explore the developed and undeveloped parts of the campus. A good place to begin is at the north end of Heller Drive. From here you can head north through a patchwork ecology of second-growth redwoods, Douglas fir, madrone, chaparral, and broad grassy meadows,

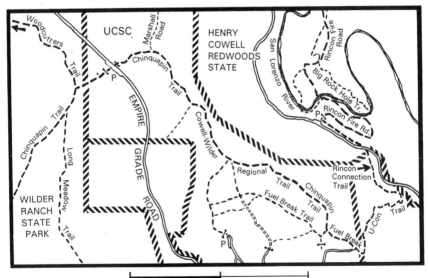

1 mile

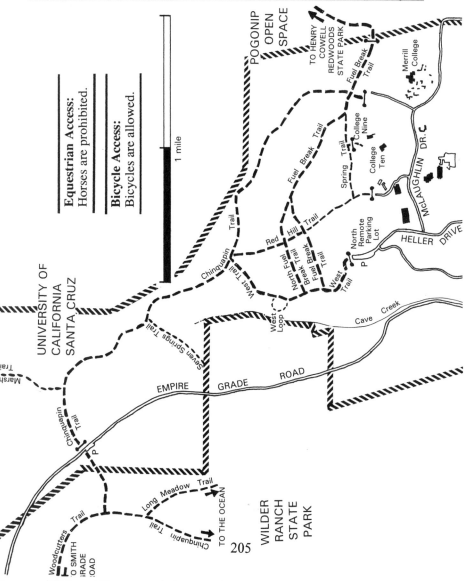

Equestrian Access:
Horses are prohibited.

Bicycle Access:
Bicycles are allowed.

1 mile

UNIVERSITY OF
CALIFORNIA
SANTA CRUZ

POGONIP
OPEN
SPACE

TO HENRY
COWELL
REDWOODS
STATE PARK

Merrill
College

Fuel Break
Trail

Fuel Break Trail

College Nine

Spring Trail

College
Ten

McLAUGHLIN DR. C

HELLER DRIVE

Red Hill Trail

Chinquapin Trail

West Trail

North Fuel
Break Trail

Fuel Break
Trail

North
Remote
Parking
Lot

P

West
Trail

West
Loop

Cave Creek

Marshall
Trail

Chinquapin Trail

Seven Springs Trail

EMPIRE GRADE ROAD

P

WILDER RANCH
STATE PARK

Long Meadow Trail

TO THE OCEAN

Chinquapin Trail

Woodcutters Trail

TO SMITH
GRADE
ROAD

205

which are home to an endangered green insect called the Ohlone Tiger Beetle. Motor vehicles and camping are prohibited.

You can also enter this undeveloped part of the campus on Empire Grade Road 2.5 miles north of its intersection with Heller Road. Trails connect the UC campus with Wilder Ranch State Park, all the way to the beach, to the west, and Pogonip Open Space Preserve and Henry Cowell Redwoods State Park to the east. Because limestone is common in this area, limestone caves have developed. The easy to reach caverns, such as the one on the east side of Empire Grade Road, have been heavily vandalized.

The UCSC Campus Natural Reserve covers 400 acres of protected natural landscape on the campus. Tours of the Natural Reserve are offered by undergraduate students.

For more information, call (831) 459-4971 (www.ucsc.edu).

SPECIAL SECTION
Mountain Lions

With its diverse ecology, abundant deer, and mild climate, the Santa Cruz Mountains are ideal mountain lion habitat. You may notice that signs are posted at many trailheads warning of the presence of these native cats, and advising visitors to take precautions.

How concerned should you be?

I have been exploring these mountains for many years, and have never seen a mountain lion. I know they are there because I have seen their tracks and have talked to people who have seen them. They are extremely reclusive and avoid contact with people. Mountain lion attacks throughout California are very rare. There is no record of anyone being attacked by a lion in the Santa Cruz Mountains. The statistics are clear: you are much more likely to be injured or killed driving your car to the local supermarket than being attacked by a mountain lion in any wildland in California.

However, the California Department of Fish and Game recommends you take the following precautions:

1) Don't hike alone.
2) Keep children close.
3) Do not run from a mountain lion.
4) Fight back if attacked.

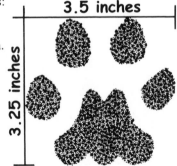

206

Upper Stevens Creek County Park

TO GET THERE... The park is accessible from the Charcoal Road and Grizzly Flat entrances along the east side of Skyline Boulevard north of Saratoga Gap.

There are so many open space preserves along Skyline Boulevard that it is easy to overlook this 1,276-acre Santa Clara County Park.

For many trail users this park is only known as a link along the Canyon Trail between Page Mill Road (See Monte Bello O.S.P chapter) and Saratoga Gap. Unfortunately, the Grizzly Flat and Table Mountain/Charcoal Road Trails don't form a convenient loop. If you don't want to backtrack or walk 2 miles along Skyline Boulevard, consider adding 3.5 miles of trails in Long Ridge Open Space Preserve to your trip. Be aware that bicycles are only allowed to go uphill on the Table Mountain and Charcoal Road Trails.

The hiking-only route offers an interesting variety of chaparral, but it is quite narrow and there is lots of poison oak along the way. At the downhill end of this trail is a large, fairly flat, open area called Table Mountain. Look for young giant sequoias and other non-native trees here.

This is a steep canyon park, forested with canyon oak, black oak, coast live oak, tanbark oak, buckeye, madrone, bay, maple, and Douglas fir. There are also areas of chaparral. The park crosses the San Andreas Fault, as evidenced by linear valleys and pressure ridges. There is an Ohlone Indian acorn grinding stone a short walk down Charcoal Road from Skyline Boulevard.

The park is open from 8 a.m. until half an hour after sunset. For more information, call (408) 867-3654 or (408) 358-3741.(www.parkhere.org).

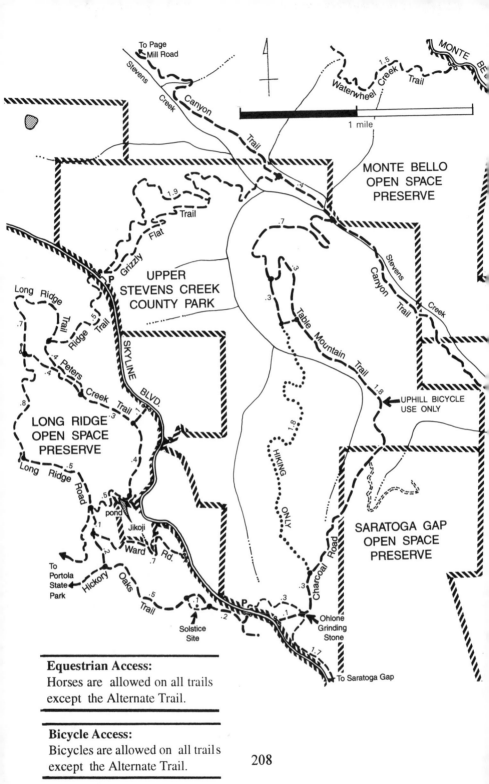

To Page
Mill Road

MONTE BE

Stevens

Creek

Canyon

Trail

Waterwheel Creek Trail

1.5

1 mile

MONTE BELLO
OPEN SPACE
PRESERVE

.4

1.9

Trail

Grizzly

Flat

.7

.3

P

UPPER
STEVENS CREEK
COUNTY PARK

.3

Stevens

Canyon

Trail

Creek

Long Ridge Trail

.7

.5

Ridge Trail

.4

Peters

.4

Creek

Trail

.8

SKYLINE

BLVD

.3

.1

Table Mountain Trail

1.8

UPHILL BICYCLE
USE ONLY

LONG RIDGE
OPEN SPACE
PRESERVE

1.8

.4

Long Ridge Road

.5

HIKING ONLY

.5

pond

Jikoji

1

Ward Rd.

.7

.2

SARATOGA GAP
OPEN SPACE
PRESERVE

To
Portola
State
Park

Hickory Oaks Trail

.5

.1

Solstice
Site

.2

P

.3

Charcoal Road

.3

.7

.7

Ohlone
Grinding
Stone

1.7

To Saratoga Gap

Equestrian Access:
Horses are allowed on all trails
except the Alternate Trail.

Bicycle Access:
Bicycles are allowed on all trails
except the Alternate Trail.

208

The waterfalls of Uvas Canyon are best in winter and early spring.

Uvas Canyon County Park

TO GET THERE... From Highway 101 take Bernal Road west, turn left on Santa Teresa Boulevard, right on Bailey Avenue, left on McKean Road (which turns into Uvas Road), and right on Croy Road.

This 1,133-acre wooded park is tucked into a beautiful canyon west of Morgan Hill. Here you can escape the crowds and hike about 7 miles of trails along shady creeks and through wonderfully diverse forests of second-growth redwood, Douglas fir, bay, madrone, sycamore, bigleaf maple, buckeye, and several kinds of oak.

A great day hike can be taken on the loop trail that begins at the Nature Trail about a quarter mile beyond the bridge on the left side of the road. Follow the Swanson Creek Trail until it crosses Swanson Creek beyond the Old Hot House Site. This part of the route becomes the Contour Trail, which gains elevation and eventually intersects Alec Canyon Trail. Turn left here and return to the starting point. This loop is only about 3 easy miles and involves just a little uphill hiking. Short sidetrips from the loop can be taken to Black Rock Falls and Basin Falls. Late winter through early spring is the best time to enjoy the waterfalls, which nearly dry up in summer.

To make this route longer, turn right on Alec Canyon Trail to explore the deep and shady second-growth redwoods along Alec Creek.

For an even more vigorous walk, climb Nibbs Knob by way of the Nibbs Knob Trail, which gains about 1,800 feet in less than 2 miles. Exposed to the sun, this is a tough trek on hot summer days. Take plenty of water. Great views of Loma Prieta, the Santa Clara Valley, and the Diablo Range will reward your efforts.

You can continue on Nibbs Knob Trail to Summit Road and on south to Mount Madonna County Park.

   The park has a campground with 25 individual campsites and a youth group camping area for non-profit youth groups of up to 40 people, available on a first-come, first-served basis. There are also individual and group picnic facilities. For more information, call (408) 779-9232.

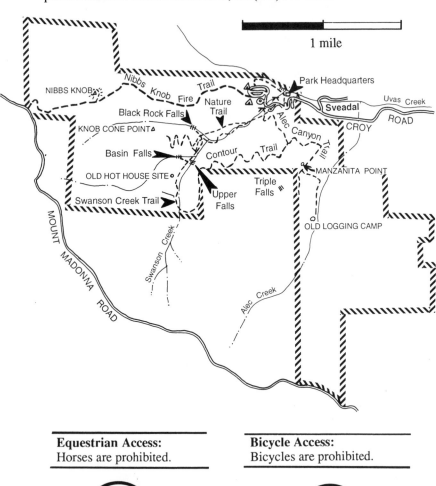

Equestrian Access:
Horses are prohibited.

Bicycle Access:
Bicycles are prohibited.

Villa Montalvo Arboretum & County Park

TO GET THERE. . . take Saratoga-Los Gatos Road south of Highway 9 in Saratoga and turn southwest on Montalvo Road.

Villa Montalvo is a 175-acre cultural center, arboretum, and wildlife refuge in the hills west of Saratoga. The mansion is maintained by the Montalvo Association, and the remainder of the grounds have been under Santa Clara County jurisdiction since 1960. Plays, concerts, recitals, and artistic displays are often open to the public.

Villa Montalvo is a very unique park. Because it is more of an educational than a recreational facility, there are no picnicking or camping facilities available. An easy 1.5 mile self-guided nature loop climbs about 400 feet through redwoods, mixed evergreen forest, and chaparral. The park has only about 3 miles of trails, making it a good place for casual saunters and an excellent place to study the ecology of the east side of the Santa Cruz Mountains.

From Lookout Point you can enjoy views of the Santa Clara Valley.

The grounds and mansion were bought by California Senator and San Francisco Mayor James Phelan in 1911. Rooms on the estate are now rented to promising artists.

The park is open from 8:00 a.m. to 5:00 p.m. Monday through Friday and from 9:00 a.m. to 5:00 p.m. weekends and holidays. For more information, call (408)961-5800 (www.parkhere.org).

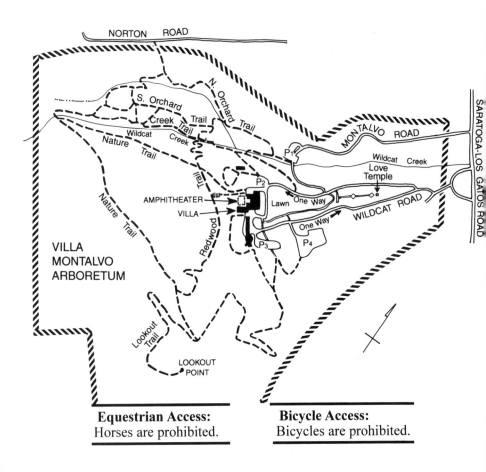

NORTON ROAD

SARATOGA-LOS GATOS ROAD

MONTALVO ROAD

N. Orchard Trail

S. Orchard Trail

Creek Trail

Wildcat Creek

Nature Trail

Wildcat Creek

Love Temple

P1

P2

Redwood Trail

AMPHITHEATER

VILLA

Lawn

One Way

One Way

WILDCAT ROAD

P3

P4

Nature Trail

VILLA MONTALVO ARBORETUM

Lookout Trail

LOOKOUT POINT

Equestrian Access:
Horses are prohibited.

Bicycle Access:
Bicycles are prohibited.

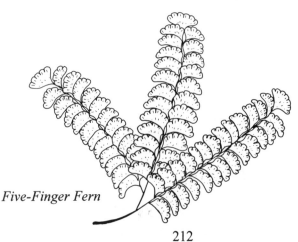

Five-Finger Fern

212

Wilder Ranch State Park

TO GET THERE... The main entrance is 2 miles west of Santa Cruz and 42 miles south of Half Moon Bay on Highway 1. There is an entrance fee and a large parking lot, though you can park along the highway for free. The park continues along both sides of Highway 1 for about 4.5 miles. There is an entrance on Smith Grade Road with limited parking. There is also an unmarked entrance on the inland side of Highway 1 between Baldwin Creek and Majors Creek with limited parking.

From the wild and rugged coast this 6,219-acre park sweeps gently upward through grasslands and oakwoods and steep valleys filled with redwood and Douglas fir. An excellent trail system, totaling 34 miles, is open to walkers, mountain bikers, and equestrians. It is particularly popular with offroad bicyclists.

The best place to begin your visit is at the historic Wilder Ranch Cultural Preserve complex. Here you will find visitor information and see historic buildings and antique farming methods.

This land was once the Wilder Ranch, a prosperous dairy operation headquartered in a cluster of 19th-century buildings just off Highway 1. The oldest of these structures is an 1830's adobe built when this was Rancho Refugio, a Mexican land grant. A workshop with water-powered machinery, a dairy barn built of hand-hewn timbers held together with wooden pegs, a horse barn, 2 houses, and several other historic buildings remain from the period before 1900. These buildings are being restored as a park interpretive center and agricultural history exhibit. Antique agricultural methods are sometimes demonstrated at Wilder Ranch, especially at the annual Harvest Festival in October. Call (831) 426-0505 for exact date.

The Fern Grotto, a beach cave with ferns growing from the ceiling, is one of many wonderful sights along the Old Cove Landing Trail.

There are too many potential trail combinations to mention here. Some of the trails are identified as loops and some of these loops can be combined to form larger loops. There are public access restrictions at the marsh at the mouth of Meder Creek, and about 600 acres of farmland.

The Old Cove Landing Trail can be combined with the Ohlone Bluff Trail for a 3.75-mile (one-way) adventure that parallels a rugged stretch of coast characterized by precipitous cliffs, sea caves, and isolated pocket beaches that are sometimes used by nude sunbathers. A beach cave with ferns growing from the ceiling is one of the many attractions. Be sure to look for seals, sea lions, and sea otters just offshore. Horses are not allowed on this route.

Here are the mileages for some of the loop options:

Baldwin Loop: 3.25 miles   **Cowboy Loop:** 1.5 miles
Enchanted Loop: 1.5 miles   **Englesman Loop:** 3.0 miles
Eucalyptus Loop: 3.75 miles   **Wilder Ridge Loop:** 6.25 miles

From the Woodcutters Trail, in the northern part of the park, you can take the Chinquapin Trail into the University of California, Santa Cruz campus. From there you can continue through Pogonip Open Space Preserve and on to Henry Cowell Redwoods State Park. Most of the trails in this park are old ranch roads.

As you travel into the backcountry of the park you will climb through a progression of nearly level areas followed by steep rises, creating a step-like effect. The flat areas are ancient marine terraces. The steep rises are remnants of ancient sea cliffs. As the landscape was uplifted by earthquakes new marine terraces and sea cliffs were formed that now comprise this amazing staircase up the mountains.

A new parcel of land was added to this park between Baldwin Creek and Majors Creek. An excellent road-trail follows a gentle grade for less than 2 miles from Highway 1 to a beautiful little reservoir on Majors Creek.

As of this writing there is only room for a few cars near the metal gate entrance on the inland side of Highway 1 between Baldwin and Majors Creeks. Climb through the locked gate. The trail starts out as a paved road. The pavement soon breaks up and it is gravel the rest of the way. The route ascends through the coastal prairie from one marine terrace to the next. This is a great place to see birds of prey. It then drops into the Majors Creek canyon, which is wooded with bay, Douglas fir, and oak, all festooned with copious lichen. Because lichen absorbs airborne particulates, it is very sensitive to pollution. The cleaner the air the more lichen. Second-growth redwoods predominate farther up the canyon.

This route ends at a small Santa Cruz Water Department pump station and reservoir on Majors Creek. You may be tempted to take a dip in the reservoir on a warm day. A short footpath will take you to a bench stating that you are in the "PAUL AND BOB GERSTLEY MEMORIAL GROVE."

Wilder Ranch State Park is open from 8 a.m. to Sunset. Dogs are not allowed on the trails. For more information, call park headquarters at (831) 423-9703 (www.parks.ca.gov).

MARINE TERRACES

Fault movement has rapidly uplifted the Santa Cruz Mountains, leaving step-like formations of marine terraces well above the high tide line. Formed by wave erosion, these terraces are particularly noticeable along the coast between Half Moon Bay and Santa Cruz.

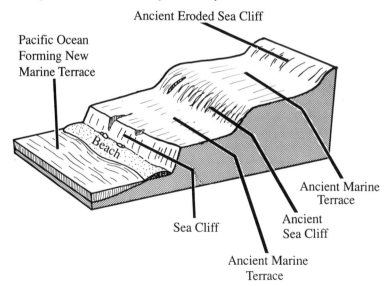

Ancient Eroded Sea Cliff

Pacific Ocean
Forming New
Marine Terrace

Beach

Sea Cliff

Ancient
Sea Cliff

Ancient Marine
Terrace

Ancient Marine
Terrace

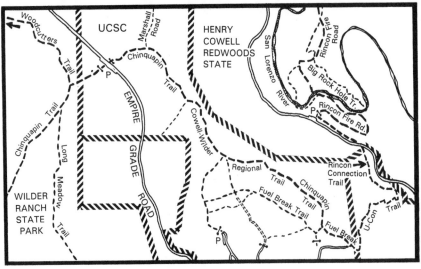

With gentle grades and 34 miles of bike trails,
Wilder Ranch is the best mountain biking park
in the Santa Cruz Mountains. There is also a
trail connection to The University of California,
Santa Cruz campus (see page 204), which
continues on to Henry Cowell Redwoods
State Park (see page 86).

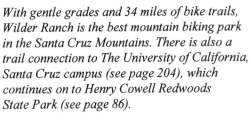

Bicycle Access:
Bicycles are allowed on all trails.

Equestrian Access:
Horses are allowed on all trails.

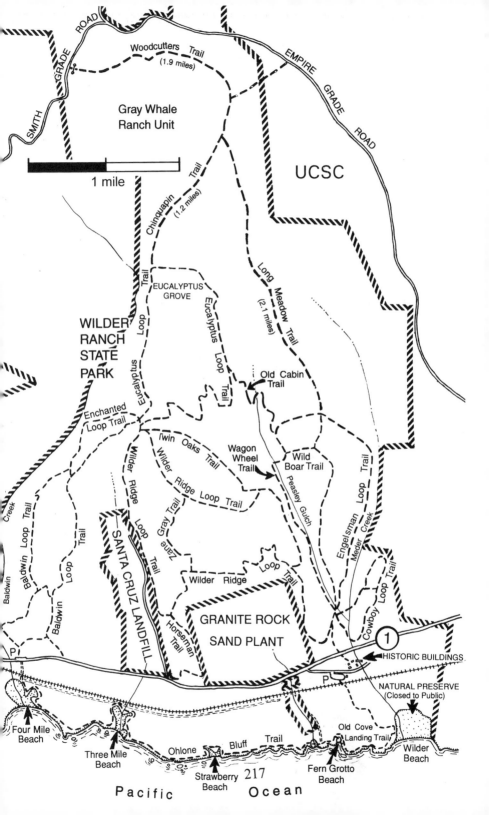

SMITH GRADE ROAD

EMPIRE GRADE ROAD

Woodcutters Trail
(1.9 miles)

Gray Whale
Ranch Unit

UCSC

1 mile

Chinquapin Trail
(1.2 miles)

WILDER
RANCH
STATE
PARK

Eucalyptus Loop Trail

EUCALYPTUS
GROVE

Eucalyptus Loop Trail

Long Meadow Trail
(2.1 miles)

Old Cabin
Trail

Enchanted
Loop Trail

Wilder Ridge Loop Trail

Twin Oaks Trail

Wagon
Wheel
Trail

Wild
Boar
Trail

Engelsman Loop Trail

Creek

Baldwin Loop Trail

Wilder Loop Trail

SANTA CRUZ LANDFILL

Zane Gray Trail

Wilder Ridge Loop Trail

Peasley Gulch

Meder Creek

Baldwin

Baldwin Loop Trail

Wilder Ridge

Wilder Ridge Loop Trail

GRANITE ROCK
SAND PLANT

Cowboy Loop Trail

P

Horseman Trail

(1)

P

HISTORIC BUILDINGS

NATURAL PRESERVE
(Closed to Public)

Four Mile
Beach

Three Mile
Beach

Ohlone Bluff Trail

Strawberry
Beach

Old Cove
Landing Trail

Fern Grotto
Beach

Wilder
Beach

217

Pacific   Ocean

Windy Hill Open Space Preserve

TO GET THERE... Take Skyline Boulevard 4.9 miles north of the PageMill Road intersection and 2.3 miles south of the Highway 84 (La Honda Road) intersection. Park at the picnic area on the east side of Skyline Boulevard. To reach the east (downhill) entrance from Highway 280, take Alpine Road south to Portola Road and turn right. The trailhead is at the parking lot just north of The Sequoias on Portola Road.

If ever a hill lived up to its name, this is it. This 1,308-acre preserve includes an area of high grassy hills, seen from much of the Bay Area and exposed to steady currents of wind that bombard the coast and prevent trees from growing on its windier parts. Much of the rest of the preserve, which swoops down to Portola Valley to the east, is densely wooded with oak, bay, and Douglas fir. The preserve has about 12 miles of trails.

Take the short Anniversary Trail from the picnic area along Skyline Boulevard to the top of Windy Hill. Here you will find one of the Santa Cruz Mountains' great views, and a complete cross section of The Peninsula, with San Francisco Bay and its cities spread out below to the east, and the ocean to the west. This windswept summit is also perfect for kite flying, with no entangling trees or telephone wires.

The grove of Monterey cypress trees just below and to the east of the Windy Hill summit was planted as a wind break bordering the old Orton ranchhouse, which is no longer there.

For a good workout, and to get out of the wind, combine the Spring

Bicycle Access:
Bicycles are prohibited on Anniversary Trail, Eagle Trail, Hamms Gulch Trail, Razorback Ridge Trail, and Lost Trail.

Equestrian Access:
Horses are allowed on all trails except the Anniversary Trail.

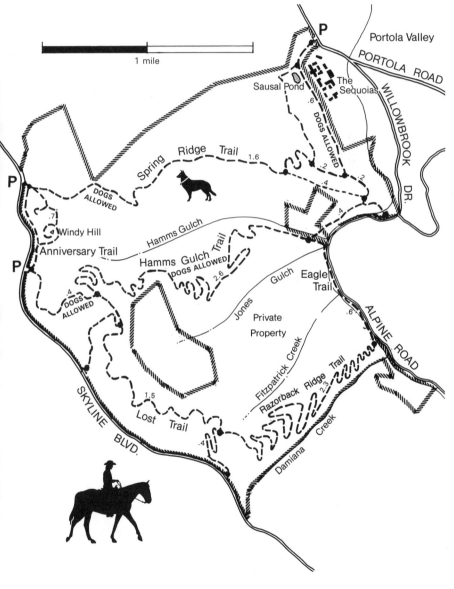

1 mile

Portola Valley

PORTOLA ROAD

WILLOWBROOK DR.

Sausal Pond

The Sequoias

DOGS ALLOWED

.6

P

Spring Ridge Trail 1.6

.2

.2

.4

.4

P

DOGS ALLOWED

Windy Hill

Anniversary Trail

P

Hamms Gulch

Hamms Gulch Trail

DOGS ALLOWED 2.6

.4 DOGS ALLOWED

Jones Gulch

Eagle Trail

.6

ALPINE ROAD

Private Property

Fitzpatrick Creek

Razorback Ridge Trail 2.3

1.5

Lost Trail

.4

Damiana Creek

SKYLINE BLVD.

219

Ridge and Hamms Gulch Trails to form a loop of 6 miles and an elevation range of 1,200 feet. Near the bottom of the loop you can make a side trip to Sausal Pond, next to the Sequoias retirement community.

The southern part of the preserve is largely covered with chaparral, and madrone, bay, and Douglas fir woodlands. To explore this area, take the Lost Trail 2.1 miles south from the picnic area to the Razorback Ridge Trail. This trail rapidly descends 1,000 feet to Alpine Road, where it can be combined with the Eagle Trail to connect with Hamms Gulch Trail, which makes a steep 900-foot ascent through an oak and Douglas fir woodland to the Lost Trail. The entire loop, beginning at the picnic area parking lot, is 8 fairly strenuous miles.

The western slopes of Windy Hill have been designated for use by non-motorized model gliders by permit only.

Dogs on leash are allowed on designated areas, including the Anniversary Trail, Spring Ridge Trail, Eagle Trail, Hamms Gulch Trail, and the Lost Trail segment between the picnic area parking lot and Hamms Gulch Trail.

For more information, call the Midpeninsula Regional Open Space District at (650)691-1200 (www.openspace.org).

These ancient, moss-clad Douglas firs are near the uphill end of the Hamms Gulch Trail.

Wunderlich County Park

TO GET THERE... From Highway 280 take Woodside Road west and south. The park entrance is about 2 miles beyond the town of Woodside. The uphill entrance is on Skyline Boulevard just south of where it intersects Bear Gulch Road (3.1 miles south of Kings Mountain Road).

This 942-acre park is one of the most ecologically diverse and scenically beautiful parks east of Skyline Boulevard. It is especially popular with equestrians from nearby Woodside. Bicycles are prohibited.

From the park entrance parking lot, at the old Folger Stable buildings, this looks like a bay/oakwood park. But a short saunter up the hillside reveals dark, cool groves of second-growth redwoods, open grassy meadows, and nearly pure stands of Douglas fir. This is a steep park, with an elevation range of more than 1,650 feet; but it has about 15 miles of excellent trails that are graded to avoid excessively strenuous climbs.

A beautiful 4.75-mile excursion can be enjoyed by combining the Bear Gulch and Alambique Trails. From the Woodside Road parking lot hike uphill on Bear Gulch Trail, passing through groves of live oak and on to second-growth redwoods in shady creek beds. Along the trail stands the rotting remains of a fence built when Simon Jones owned the property in the later part of the nineteenth century. You will also find a long trough running up the hill. This is one of several skid trails created by oxen dragging redwood logs down the mountain between about 1850 and 1865 when the original redwood forest was logged to provide lumber for Bay Area cities. The property was bought in 1902 by James Folger II, who built the house and stable.

You will also see large Douglas fir trees with low sprawling branches,

---

The Folger Estate Stables, built in 1905, was part of the country estate of coffee magnate James Folger II. It is not open to the public at this time.

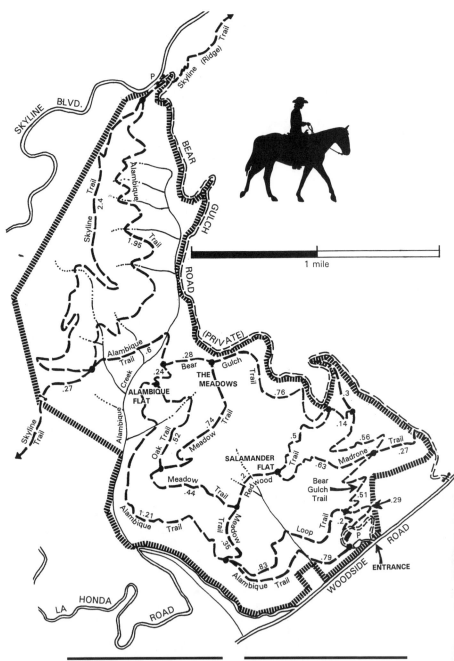

SKYLINE BLVD.

P

Skyline (Ridge) Trail

BEAR GULCH ROAD

Skyline Trail 2.4

Alambique

Trail 1.95

1 mile

Skyline Trail

(PRIVATE)

Alambique Trail .6

Alambique Creek

.27

ALAMBIQUE FLAT

.24

.28 Bear Gulch Trail

THE MEADOWS

.76

.3

Oak Trail .52

Meadow Trail .74

SALAMANDER FLAT

.5

.14

.56 Madrone Trail

.27

Meadow .44 Trail

Redwood Trail

2.1

Bear Gulch Trail

.63

.51

.29

Alambique Trail 1.21

Meadow Trail .35

Loop Trail

.2

P

.83

Alambique Trail

.79

WOODSIDE ROAD

ENTRANCE

LA HONDA ROAD

Equestrian Access:
Horses are allowed on all trails.

Bicycle Access:
Bicycles are prohibited.

222

indicating that at one time these trees were at the edge of a meadow which became a woodland when cattle grazing ceased. Suddenly the forest gives way to a beautiful meadow, which is covered with native bunch grasses and introduced perennials. There are sweeping views that make this a great place to stop and relax for awhile.

The Alambique Trail heads downhill through all the park's native plant communities, and passing such introduced species as Monterey cypress, eucalyptus, and olve trees. Be sure to pause and admire the enormous old-growth redwood on the north side of the trail; the kind you wouldn't expect to see east of Skyline. You will also see the ruins of old nineteenth century wagon bridges along the way.

If you have a few hours take the 5-mile round trip from the meadows to Skyline Boulevard and back. From Bear Gulch Trail, head uphill on Alambique Trail to the top of the ridge and then gambol down the Skyline Trail and back to Alambique Creek, which flows along the course of a branch of the Pilarcitos Fault. Notice that the rock suddenly changes from sandstone to shale as you cross the fault.

Salamander Flat, a small reservoir once used for agricultural water storage, is now a popular hangout for newts.

The Skyline Trail heads northward, out of the park for 4.7 miles to Huddart County Park and Kings Mountain Road. See the Skyline Trail chapter for details.

This park is open for day use only. For more information, call the San Mateo County Parks Department at (650) 851-1210 or (650) 851-0326. (www.eparks.net).

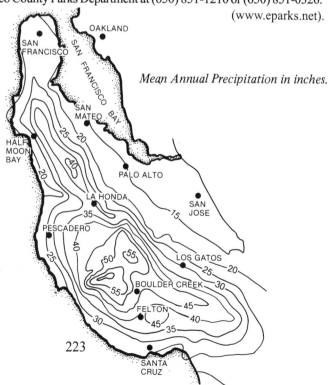

Mean Annual Precipitation in inches.

223

Coastal Access Guide

The Santa Cruz Mountains come right down to the ocean in San Mateo and Santa Cruz Counties. The following 15 pages are a guide to coastal access along this stretch of coast.

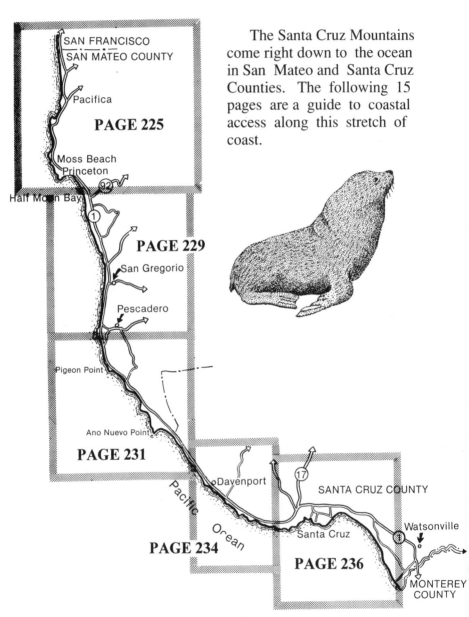

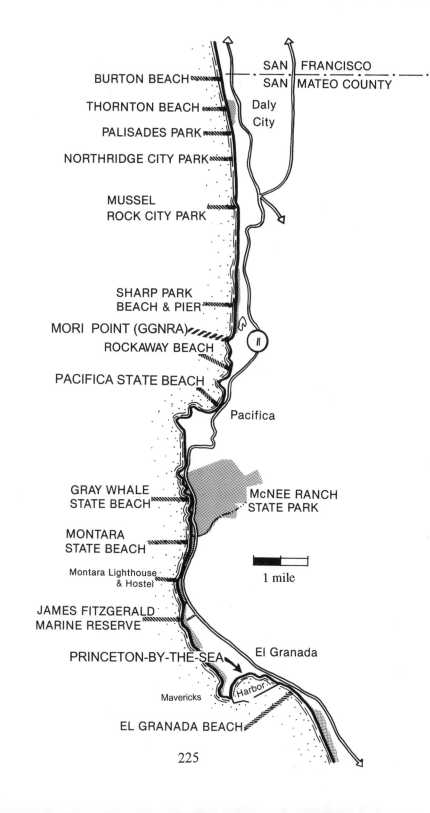

BURTON BEACH

SAN FRANCISCO
SAN MATEO COUNTY

THORNTON BEACH

Daly
City

PALISADES PARK

NORTHRIDGE CITY PARK

MUSSEL
ROCK CITY PARK

SHARP PARK
BEACH & PIER

MORI POINT (GGNRA)

ROCKAWAY BEACH

II

PACIFICA STATE BEACH

Pacifica

GRAY WHALE
STATE BEACH

McNEE RANCH
STATE PARK

MONTARA
STATE BEACH

1 mile

Montara Lighthouse
& Hostel

JAMES FITZGERALD
MARINE RESERVE

PRINCETON-BY-THE-SEA

El Granada

Mavericks

Harbor

EL GRANADA BEACH

225

Mussel Rock City Park

TO GET THERE... From Highway 1 in Pacifica take Palmetto Avenue north and turn left on Westline to the parking lot.

From the parking lot area you will enjoy awesome views up and down the coast. Be sure to bring your binoculars to view seabirds on the offshore rocks and migrating gray whales in winter.

Take the walkway northward downhill and climb over the concrete blocks to the beach. On your way down, to your right, you will see a large area where it appears the land has collapsed. This is the result of movement on the San Andreas Fault. You are very near where it goes out to sea.

Sharp Park Beach and Pier

TO GET THERE... From Highway 1 in Pacifica take Paloma Avenue west and Beach Boulevard south.

This popular sandy beach has picnic tables, barbeque grills and a 1,140-foot pier that some say is the the best fishing pier in California.

Mori Point Unit, GGNRA

SEE GOLDEN GATE NATIONAL RECREATION AREA CHAPTER.

Rockaway Beach

TO GET THERE... From Highway 1 in Pacifica take Rockaway Beach Avenue west.

This small sandy beach, popular with surfers, is tucked between rocky headlands. A pedestrian walkway connects this beach with Pacifica beach to the south. Dogs on leash are allowed.

PACIFICA STATE BEACH

TO GET THERE... It is in Pacifica along Highway 1 where it intersects Linda Mar Boulevard.

This mile-long sandy beach can be packed on those rare warm weekend days. It is popular with surfers, but not recommended for swimming because of cold water and rip currents. Dogs on leash are allowed.

Gray Whale Cove State Beach
TO GET THERE... It's south of Pacifica and just south of Devil's Slide. From the parking lot on the east side of Highway 1, cross the road and walk a narrow road downhill to a wooden stairway to the beach.

This small, beautiful crescent-shaped sandy beach is tucked out of sight by steep cliffs and bracketed by granite outcrops. Though this is a clothing optional beach, the weather is often not conducive to nudity.

Montara State Beach
TO GET THERE... It's just west of Highway 1 south of Devil's Slide and 7.7 miles north of Highway 92. Park at the Chart House restaurant or at a small dirt parking lot half a mile north.

Half a mile of golden orange sand make this a popular beach with volleyball players, sandcastle builders, and surfcasters. Just south of the beach are sea caves exposed at minus tide.

Montara Lighthouse Hostel
TO GET THERE... It's on Highway 1 about 7 miles north of Highway 92 and .7 miles south of the Chart House restaurant.

You can spend a night in a dramatic coastal hostel setting adjacent to the old Montara lighthouse. There are 30 beds plus a kitchen in an old victorian house near the lighthouse. The hostel is closed from 9:30 a.m. to 4:30 p.m. It is 25 bicycle miles south of San Francisco's Fort Mason hostel. For more information call (650) 728-7177(www.norcalhostels.org).

James Fitzgerald Marine Reserve
TO GET THERE... Take Highway 1 to the town of Moss Beach and turn west on California Avenue. It's about 10 miles south of Pacifica and 6.3 miles north of Highway 92.

A large rocky reef exposed at low tide makes this 3-mile long beach one of the best places in California to enjoy the amazing diversity of marine life. Get a tide table from a bait shop or sporting goods store and then head for this reserve when the tide is low. Tidepool walks are conducted at low tide by rangers or docents. Special group tours can also be arranged.

Remember that it is illegal to remove or disturb marine life.

There is a hiking trail along the bluffs to the south of the parking lot, and there are picnic tables and a restroom amid the cypress grove near the parking lot. The Seal Cove earthquake fault can be seen in the cliff about 100 feet north of San Clemente Creek.

For more information, call (650) 728-3584(www.co.sanmateo.ca.us).

Princeton-by-the-Sea
TO GET THERE... Just north of Half Moon Bay, take Capistrano Road west from Highway 1, continue west on Harvard Avenue or Princeton Avenue to West Point Avenue.

A peninsula juts westward from the town of Princeton, forming the north end of Half Moon Bay. From the parking lot on West Point Avenue take the trail that contours along the south side of the peninsula, passing a brackish marsh and the Pillar Point Harbor. Upon reaching the end of the peninsula, continue north to the southern end of the Fitzgerald Marine Preserve at low tide. Even at high tide this is a good place to see seals, sea lions, and sea birds offshore.

Offshore from the end of the peninsula is an underwater rock shelf that forms some of the biggest waves anywhere. Maverick's has become a world famous big wave surfing destination, drawing serious surfers from around the world when conditions are right. The best place to witness Maverick's surfing is on the bluffs overlooking the beach at the end of the peninsula, especially near the red and white tower.

228

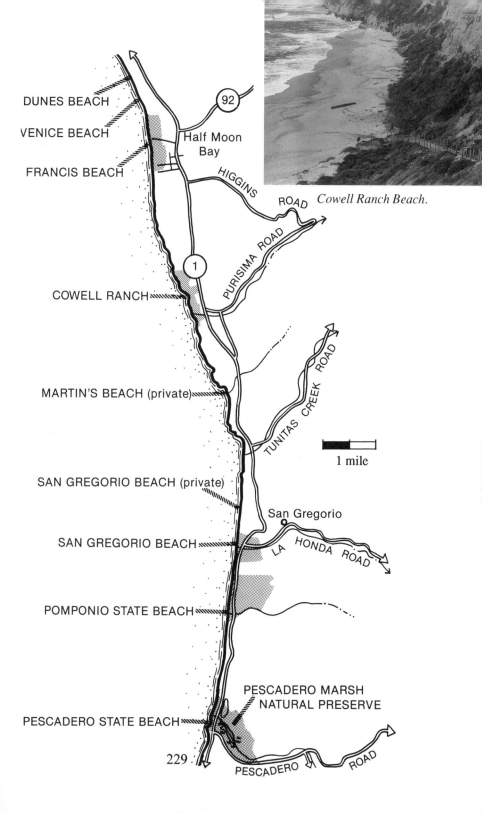

DUNES BEACH

VENICE BEACH

FRANCIS BEACH

Half Moon
Bay

92

Cowell Ranch Beach.

HIGGINS ROAD

PURISIMA ROAD

1

COWELL RANCH

MARTIN'S BEACH (private)

TUNITAS CREEK ROAD

1 mile

SAN GREGORIO BEACH (private)

San Gregorio

SAN GREGORIO BEACH

LA HONDA ROAD

POMPONIO STATE BEACH

PESCADERO MARSH
NATURAL PRESERVE

PESCADERO STATE BEACH

229

PESCADERO ROAD

Francis Beach
TO GET THERE... Take Highway 1 to Half Moon Bay and turn west on Kelly Avenue.

This unit of Half Moon Bay State Beach has a campground with 52 campsites. To reserve a campsite call (800) 444-PARK or go to the website at www.reserveamerica.com.

Cowell Ranch State Beach
TO GET THERE... The parking lot is on the west side of Highway 1 just south of Half Moon Bay and 3 miles south of Highway 92.

Most of this 1,300-acre ranch will be kept in agriculture. From the parking lot walk a half-mile dirt road trail to a viewpoint overlooking the sea cliffs. A stairway trail descends to a beautiful secluded beach. There is no access to the next beach south where harbor seals breed.

Martin's Beach
TO GET THERE... Take Highway 1 about 7 miles south from Highway 92

A fee is charged to drive the private-access toll road west from Highway 1 to a small seaside community and private beach. Impressive rock outcroppings and sandy beaches make this a pleasant area for beach relaxation and exploration.

There are some sea caves accessible at low tide. The Rocky islands offshore are popular rest stops for harbor seals. Pups are born from late May through July. Surf fishing and surf netting are also popular.

San Gregorio Private Beach
TO GET THERE... From Highway 1 it's at the end of a paved toll road about 1.5 miles north of San Gregorio State Beach.

There is an admission fee to visit this clothing optional beach. It is open most weekends.

San Gregorio State Beach
TO GET THERE... It's at the mouth of San Gregorio Creek along Highway 1 about 11 miles south of Half Moon Bay.

This beach has a large paved parking lot, a restroom, and picnic facilities. There is a small lagoon, good for wading, along San Gregorio Creek. There is a freshwater marsh east of Highway 1. The Portola expedition camped here in 1769.

Pomponio State Beach
TO GET THERE... take Highway 1 13 miles south from Half Moon Bay.

With a big parking lot, picnic facilities, and restrooms, this beach is ready for lots of visitors. Steep coastal bluffs overlook this long straight beach, which was named for an Ohlone Indian outlaw.

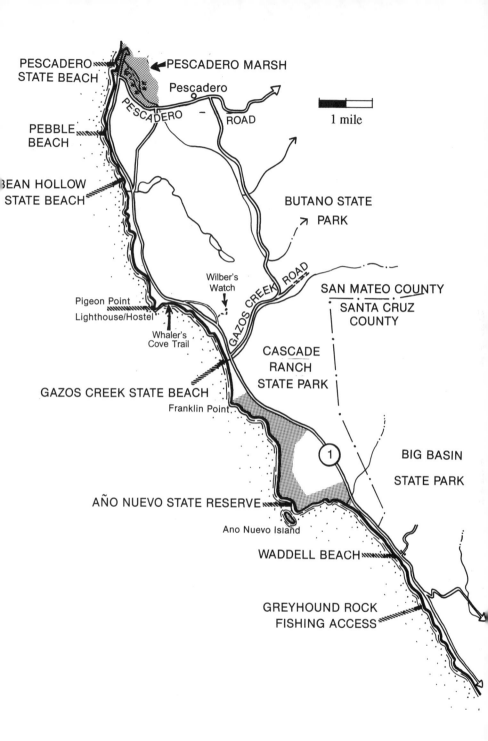

PESCADERO STATE BEACH

← PESCADERO MARSH

Pescadero

PESCADERO — ROAD

1 mile

PEBBLE BEACH

BEAN HOLLOW STATE BEACH

BUTANO STATE PARK

Wilber's Watch

GAZOS CREEK ROAD

SAN MATEO COUNTY

SANTA CRUZ COUNTY

Pigeon Point Lighthouse/Hostel

Whaler's Cove Trail

CASCADE RANCH STATE PARK

GAZOS CREEK STATE BEACH

Franklin Point

1

BIG BASIN STATE PARK

AÑO NUEVO STATE RESERVE

Ano Nuevo Island

WADDELL BEACH

GREYHOUND ROCK FISHING ACCESS

231

Pescadero State Beach
TO GET THERE... It stretches for about a mile along the coast near the intersection of Highway 1 and Pescadero Road.

Sand dunes, a wide beach, tidepools, and the mouth of Pescadero Creek are a few of the attractions of this popular beach. Steelhead spawn up Pescadero Creek during the rainy season. It's just across Highway 1 from Pescadero Marsh. See the Pescadero Marsh chapter.

Pebble Beach
TO GET THERE... It's just west of Highway 1 about 1 mile north of Bean Hollow Beach and 16 miles south of Half Moon Bay.

This small cove beach is covered with wave-smoothed agate, carnelian, quartz, serpentine, and other beautiful pebbles formed from an offshore quartz reef. There are good tidepools at low tide.

Bean Hollow State Beach
TO GET THERE... It's just west of Highway 1 about a mile south of Pebble Beach.

This small and intimate beach has a paved parking lot, picnic tables, and a restroom, There are good tidepools at low tide.

Pigeon Point
TO GET THERE... Look for the tall lighthouse just west of Highway 1 between Pescadero Road and Ano Nuevo State Reserve.

You can't miss Pigeon Point. It's marked by one of the most picturesque lighthouses on the west coast. At a height of 115 feet, no other west coast lighthouse is taller, and only one other is as tall. This classic structure, built in 1872, will guide you to a rocky stretch of coast that is popular for tidepooling, surf fishing, and scuba diving. Just east of the lighthouse the Whaler's Cove trail will take you to a small sandy beach.

You can stay the night here at the inexpensive and comfortable Pigeon Point Lighthouse Hostel, which is located in a series of cottages adjacent to the historic light. There are 40 beds, most in dormitory rooms, and private accommodations for families are also available. Daily check-in hours

232

are 4:30 p.m. to 9:30 p.m. It is closed daily from 10 a.m. until 4:30 p.m. Reservations are recommended by calling (650) 879-0633; www.norcalhostels.org.

Wilbur's Watch Trail
TO GET THERE... From Highway 1 turn east (inland) on Pigeon Point Road near Pigeon Point Lighthouse.

The Wilbur's Watch Trail gently ascends slightly more than a mile eastward to a lookout replete with benches, a telescope for enjoying the coastal panorama, and a display that describes what you are seeing. At this time this is the only public trail in the 5,600-acre Cloverdale Ranch, which is owned by Peninsula Open Space Trust (POST). The trail is named after Colburn Wilbur, open space advocate.

Gazos Creek State Beach
TO GET THERE... Look for the turnoff to the parking lot just west of Highway 1 near its intersection with Gazos Creek Road.

This is a good starting point for people who like long saunters along a remote wild seashore. Franklin Point, in Ano Nuevo State Reserve, is a short walk to the south. Wild salmon and steelhead spawn up Gazos Creek during the rainy season.

Ano Nuevo State Reserve
SEE SEPARATE CHAPTER ON PAGE 18.

Wilbur's Watch

Waddell Beach
TO GET THERE... This beach is adjacent to the Highway 1 entrance to Big Basin Redwoods State Park. It is just south of the high coastal bluffs that form the boundary between San Mateo and Santa Cruz Counties.

The most northerly beach in Santa Cruz County is located where Waddell Creek flows out to sea. This sandy beach is popular for windsurfing.

Greyhound Rock
TO GET THERE... Look for the parking lot along Highway 1 about 19 miles north of Santa Cruz and 7 miles north from Davenport. it is 1.4 miles south of Waddell Beach.

A steep, paved trail leads down the rugged bluffs to a magnificent beach and rocky shore with rock outcroppings just offshore. An outstanding place for rock fishing, surf netting, scuba diving, and beach combing, this is a California State Fish and Game Reserve. There are picnic

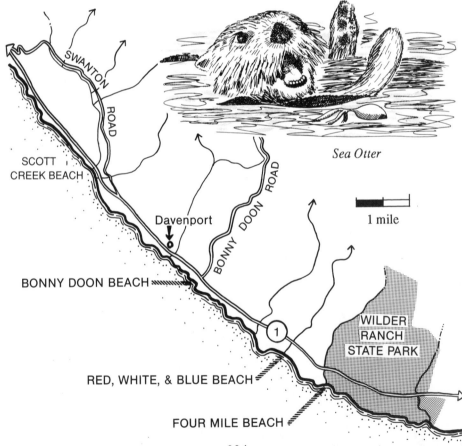

Sea Otter

1 mile

SWANTON ROAD

SCOTT CREEK BEACH

Davenport

BONNY DOON ROAD

BONNY DOON BEACH

1

WILDER RANCH STATE PARK

RED, WHITE, & BLUE BEACH

FOUR MILE BEACH

234

tables and a restroom on the bluff overlooing the beach. The reserve is open from 6 a.m. until 10 p.m.

Scott Creek Beach
TO GET THERE... It's at the mouth of Scott Creek, 3.6 miles south of Greyhound Rock.

This broad sandy beach is popular with hang gliders. it has an exceptional freshwater wetland just east of Highway 1.

Davenport

Across from this town's shops and restaurants along Highway1 is a parking lot where you can follow paths along the rim of a bluff overlooking the sea. This is a good place to see gray whales on their annual southbound winter migration. To the south a path descends to an inviting sandy beach bordered by impressive veritcal cliffs. Even more impressive is a large man-made tunnel cut through solid rock where a creek now flows.

Bonny Doon Beach
TO GET THERE... About a mile south of Davenport, park at the intersection of Highway 1 and Bonny Doon Road. Cross the railroad tracks and continue down to the beach.

This is a beautiful and fairly small rounded sandy beach partly enclosed by rock outcroppings which protect it from wind. Clothing is optional.

Red, White, and Blue Beach
TO GET THERE... Take Highway 1 north 7 miles from Santa Cruz or 4.2 miles south from Davenport and watch for a red, white, and blue mailbox. Take Scaroni Road toward the ocean.

This is a private clothing optional beach which is protected from wind by rocky headlands. An entrance fee is charged to use camping and picnicking facilities, restrooms, and showers. No dogs or cameras are allowed. For more information, call (831) 423-6332.

Four Mile Beach

TO GET THERE... Park along Highway 1 four miles north of the junction with Mission Street in Santa Cruz. Park near the where Highway 1 crosses Baldwin Creek.

Take the dirt road across the railroad tracks and downhill to the wide sandy beach, which is part of Wilder Ranch State Park. This clothing optional beach is considered an exceptional surfing destination. There is a large freshwater marsh at the beach.

Wilder Ranch State Park
SEE PAGE 213

Long Marine Laboratory

TO GET THERE... From Highway 1 in Santa Cruz turn south (seaward) on Western, right on Mission, left on Natural Bridges Drive, then right on Delaware.

Anyone interested in marine biology will enjoy a free docent-led tour of this marine research facility operated by the University of California Center for Coastal Marine Studies. Don't miss the 87-foot long blue whale skeleton. The Seymore Marine Discovery Center is open Tuesdays through

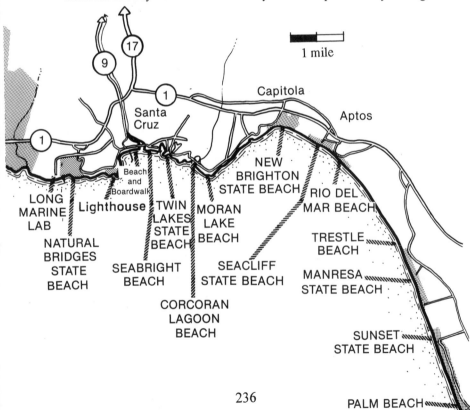

236

Saturdays from 10 a.m. to 5 p.m. and Sundays from noon to 5 p.m. The first Tuesday of each month is free.

For more information call (831) 459-3800.

Natural Bridges State Beach
TO GET THERE... Take Highway 1 to near the west end of Santa Cruz, turn south on Swift Street, and turn right on West Cliff Drive.

This small park has many attractions, including a crescent-shaped beach, tidepools, good surfing, picnic sites, and of course the famous monarch butterfly overwintering grove. Despite its name, all but one of the natural stone arches at the beach have collapsed.

Monarch butterflies west of the Rocky Mountains, some from as far away as western Canada, migrate each fall to ancestral groves along the California coast to avoid freezing in the winter. They are first seen at Natural Bridges in October and most are gone by March. The Eucalyptus grove in the small ravine near the visitors center hosts one of the largest overwintering colonies in the state, greatly surpassing the more famous assemblage at Pacific Grove. The eucalyptus not only provide support for large clusters of butterflies and protection from ocean winds, but their winter blossoms provide a valuable food source. This grove is the only official Monarch Natural Preserve in California.

Because monarchs have a hard time flying when the temperature dips below 55 F, on cool days look for multitudes of the insects clustered together on branches hanging down under their weight. These clusters may be so motionless that at first you may not even recognize them as being composed of butterflies. As the temperature rises, these inanimate butterfly clusters come to life and the air is filled with countless orange and black insects. For this reason, calm and mild days are best for viewing. For more information, call (831) 423-4609(www.parks.ca.gov).

Santa Cruz City Beaches

At **Lighthouse Point** is the **Mark Abbott Memorial Lighthouse**, now operated as a surfing museum. Call (831)420-6289 for details. This is a great place to watch surfers. Sea lions hang out on the offshore rocks.

Santa Cruz Beach, along Beach Street next to the Boardwalk, is the most popular and crowded beach in the city. Be sure to visit the half-mile long **Municipal Pier**. The beach has public restrooms and lifeguards.

Seabright Beach, between the Boardwalk and Santa Cruz Harbor along East Cliff Drive, has public restrooms and summer lifeguards. Call (408)688-3241 for more information. **Twin Lakes State Beach**, along East Cliff Drive just south of the Santa Cruz Harbor, covers 110 acres, including a lagoon behind the beach. For details call (831)688-3241.

Moran Lake Beach, near Lake Avenue, **Sunny Cove Beach**, at the end of Johans Beach Drive, and **Lincoln Beach**, at the end of 14th Avenue, are all in residential areas and are less crowded than other beaches. They are along East Cliff Drive.

New Brighton State Beach

TO GET THERE... It's just west of Highway 1 in Capitola, about 4 miles south of Santa Cruz. Take the New Brighton/Park Avenue exit from Highway 1.

This popular sandy beach, adjoining Seacliff Beach, has interpretive nature trails on the bluff, showers, firepits, and more than 100 well developed campsites amid a Monterey pine forest. For reservations call (800)444-7275. Look for seashell fossils in the cliff.

For more information, call (831)464-6330(www.santacruzstateparks.org).

Seacliff State Beach

TO GET THERE... In Aptos, it is off Highway 1 about 5 miles south of Santa Cruz.

This popular 85-acre beach stretches for about 2 miles along the coast. It is often crowded on warm days. There are 26 campsites available. For reservations call (800)444-7275. There are also picnic tables.

The fishing pier leads to a 435-foot-long concrete ship, the Palo Alto, which was built during World War I. There was once a dance floor on the ship deck before the vessel broke up in a storm. This beach is at the northernmost range of the pismo clam. For more information call (831)685-6442.

Manresa State Beach

TO GET THERE... From Highway 1 take Mar Monte Avenue to San Andreas Road.

Take the long, steep, wooden stairway down to this long sandy beach from the parking lot. It is popular with pismo clam diggers from September through April, and with surfers and sunbathers. There are restrooms and outdoor showers. There are 64 walk-in tent only campsites at the Manresa Uplands Campground about a mile to the south. The campground is opened from March through November.

For more information, call (831)688-3241 or (831)724-1266 (www.santacruzstateparks.org).

Sunset State Beach

TO GET THERE... Take the Mar Monte exit from Highway 1 and head south on San Andreas Road. Then take Sunset Beach Road or Beach Road toward the ocean.

This 218-acre beach spreads across 7 miles of sandy beachfront. It has picnic tables and 90 campsites. For camping reservations call (800)444-7275. Spring wildflowers are abundant on the bluffs. Usually foggier than Seacliff Beach, this beach is popular for surf fishing. Pismo clams are gathered from september until April. The Palm Beach Unit, at the end of Beach Road, has a broad sandy beach backed by low dunes.

For more information, call (831)763-7063 or (831)763-7062 (www.santacruzstateparks.org).

The Mountain Charlie Big Tree

is the last of the giant old-growth redwoods in the Glenwood area. From Highway 17 between Los Gatos and Santa Cruz, take the Glenwood exit and drive about 2 miles on The Old Highway (Glenwood Drive) to the sign that says "BIG REDWOOD PARK A RESIDENTIAL COMMUNITY". There are a few places to park at the intersection of Glenwood Drive and Main Blvd. Facing north, cross Glenwood Drive and take the unmarked dirt road trail that veers to the right and goes uphill. The big tree is about a thousand feet up the trail. Because the Mountain Charlie Tree is on private land, please do not stray from this route.

Mountain Charlie didn't spare this tree out of any environmental ethic, After his long struggle to fell the nearby Queen of the Forest, Charlie decided that it would be just too much effort to cut down a tree that was even bigger. A plaque next to the tree explains:

"This Sequoia Sempervirens was originally over 300 feet high. The tree stands today at 260 feet from the ground, having been broken off in a storm years ago. It is 18 feet in diameter at the base, 60 feet in circumference, and over 5 feet in diameter at the top. In 1880 when Mountain Charlie began to timber this area, he planned to cut both the big tree, known then as "King of the Forest", and the "Queen", whose stump remains as a testimony to the grand tree. Problems with the "Queen" changed that decision and the "King" still stands today as it has for over a thousand years."

See page 26 for more information about Mountain Charlie.

240

Resources

Audubon Society: (Outings and conservation); Sequoia Chapter; P.O. Box 620292, Woodside, CA 94062; (650) 529-1454; www.sequoia-audubon.org;. Santa Clara Valley Chapter; 22221 McClellan Rd., Cupertino, CA 95014; (408) 252-3747;www.scvas.org.

California Department of Parks and Recreation, Santa Cruz District (State Parks information); 303 Big Trees Park Road, Felton, CA 95018; (831) 429-2850; www.santacruzstateparks.org.

California Native Plant Society: (Native plant conservation and education); 2707 K Street, Suite 1, Sacramento, CA 95816; (916) 447-2677; www.cnps.org.

Committee For Green Foothills: (Conservation); 3921 E. Bayshore Rd., Palo Alto, CA 94303; (650) 968-7243; www.greenfoothills.org.

Coyote Point Museum: (Environmental Education); Coyote Point, CA 94401; (650) 342-7755; www.coyoteptmuseum.org.

Environmental Volunteers: (Nature education for children); 3921 E. Bayshore Rd., CA 94303; (650) 961-0545; www.evols.org.

Friends of Edgewood Natural Preserve: (Edgewood habitat restoration); P.O. Box 3422, Redwood City, CA 94064; (866) GO-EDGEWOOD; www.friendsofedgewood.org.

Friends of Filoli: (Tours and special events at the Filoli estate); Canada Road, Woodside, CA 94062; (650) 364-8300; www.filoli.org.

Golden Gate National Recreation Area (GGNRA information); Fort Mason, Building 201, San Francisco, CA 94123; (415) 561-4700; www.nps.gov/goga/.

Hidden Villa Association: (Environmental Education and hostel); 26870 Moody Rd., Los Altos Hills, CA 94022; (650) 949-8650; www.hiddenvilla.org.

Midpeninsula Regional Open Space District: (Docent walks and open space preserve information); 330 Distel Circle, Los Altos, CA 94022; (650) 691-1200; www.openspace.org.

Mountain Parks Foundation: (Environmental Education); 525 N. Big Trees Park Road, Felton, CA 95018; (408) 335-3174; www.mountainparks.org.

Mountain View Recreation Department: (Deer Hollow Farm); P.O. Box 7540, Mountain View, CA 94039; (650) 903-6430; www.ci.mtnview.ca.us.

New Almaden Quicksilver County Park Association: (Historic and recreation activities); P.O. Box 124, New Almaden, CA 95042; www.newalmaden.org.

Peninsula Conservation Center Foundation: (Conservation activities and environmental library); 3921 E. Bayshore Rd., Palo Alto, CA 94303; (650) 962-9876; www.volunteerinfo.org.

Peninsula Open Space Trust: (Acquisition and protection of open space); 3000 Sand Hill Rd., Menlo Park, CA 94025; (650) 854-7696; www.openspacetrust.org.

Rancho Del Oso Nature & History Center: (Natural history programs and exhibits); 3600 Highway 1, Davenport, CA 95017; (408) 427-2288; www.santacruzstateparks.org.
Responsible Organized Mountain Pedalers (ROMP): (Off-road bicycle advocacy); P.O. Box 1723, Campbell, CA 95009; (408) 380-2271, ext.2171; www.romp.org.
San Bruno Mountain Watch: (Outings and conservation on San Bruno Mountain); P.O. Box 53, Brisbane, CA 94005; (415) 467-6631; www.mountainwatch.org.
San Mateo County Parks Department: County Office Building, Redwood City, CA 94063; (650) 363-4020; www.co.sanmateo.ca.us.
San Mateo County Parks & Recreation Foundation: (Raise funds for San Mateo County Parks); 215 Bay Road, Menlo Park, CA 94025; (650) 321-5812; www.supportparks.org.
Santa Clara County Open Space Authority: (Open space preserve information); 6830 Via Del Oro, Suite 200, San Jose, CA 95119; (408) 224-7476; www.openspaceauthority.org.
Santa Clara County Parks Department: 298 Garden Hill Dr., Los Gatos, CA 95030; (408) 358-3751; www.parkhere.org.
Sempervirens Fund: (Parkland acquisition); P.O. Drawer BE, Los Altos, CA 94023; (650) 968-4509; www.sempervirens.org.
Sierra Club: (Outings and conservation); Loma Prieta Chapter; 3921 E. Bayshore Rd., Palo Alto, CA 94303; (650) 390-8411; www.lomaprieta.sierraclub.org.
Trail Center: (Trail building, maintenance, and information); 3921 E. Bayshore Rd., Palo Alto, CA 94303; (650) 968-7065; www.trailcenter.org.
Youth Science Institute: (Wilderness instruction and leadership development in Santa Clara County); 296 Garden Hill Drive, Los Altos, CA 95030; (408) 356-4945; www.ysi-ca.ca.

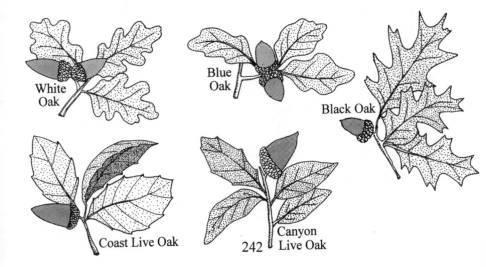

White Oak

Blue Oak

Black Oak

Coast Live Oak

Canyon Live Oak

242

The Best of the
Santa Cruz Mountains

Places that are significantly better than the others are underlined. This is an incomplete list.

Birds:

Ano Nuevo State Reserve (sea and shore birds), Pescadero Marsh Preserve (shore birds), Russian Ridge O.S.P. (raptors), Skyline Ridge O.S.P. (acorn woodpeckers, etc.).

Earthquake Faults:

Ano Nuevo State Reserve, Forest of Nisene Marks State Park, Los Trancos O.S.P., Monte Bello O.S.P., Sanborn Skyline County Park, San Francisco Fish & Game Refuge.

Ecological Diversity:

Ano Nuevo State Reserve, La Honda Creek O.S.P., Monte Bello O.S.P., Mount Madonna County Park, Russian Ridge O.S.P.

Fall Foliage:

Henry Cowell Redwoods State Park (Fall Creek Unit), Mount Madonna County Park, Sam McDonald County Park, Sanborn Skyline County Park, Uvas Canyon County Park.

Oak Trees:

Castle Rock State Park, Long Ridge O.S.P., Russian Ridge O.S.P., Skyline Ridge O.S.P.

Ponds:

Arastradero Preserve, Long Ridge O.S.P., Mount Madonna County Park, Rancho San Antonio O.S.P., Sanborn Skyline County Park, Skyline Ridge O.S.P., Windy Hill O.S.P.

Redwoods (old growth):

Big Basin Redwoods State Park, Henry Cowell Redwoods State Park (Southern Unit, Redwood Loop Trail), Portola State Park (Peters Creek grove), San Mateo County Memorial Park.

Reptiles:

Almaden Quicksilver County Park, La Honda Creek O.S.P., Monte Bello O.S.P., Rancho San Antonio O.S.P.

Rock Outcroppings:

Bonny Doon Ecological Preserve, Castle Rock State Park, El Corte de Madera Creek O.S.P., Sanborn Skyline County Park.

Serpentine Grasslands (for native plants):

Almaden Quicksilver County Park, Edgewood County Park & Preserve, Jasper Ridge Biological Preserve, Santa Teresa County Park, Sierra Azul O.S.P.

Waterfalls (best in winter and early spring):

Big Basin Redwoods State Park, Castle Rock State Park, Forest of Nisene Marks State Park, Portola State Park, San Pedro Valley County Park, Uvas Canyon County Park.

Wildflowers (best in spring, especially April):
Almaden Quicksilver County Park, Castle Rock State Park, Edgewood County Park & Preserve, Jasper Ridge Biological Preserve, McNee Ranch State Park, Russian Ridge O.S.P., San Bruno Mountain County Park, Santa Teresa County Park, Windy Hill O.S.P.

Backpack Camping:
Big Basin Redwoods State Park, Butano State Park, Forest of Nisene Marks State Park, Monte Bello O.S.P., Pescadero Creek County Park, Portola State Park.

Car Camping:
Big Basin Redwoods State Park, Butano State Park, Henry Cowell Redwoods State Park (southern unit), Mount Madonna County Park, Portola State Park, San Mateo County Memorial Park, Uvas Canyon County Park.

Dog Walking (on trails):
Almaden Quicksilver County Park, Golden Gate National Recreation Area, Mount Madonna County Park, Pulgas Ridge O.S.P., Santa Teresa County Park, Uvas Canyon County Park.

Easy Walks (short & nearly level):
Big Basin Redwoods State Park (Redwood Trail), Henry Cowell Redwoods State Park (Redwood Loop), Pescadero Marsh Preserve, Purisima Creek O.S.P. (Redwood Trail), Rancho San Antonio O.S.P. (to Deer Hollow Farm), San Mateo County Memorial Park (Creek Trail), San Pedro Valley County Park (Ranch Road Trail), Skyline Ridge O.S.P. (trail around Alpine Pond).

Horseback Riding:
Almaden Quicksilver County Park, Arastradero Preserve, Big Basin Redwoods State Park, Fremont Older O.S.P., Huddart County Park, Monte Bello O.S.P., Pescadero Creek County Park, Sam McDonald County Park (horse camp), Skyline Ridge O.S.P., Wunderlich County Park.

Hostels & Hikers Hut:
Hidden Villa Ranch, Pigeon Point Lighthouse, Point Montara Lighhouse, Sam McDonald County Park, Sanborn Skyline County Park

Kite Flying:
La Honda Creek O.S.P.,Russian Ridge O.S.P., San Bruno Mountain County Park, Windy Hill O.S.P.

Solitude:
Big Basin Redwoods State Park, Butano State Park, Henry Cowell Redwoods State Park (Fall Creek Unit), La Honda Creek O.S.P., Pescadero Creek County Park, Portola State Park, Sierra Azul O.S.P.

Strenuous Hikes (more than 10 miles):
Big Basin Redwoods State Park (loop to Berry Creek Falls), Butano State Park (Butano Fire Trail/Olmo Fire Road loop), Forest of Nisene Marks State Park (West Ridge Trail/Aptos Creek Fire Road loop),

Long Ridge O.S.P./Upper Stevens Creek County Park loop, Pescadero Creek County Park (any loop that includes Butano Ridge Trail), Purisima Creek O.S.P. (loop from top to bottom and back), Sierra Azul O.S.P. (one way from Mt. Umunhum Road to Lexington Reservoir), Skyline-to-the-Sea Trail, Wilder Ranch State Park (many loops).

Swimming Holes (dry season, warm weather):
Big Basin Redwoods State Park (where Hihn Hammond Road crosses Opal Creek, East Waddel Creek), Henry Cowell Redwoods State Park (Big Rock Hole), Pescadero Creek County Park (several deep pools in the creek), Portola State Park, San Mateo County Memorial Park (creek dammed in summer),

Views:
Castle Rock State Park, Golden Gate National Recreation Area (Sweeney Ridge), Long Ridge O.S.P., McNee Ranch State Park, Russian Ridge O.S.P., Sierra Azul O.S.P., Skyline Ridge O.S.P. Windy Hill O.S.P.

Archaelogical Sites:
Ano Nuevo State Reserve (shell mounds), Filoli Estate (archaelogical excavation and museum), San Bruno Mountain County Park (shell mound), Skyline Ridge O.S.P. (acorn grinding stones), Upper Stevens Creek County Park (acorn grinding stone).

Fruit & Nut Orchards (abandoned but still producing):
Fremont Older O.S.P., Long Ridge O.S.P.,Monte Bello O.S.P., Picchetti Ranch O.S.P.

Historic Buildings & Relics:
Almaden Quicksilver County Park, Ano Nuevo State Reserve, Burleigh Murray Ranch State Park, Forest of Nisene Marks State Park, Fremont Older O.S.P., Henry Cowell Redwoods State Park (Fall Creek unit), Mount Madonna County Park, Picchetti Ranch O.S.P., Pogonip O.S.P., Portola State Park, Purisima Creek O.S.P., Quail Hollow Ranch County Park, Rancho San Antonio O.S.P., Sanborn Skyline County Park, Skyline Ridge O.S.P., Wilder Ranch State Park, Wunderlich County Park.

Beautiful Beaches:
Ano Nuevo State Reserve, Bean Hollow State Beach, Bonny Doon Beach, Cowell Ranch Beach, Four Mile Beach, Greyhound Rock Beach, Martin's Beach, Pebble Beach.

Clothing Optional Beaches:
Bonny Doon Beach, Four Mile Beach, Gray Whale Cove Beach, Red White & Blue Beach, San Gregorio Private Beach.

Coastal Trails (away from Highway 1):
Ano Nuevo State Reserve, Wilder Ranch State Park.

Tidepools:
Ano Nuevo State Reserve, Bean Hollow State Beach, Fitzgerald Marine Preserve, Pescadero State Beach, Wilder Ranch State Park.

Wildlife Tracks

Most wild animals avoid people, but their tracks are often seen in muddy and dusty places. Here are some tracks you are likely to see in the Santa Cruz Mountains:

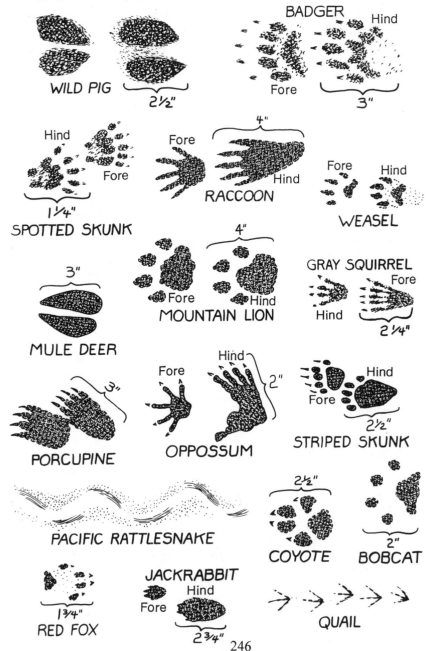

WILD PIG 2½"

BADGER
Hind
Fore 3"

Hind
Fore
1¼"
SPOTTED SKUNK

Fore
4"
Hind
RACCOON

Fore Hind
WEASEL

3"
MULE DEER

4"
Fore Hind
MOUNTAIN LION

GRAY SQUIRREL
Fore
Hind 2¼"

PORCUPINE 3"

OPPOSSUM
Fore
Hind 2"

STRIPED SKUNK
Fore Hind
2½"

PACIFIC RATTLESNAKE

COYOTE 2½"

BOBCAT 2"

RED FOX 1¾"

JACKRABBIT
Fore Hind
2¾"

QUAIL

A few of the intertidal creatures you may see:

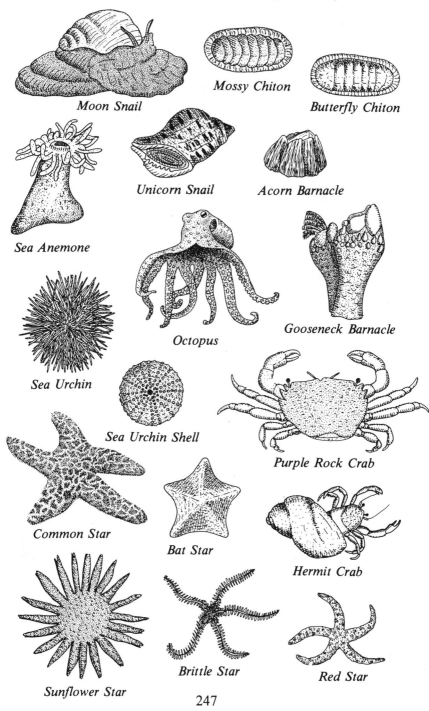

Moon Snail

Mossy Chiton

Butterfly Chiton

Unicorn Snail

Acorn Barnacle

Sea Anemone

Octopus

Gooseneck Barnacle

Sea Urchin

Sea Urchin Shell

Purple Rock Crab

Common Star

Bat Star

Hermit Crab

Sunflower Star

Brittle Star

Red Star